THE PROFESSIONAL PRACTICE SERIES

The Professional Practice Series is sponsored by the Society for Industrial and Organizational Psychology (SIOP). The series was launched in 1988 to provide industrial/organizational psychologists, organizational scientists and practitioners, human resource professionals, managers, executives, and those interested in organizational behavior and performance with volumes that are insightful, current, informative, and relevant to organizational practice. The volumes in the Professional Practice Series are guided by five tenets designed to enhance future organizational practice:

1. Focus on practice, but grounded in science
2. Translate organizational science into practice by generating guidelines, principles, and lessons learned that can shape and guide practice
3. Showcase the application of industrial/organizational psychology to solve problems
4. Document and demonstrate best industrial and organizational-based practices
5. Stimulate research needed to guide future organizational practice

The volumes seek to inform those interested in practice with guidance, insights, and advice on how to apply the concepts, findings, methods, and tools derived from industrial/organizational psychology to solve human-related organizational problems.

Previous Professional Practice Series volumes include:

Published by Jossey-Bass

Creating, Implementing, and Managing Effective Training and Development
Kurt Kraiger, Editor

The 21st Century Executive
Rob Silzer, Editor

Managing Selection in Changing Organizations
Jerard F. Kehoe, Editor

Evolving Practices in Human Resource Management
Allen I. Kraut, Abraham K. Korman, Editors

Individual Psychological Assessment
Richard Jeanneret, Rob Silzer, Editors

Performance Appraisal
James W. Smither, Editor

Organizational Surveys
Allen I. Kraut, Editor

Employees, Careers, and Job Creation
Manuel London, Editor

Published by Guilford Press

Diagnosis for Organizational Change
Ann Howard and Associates

Human Dilemmas in Work Organizations
Abraham K. Korman and Associates

Diversity in the Workplace
Susan E. Jackson and Associates

Working with Organizations and Their People
Douglas W. Bray and Associates

Organization Development

Organization Development

A Data-Driven Approach to Organizational Change

Janine Waclawski

Allan H. Church

Editors

Foreword by Eduardo Salas

JOSSEY-BASS
A Wiley Company
www.josseybass.com

Published by Jossey-Bass
A Wiley Imprint
989 Market Street, San Francisco, CA 94103-1741   www.josseybass.com

Library of Congress Cataloging-in-Publication Data

Organization development : a data-driven approach to organizational change / Janine Waclawski, Allan H. Church, Editors.
   p. cm.—(The professional practice series)
   Includes bibliographical references and index.
   ISBN 0-7879-5718-6
   1. Organizational change.   I. Waclawski, Janine, 1966-   II. Church, Allan H., 1966-
III. Series.
HD58.8 .O72833 2001
658.4'063—dc21

2001004593

Printed in the United States of America
FIRST EDITION
HB Printing   10 9 8 7 6 5 4 3

The Jossey-Bass
Business & Management Series

The Professional Practice Series

Contents

Part Two: Process-Based Approaches to Organization Development

Part Three: Major Developments in Organization Development

Foreword

Change. Data-driven change. This is at the core of what this book is about. This book is about moving organizations forward—about planning, diagnosing, implementing, and evaluating organization development interventions. It is about providing those who manage change with scientifically based information, tools, tips, and guidelines such that they can succeed in their efforts. It is about understanding the processes, approaches, and strategies that seem to work in managing organizational change. It is about organizational change and how to succeed at it.

Who is not in favor of developing organizations? Frankly, I do not know anyone who is not. And I hope all of us are in favor of change when organizations are confronted with socioeconomic, political, and global pressures. Industrial/organizational (I/O) psychologists, human resource executives, managers, and chief executive officers should all support change when it is needed in organizations so that they can remain viable and competitive. What helps in a small way to do our job—advise, support, and direct organizational change—is the information contained in these chapters.

In my opinion, Janine Waclawski and Allan Church (and the chapter authors) have provided a good service to our profession. They have put together a remarkable collection of chapters that are easy to read; directly relevant to the topic of how, when, and why change; and, most important, with suggestions and advice. This is clearly a must-read book for organization development practitioners.

I/O psychologists in general, graduate students, academicians interested in organizational issues, managers, human resource development executives, and even chief executive officers or CLOs should read this book. It illustrates how theory, supported by data, can be powerful in transforming organizations.

This book series is also about change. One of the main objectives of the SIOP Professional Practice Series is to change how I/O psychologists are viewed in the world of work. The Professional Practice Editorial Board continues to work at achieving that goal, and this book is a step in that direction. We also hope this book reaches those who promote, manage, and support change in organizations.

Thanks to Janine Waclawski and Allan Church for their efforts and to all the authors of the chapters for their contributions.

September 2001

EDUARDO SALAS
University of Central Florida
Series Editor

Preface

Although many practitioners, researchers, and leaders may not think of organization development (OD) as a data-driven process for organizational improvement and change, OD is at its very foundation just that. OD is about using interpersonal process and social science data (such as behaviors, attitudes, opinions, perceptions, and observations) to diagnose and ultimately help fix organizations. This use of human data is what differentiates OD work and OD consultation from many other types of approaches to organizational intervention and problem solving such as the closely aligned fields of industrial/organizational (I/O) psychology, organization behavior (OB), and human resource development (HRD), not to mention the more ubiquitous and nebulous realm of management consulting. In short, focusing on the softer, interpersonal side of data to drive improvement and change is both a strength and a core competency of OD practice and research.

In our opinion (as practitioners who attempt to bridge the gap among the fields of OD, OB, HRD, and I/O psychology), a book that focuses on and delineates the processes and interventions by which human data are used as an integral part of large-scale organizational change and development is long overdue. Practitioners have known for years that data are essential to all that we do, but this reality lags behind public perception based on images and stereotypes forged in the 1960s that OD is just that "touchy-feely stuff" and is driven largely by the whims and idiosyncrasies of those who practice it.

At the most basic level, the purpose of this book is to address this need in the literature by focusing on the unique contribution of data-driven OD practitioners. Before detailing our approach to this contribution, however, it is important to have a basic understanding of the core constituents of and mind-sets that people have toward the field of OD in general. Our experience has been that perceptions of and attitudes about OD fall into two broad categories: those who are proponents of OD and those who are skeptical or unaware of OD.

Proponents of OD

With respect to the first category of individuals, proponents of OD, although there certainly is a core constituency of what we like to call *card-carrying ODers* (those whose primary allegiance is to the study and practice of OD), this group represents a relatively small percentage of individuals, even within the OD community. In fact, the joint membership of the three major professional organizations for ODers (in the United States)—the Organization Development Institute, the Organization Development Network, and the Organization Development and Change division of the Academy of Management—do not even have a combined membership of ten thousand individuals. Moreover, these numbers do not reflect unique memberships; many practitioners belong to all three organizations, making the total number of card-carrying ODers even smaller.

In addition, there are others who would be considered proponents of the OD approach but whose allegiance to the field itself is not as strong; we call these practitioners *dabblers in OD*. This group consists of individuals such as I/O psychologists, management consultants, HRD specialists, counseling psychologists, and others who engage in certain types of OD work but do not consider themselves to be primarily OD practitioners (for a more data-based comparison of some of these professional groups, see Church & Burke, 1992, 1993). While these dabblers probably represent a larger percentage of the total professional population than the card-carrying ODers, this group is by no means large.

Skeptical or Unaware of OD

A considerably larger percentage of the population fits the second category: individuals who are skeptical or totally unaware of OD. The vast majority of people working in and with organizations are either not well versed in or are unsure of the potential impact and contribution of data-driven OD tools and techniques. Many who do not practice OD view it as an unproven technique for organizational improvement.

If we were to classify these types of individuals further, we would notice four subgroups of resisters to the OD approach. More specifically, nonpractitioners (and often clients or professionals belonging to other disciplines) usually reflect one of the following groups with respect to their opinions about OD:

- OD is irrelevant to the way organizations work and has never been particularly useful.
- OD is dead; it represents a failed experiment from the 1960s that sought to get organizations to consider the implications of the human side of change.
- OD is only marginally useful as a technique for helping groups deal with issues such as interpersonal dynamics that might be interfering with work.
- OD is simply an enigma; people have heard the term but do not really know what it means.

Given this plethora of potential detractors, resisters, and the simply clueless, one important goal of this book is to demonstrate the importance and power of the theory and practice of OD as a data-driven tool for organization improvement and change. To this end, the chapters are intended to represent both the cutting edge and best practice with respect to the art and science of OD. Thus, this book is targeted not only at those who are skeptical or unaware of the nature of OD work, but also at those who may currently be dabblers in the field but want to expand their OD repertoire, and even some experienced card-carrying ODers.

If recent trends in interest and practice (Waclawski & Church, 2000a) are any indication of the future, the contribution of OD is both enticing and exciting. Experience has shown, for example, that when done well, OD can be a highly effective means for transforming organizations, and thus, contrary to the perceptions of many, it is here to stay. In short, to paraphrase Mark Twain, "The reports of OD's death are greatly exaggerated." If, as we believe, organizational change is truly a constant state from which new organizational forms are emerging daily, then understanding, facilitating, and helping leaders manage the human side of change will continue to be an essential skill for practitioners working in all aspects of organizations (Howard, 1995; Kraut & Korman, 1999).

Perceptions about the field of OD, however, are not the only forces and factors contributing to its current state as a fractured and often disjointed approach. Much of the current state of OD has to do with its origins and development over the past forty or so years.

The State of OD

In general, OD is one of the most popular and widely used approaches for implementing organizational change. Year after year, the field continues to experience phenomenal growth in practitioners; for example, membership in the National OD Network has risen from 2,800 in 1992 (Thorne & Hogan, 1993) to 4,031 at last count (K. Yaeger, e-mail to A. H. Church, Nov. 8, 1999), representing an almost 70 percent increase in seven years. Despite its continued popularity, however, and somewhat paradoxically, OD is also one of the most misunderstood and underappreciated fields as well (Waclawski & Church, 2000b). More specifically, there is a considerable lack of understanding regarding exactly what is and what is not OD. This situation is apparent with both clients—those leaders, managers, and employees who are the potential recipients of OD interventions—and some of those who profess to be practitioners and consultants (including dabblers and even card-carrying ODers), as research on attitudes regarding the field has shown (Church & Burke, 1995).

Unfortunately, this is a major concern for all of those in the field, from students in formal OD-centered academic programs (such as those at Pepperdine University and Loyola University, both in California, and Bowling Green State University in Ohio) to experienced practitioners who continue to struggle with an identity crisis regarding an evolving field. Although many factors have contributed to the complexity of understanding and defining OD, two issues in particular continue to prevent OD from making a difference in organizations and from coming together as a unified entity in general.

First, although seen as a major strength by many individuals, particularly during its initial growth in the 1970s and 1980s, the diversity of theoretical influences, approaches, and tools in doing OD work has resulted in considerable confusion and misunderstanding regarding the goals, values, and types of practice that should typify this method of working with organizations and those who work in them (Church, Burke, & Van Eynde, 1994; Sanzgiri & Gottlieb, 1992). For example, is OD large scale or small? Is it focused on data or focused on process? What does OD stand for? How does OD differ from training and development efforts, corporate opinion surveys, team-building wilderness exercises, or executive coaching?

Second, there is considerable inconsistency and often even concerted inattention by many practitioners in the field regarding the importance of and need to demonstrate the impact of OD-related efforts on improving individual and organizational performance (Cady, 1998; Church, Waclawski, & Burke, 1996). Historically, the field has been slow to demonstrate significant results from OD efforts and has been criticized extensively for it (Porras & Robertson, 1992). While some professionals clearly value the importance of making a significant difference for their internal or external clients, relatively few accounts of such results are evident. Moreover, many practitioners have unfortunately focused on concerns other than impact, such as specialization in a specific technique, promotion of new model, or finding novel ways to make OD unique, such as through the use of musical instruments or custom-colored Silly Putty. Such efforts have contributed further to the diffusion and disillusionment of OD as a profession and as a field by many both within and outside its boundaries (Church & Burke, 1992, 1995).

The Purpose of This Book

Given the state of the field as we have just described it and the variety of perceptions (both negative and indifferent), the purpose of this book is to provide a unified framework for understanding and unifying OD and demonstrating its organizational impact through data-driven methods. We offer readers a fresh resource for exploring the primary theoretical influences on OD, the major categories of hard and soft measurement methodologies employed and the nature of the underlying assumptions inherent in their use, and an overview of major issues and trends in the field.

This book was compiled for three objectives. The first objective is to establish the importance of using applied data—whether from perceptions, observations, opinions, culture ratings, learnings, multisource feedback assessments, or personality preferences—to identify specific issues, create energy and motivation, target areas for improvement, and ultimately drive individual and organizational change efforts.

Second, we seek to underscore the importance of demonstrating impact—including planning, measuring, analyzing, and demonstrating the effects of OD efforts—on individual and organizational performance improvement. Finally, we seek to show the importance of defining and maintaining a clear and consistent set of boundaries, norms, and values for the future of the field of OD.

Why Another Book on OD?

Although there are many other OD books in the marketplace, both those reflecting singular approaches and reviews (Burke, 1994; Cummings & Worley, 1997; French & Bell, 1998) as well as those based on various sets of contributors (Rothwell, Sullivan, & McLean, 1995; Van Eynde, Hoy, & Van Eynde, 1997; or the annual series edited by Richard Woodman and William Passmore from JAI Press titled *Research in Organizational Change and Development*), this book represents a unique contribution to the field based on the centrality of the normative themes we have outlined; the nature of the individual contributors, their cross-spectrum representation and appeal, and the level of depth they bring to their specific chapters; and the emphasis on OD as a practice grounded in data-based theory and research.

Moreover, we believe that there is a particular need for this book in the I/O psychology community. Despite the fact that roughly 23 percent of members of the Society for Industrial-Organizational Psychology (SIOP) consider themselves to be engaged in OD-related activities (Howard, 1990), recent surveys of members (Schneider & Smith, 1999; Waclawski & Church, 2000b) indicate that OD and change is one of the highest-rated areas of interest among respondents. Given this level of interest and the need to improve awareness and understanding of OD among many types of organizational practitioners, this book provides a number of different approaches and perspectives to OD in various settings. Although there are many areas of overlap with I/O and HRD practice and methodology, there are also some distinct differences, which we highlight here. As a result, the book should be of interest to a variety of professionals, academics, managers, HR personnel, and researchers interested in and engaged in OD and change interventions and research.

Although the issues we have described in detail do not necessarily represent new concerns for those who think and write about the field of OD, they do represent something with which I/O and HRD practitioners are less familiar. Moreover, OD has reached a critical point in its evolution. With the rising popularity of organizational consulting in general (Micklethwait & Wooldridge, 1996) and many subspecialties such as Total Quality Management and business process reengineering that overlap with OD principles and techniques, at least in part, there is a strong need in the field and in the literature for a concise, normative, yet well-rounded book that specifies what types of efforts and interventions should and should not represent OD. Such a book will not only help bring a greater sense of cohesion to the field; it should serve to differentiate OD practice from consulting approaches that have been heavily critiqued in recent years through such vehicles as Dilbert cartoons (Adams, 1996) and exposés detailing the excesses and abuses of much of the larger consulting industry (Micklethwait & Wooldridge, 1996; Pinault, 2000).

Organization of the Book

The book has three parts. Part One focuses on the quantitative and qualitative approaches to doing OD work and affecting performance improvement. Each of these methodologies for collecting individual information (for example, opinions, attitudes, and behaviors) in an OD context, including their respective strengths and weakness, is discussed. Case examples of best practices and additional detail are also provided.

In Chapter One, we provide an introduction and overview of OD as a data-driven process for change and focus on both theory and practice. We begin with a presentation of the theoretical underpinnings of OD and conclude with a discussion of the role of data in the OD consultation process and a new framework of OD.

In Chapter Two, Allan Church, Alan Walker, and Joel Brockner discuss an increasingly popular OD tool, multisource feedback (MSF), and its role in OD and change work. They cover such topics as the basics of multisource feedback for OD, the different organizational levels at which practitioners can use MSF data, aligning MSF with other HR processes, and using MSF for team diagnosis.

In Chapter Three, Warner Burke and Debra Noumair tackle the complex issue of the role and function of personality assessment in organization development. They highlight several personality assessment instruments that are commonly (and successfully) used in OD. They also provide many interesting case studies about the use of these assessments in OD and leadership development work.

Salvatore Falletta and Wendy Combs explore the use of organizational surveys as a tool for large-scale change in Chapter Four. Some of the issues they tackle include the four tenets for using surveys for OD work, the difference between traditional organizational surveys and surveys used for OD purposes, and using models to drive surveys for OD. Among other things, this chapter offers a good summary of some well-known and important OD consulting frameworks.

In Chapter Five, Janine Waclawski and Steven Rogelberg team up to provide an overview of how interviews and focus groups are used in OD. Although these two techniques have a myriad of other applications, their use in OD represents a somewhat unique perspective. Topics covered in this chapter include using interviews for both diagnostic and exploratory purposes, the four steps to using interviews and focus groups in OD, how to prepare for and conduct OD interviews, and focus groups and models for analyzing and interpreting interview and focus group results. This chapter also contains a case study demonstrating the use of interviews for an organizational diagnosis.

Steve Cady and Mark Lewis conclude the first part of this book with an important and up-and-coming area in OD: focusing on the bottom line by linking soft measures and hard results. This chapter discusses the importance of demonstrating the impact of OD by linking our work as practitioners to hard measures of performance, such as sales, profitability, and turnover.

Part Two describes process-based approaches to OD. Although these are more difficult to measure, they are important to include in this or any other OD book because they represent one of the major sets of original interventions in the field and a significant proportion of current practice and interest. At least two cutting-edge approaches not typically covered in traditional OD texts, appreciative inquiry and large system interventions, are examined. These approaches are part of the unique element of OD as a field and fundamentally yet another form and use of data for individual and organizational change.

This part begins with a chapter by William Kahnweiler on using process consultation (PC). For those of you who are unfamiliar with OD, this chapter highlights a cornerstone of OD practice of which you should be aware. For those of you well versed in OD, this chapter will provide you with some new insights about a familiar tool. In any event, Kahnweiler does a superb job of describing not only the nature of PC work but also pointing out those organizational factors that enable and block the successful use of PC. Finally, he provides a list of key skills that anyone doing PC should possess.

Next, in Chapter Eight, Richard Woodman and William Pasmore provide a thought-provoking look at group- and team-based interventions in OD. The understanding and facilitation of team and group functioning are fundamental to much of what is considered OD work. This chapter includes a primer on group dynamics and an in-depth look at the types of group- and team-based interventions available to OD practitioners. Moreover, the authors cover a topic that is often and unfortunately left unaddressed: the difference between what is referred to as "BIG OD" (large-scale systemwide change) and "little od" (an isolated set of interventions or techniques). The chapter concludes with an extensive list of excellent practice tips.

Victoria Marsick, Judy O'Neil, and Karen Watkins then discuss a topic that they have a great deal of experience with and knowledge about: action learning. Among other things, they discuss the difference between action learning and other OD methods, the different types of approaches to action learning, and how to choose from among them and the importance of data in this process.

Chapter Ten by Stephen Fitzgerald, Kenneth Murrell, and Lynn Newman looks at a relatively new OD approach, appreciative inquiry (Ai). It explores some of the fundamentals of Ai in terms of the steps in using this technique and its organizational applications. The authors go beyond these topics and conclude the chapter with a compelling discourse on slaying "the mythical dragons of Ai." For any of you who have come up against these mythical dragons in other types of OD work, this chapter is certain to be of interest.

In Chapter Eleven, Barbara Bunker and Billie Alban provide an excellent overview of an increasingly popular and high-impact OD technique: large system interventions (LSI). They draw on their wealth of experience in using LSI to share some of the fundamentals of this technique for working with organizations as a whole. They cover such compelling issues as why large systems interventions are important to I/O and OD, the key concepts of change in large systems, how LSI differs from organizational surveys, and emerging trends in LSI.

Part Three covers other major developments and issues in OD not related to core theory or methodologies: the role of OD in information technology and systems efforts; the future of the field, including issues of education, experience, ethics, and accreditation standards; global and international issues; and the process of evaluating and demonstrating impact. We also discuss future areas for OD work in terms of both theory development and application.

In Chapter Twelve, Nancy Tippins describes the challenges facing practitioners in implementing OD in the virtual world. She begins with a thoughtful discussion about the impact of the technological revolution and then examines the impact of information technology on the process of OD in relation to the lens of six core OD practices. She ends with a look at the impact of information technology on the content of OD.

Michael Marquardt tackles a difficult yet critical aspect of OD work in Chapter Thirteen: doing OD in the international context. He not only discusses the impact of globalization on OD but also probes at length the challenges of implementing OD in different countries. In particular, he deftly examines the plethora of issues (both explicit and implicit) that OD practitioners face in doing

OD in different cultures and provides ample practice tips to help practitioners avoid some of the common blunders in doing OD in other parts of the world.

In Chapter Fourteen, Jennifer Martineau and Hallie Preskill discuss the important topic of evaluating the impact of OD interventions. Evaluating the impact of this work is arguably one of the most important yet often overlooked areas of OD practice. The topics in this chapter include challenges to evaluating OD efforts, designing effective evaluation measures and systems, and how to make evaluation an integrated component of OD initiatives.

In Chapter Fifteen, Gary McLean and Susan DeVogel cover some of the ethical dilemmas OD practitioners face in their work and present several frameworks for ethical decision making. They devote a section of the chapter to a discussion about the changing nature of OD values and how this has led to tension within the field regarding what constitutes the ethical practice of OD.

Finally, Allan Church, Janine Waclawski, and Seth Berr take us into the trenches and present the results of interviews done with senior practitioners in the field regarding current trends and future directions in OD.

Pound Ridge, New York   JANINE WACLAWSKI
September 2001   ALLAN H. CHURCH

References
Adams, S. (1996). *The Dilbert principle.* New York: HarperBusiness.
Burke, W. W. (1994). *Organization development: A process of learning and changing* (2nd ed.). Reading, MA: Addison-Wesley.
Cady, S. H. (1998). From the guest editor: Empirically driven change: Putting rigor in organization development and change. *Organization Development Journal, 16*(4), 2–3.
Church, A. H., & Burke, W. W. (1992). Assessing the activities and values of organization development practitioners. *Industrial-Organizational Psychologist, 30*(1), 59–66.
Church, A. H., & Burke, W. W. (1993). Exploring practitioner differences in consulting style and knowledge of change management by professional association membership. *Consulting Psychology Journal: Practice and Research, 45*(3), 7–24.

Church, A. H., & Burke, W. W. (1995). Practitioner attitudes about the field of organization development. In W. A. Pasmore & R. W. Woodman (Eds.), *Research in organizational change and development* (Vol. 8, pp. 1–46). Greenwich, CT: JAI Press.

Church, A. H., Burke, W. W., & Van Eynde, D. F. (1994). Values, motives, and interventions of organization development practitioners. *Group and Organization Management, 19*(1), 5–50.

Church, A. H., Waclawski, J., & Burke, W. W. (1996). OD practitioners as facilitators of change: An analysis of survey results. *Group and Organization Management, 21*(1), 22–66.

Cummings, T., & Worley, C. (1997). *Organization development and change* (6th ed.). St. Paul, MN: West.

French, W. L., & Bell, C. H., Jr. (1998). *Organization development: Behavioral science interventions for organization improvement* (5th ed.). Upper Saddle River, NJ: Prentice Hall.

Howard, A. (Ed.). (1995). *The changing nature of work.* San Francisco: Jossey-Bass.

Kraut, A. I., & Korman, A. K. (1999). The "delta forces" causing change in human resource management. In A. I. Kraut & A. K. Korman (Eds.), *Evolving practices in human resource management: Responses to a changing world of work* (pp. 3–22). San Francisco: Jossey-Bass.

Micklethwait, J., & Wooldridge, A. (1996). *The witch doctors: Making sense of the management gurus.* New York: Times Business.

Pinault, L. (2000). *Consulting demons: Inside the unscrupulous world of global corporate consulting.* New York: HarperBusiness.

Porras, J. I., & Robertson, P. J. (1992). Organizational development: Theory, practice, and research. In M. D. Dunnette & L. M. Hough (Eds.), *Handbook of industrial and organizational psychology* (2nd ed., Vol. 3, pp. 719–822). Palo Alto, CA: Consulting Psychologists Press.

Rothwell, W. J., Sullivan, R., & McLean, G. N. (Eds.). (1995). *Practicing organization development: A guide for consultants.* San Francisco: Jossey-Bass.

Sanzgiri, J., & Gottlieb, J. Z. (1992). Philosophic and pragmatic influences on the practice of organization development, 1950–2000. *Organization Dynamics, 21*(2), 57–69.

Schneider, J., & Smith, K. (1999). SiOP 1999 member survey results. *Industrial-Organizational Psychologist, 37*(2), 24–29.

Thorne, S., & Hogan, L (1993). ODN future search: Listening to our membership. *OD Practitioner, 25*(1), 2–7.

Van Eynde, D. F., Hoy, J. C., & D. C. Van Eynde (Eds.). (1997). *Organization development classics: The practice and theory of change—The best of the OD practitioner.* San Francisco: Jossey-Bass.

Waclawski, J., & Church, A. H. (2000a). The 2000 SIOP member survey results are in! *Industrial-Organizational Psychologist, 38*(1), 59–68.

Waclawski, J., & Church, A. H. (2000b). *What is organization development? An overview of approaches, tools, and techniques for I/O psychologists.* Symposium presented at the SIOP 2000 conference, New Orleans.

Woodman, R. W., & Wayne, S. J. (1985). An investigation of positive findings bias in evaluation of organization development interventions. *Academy of Management Journal, 28,* 889–913.

The Authors

JANINE WACLAWSKI is a principal consultant in the Management Consulting Services line of business at PricewaterhouseCoopers, LLP. She was formerly a principal at W. Warner Burke Associates, Inc., for eight years. She has also worked for IBM in corporate personnel research and for the director of training in the Department of Investigations of the City of New York. She specializes in using surveys and multisource feedback for organizational change and executive development. She is also an adjunct professor at Columbia University and has taught at Hunter College in New York. Waclawski received her bachelor's degree in psychology from the State University of New York at Stony Brook and her master's and doctoral degrees in organizational psychology from Columbia University. She received the prestigious ASTD Donald Bullock Memorial Dissertation Award for her research on large-scale organizational change and performance. She has published more than twenty articles, with a primary emphasis on data-driven methods for organization development and change in a wide variety of journals. She was the editor of *Real World,* a quarterly publication in *The Industrial-Organizational Psychologist (TIP),* a professional journal, from 1998 to 2001. Actively involved in several professional organizations, Waclawski serves on several journal editorial boards and has been an invited speaker, panel chair, and discussant at many national and international conferences. Her most recent book, *Designing and Using Organizational Surveys,* written with Allan Church, was published by Jossey-Bass in 2001.

ALLAN H. CHURCH is director of organization and management development at PepsiCo. He specializes in designing customized multisource feedback systems and large-scale diagnostic surveys for organization development and change. Previously, he was employed at PricewaterhouseCoopers, LLP, in the management consulting services line of business. Prior to that, he spent nine years at W. Warner Burke Associates, Inc., and three years at IBM in the Personnel Research and the Communications Research departments. He is an adjunct professor at Columbia University and a Distinguished Visiting Scholar in the College of Business, Technology, and Professional Programs at Benedictine University. Church received his bachelor's degree with a double major in psychology and sociology from Connecticut College and his M.A., M.Phil., and Ph.D. degrees in organizational psychology from Columbia University. He has published more than ten book chapters and more than one hundred articles. With David Bracken and Carol Timmreck, he is coeditor of *The Handbook of Multisource Feedback* (Jossey-Bass, 2001). From 1998 to 2001, Church served as editor of both *The Industrial-Organizational Psychologist (TIP)* and the *Organization Development Journal;* currently, he is associate editor of the *International Journal of Organizational Analysis,* general editor of *Human Resource Development International,* and OD Forum field editor for the American Society for Training and Development (ASTD) publication *Performance in Practice.*

BILLIE T. Alban is president of Alban & Williams and an internationally known management consultant. She teaches in executive development programs at Columbia, the University of California, Los Angeles, and Pepperdine and has served on the board of the Organization Development Network. She is the coauthor, with Barbara Bunker, of *Large Group Interventions: Engaging the Whole System for Rapid Change* (Jossey-Bass, 1997). She earned her master of fine arts degree at Yale University.

SETH A. BERR is a consultant in the Management Consulting Services division at PricewaterhouseCoopers LLP, where he specializes in organization development and change initiatives, primarily in areas of multisource feedback system development, organizational surveys, and personality assessment. He has published on topics such as personality and managerial behavior relationships and the field of OD. Berr earned his M.A. in organizational psychology from Teachers College, Columbia University.

JOEL BROCKNER is the Phillip Hettleman Professor of Business at Columbia Business School. His research interests include organizational change, organizational justice, self-processes in work organizations, decision making, and cross-cultural differences (and similarities) in work attitudes and behaviors. Works describing these interests have appeared in two books and numerous journal articles in psychology. He also is the faculty director of Columbia Business School's Executive Education program, Leading and Managing People. He received his Ph.D. in social-personality psychology from Tufts University.

BARBARA BENEDICT BUNKER is professor of psychology at the State University of New York at Buffalo and a partner in the Portsmouth Consulting Group. She has taught in executive development programs at Columbia, Pepperdine, and the Harvard University School of Education and has held Fulbright lectureships in the business schools of Keio University and Kobe University in Japan. She is the coauthor, with Billie Alban, of *Large Group Interventions: Engaging the Whole System for Rapid Change* (Jossey-Bass, 1997). She has a doctoral degree in social psychology from Columbia University.

W. WARNER BURKE is professor of psychology and education at Teachers College, Columbia University, and senior adviser to the Organization and Change Strategy Group at Pricewaterhouse Coopers. He has well over one hundred publications, including fourteen books. He is a Fellow of the Academy of Management, Society of Industrial-Organizational Psychology, and the American Psychological Society; a diplomate in industrial/organizational psychology, American Board of Professional Psychology; and a recipient of the American Society for Training and Development's award for Distinguished Contribution to Human Resource Development. He received his Ph.D. degree from the University of Texas at Austin.

STEVEN H. CADY is the director of the Institute for Organizational Effectiveness and serves on the graduate faculty at Bowling Green State University. He is an expert in the fields of organizational behavior, organization development and change, and human resource management, in which he conducts research and consults internationally. He received his Ph.D. in organizational behavior from Florida State University.

WENDY COMBS manages employee development initiatives for the e-business organization at Intel Corporation and is designing competencies, skills assessments, career paths, and curriculum road maps for the e-business workforce. She earned her Ph.D. in educational research and evaluation from North Carolina State University.

SUSAN H. DEVOGEL is director of organization development at Children's Hospitals and Clinics in Minneapolis and St. Paul, Minnesota. She spent fifteen years doing organization development consulting with organizations in all sectors as president of Ivy Consulting Group. She received her Ph.D. from the University of Minnesota.

SALVATORE V. FALLETTA is a senior survey and organizational assessment manager for the HR Research group at Intel Corporation and is heading all corporate-wide employee and organization development survey initiatives. He also has considerable experience conducting applied people and organizational behavior research. He received his Ed.D. in training and human resource development from North Carolina State University.

STEPHEN P. FITZGERALD is a doctoral candidate in organizational psychology at the California School of Professional Psychology. His research is focused on transorganizational collaboration for social change.

WILLIAM M. KAHNWEILER is an associate professor and director of human resource degree programs at Georgia State University, Atlanta. For seventeen years prior to joining the faculty, he employed process consultation as a training and development manager at General Electric Company, a principal with Hay Management Consultants, and running his own consulting business. He has published over seventy-five articles.

MARK J. LEWIS is an internal consultant with a large manufacturing organization in Canada. He has been involved with large- and small-scale change initiatives, including the implementation of a talent pool development system resulting in a systematic approach to human resource planning and development and the implementation and facilitation of a group problem-solving process that was targeted at introducing a more participative approach to managing. He received his master's degree from Bowling Green State University.

MICHAEL MARQUARDT is a professor of human resource development and president of Global Learning Associates. His consulting assignments have included industry, the U.S. government, and the governments of a number of other countries. He is the author of fourteen books and over seventy professional articles in the fields of leadership, learning, globalization, and organizational change.

VICTORIA J. MARSICK is a professor of adult education and organizational learning in the Department of Organization and Leadership at Columbia University, Teachers College. She codirects the J. M. Huber Institute on Learning in Organizations. Her most recent publications are *Action Learning: Successful Strategies for Individual, Team, and Organizational Development, Facilitating the Learning Organization,* and *Informal Learning on the Job.* She received her Ph.D. in adult education from the University of California, Berkeley.

JENNIFER W. MARTINEAU is a research scientist at the Center for Creative Leadership, where she works with CCL staff, clients, and external evaluators to create new evaluation methods for CCL programs and extend the center's capabilities in this area. She is the author of *Maximizing the Value of 360 Degree Feedback* (1998) and coauthor of *In Action: Measuring Learning and Performance* (1999) as well as refereed journal articles and reports. She received her Ph.D. from Pennsylvania State University.

GARY N. MCLEAN is professor and coordinator of human resource development and adult education and Morse Alumni Distinguished Teaching Professor at the University of Minnesota, St. Paul. He is the general editor of *Human Resource Development International* and the North American editor of *Journal of Transnational Management Development;* president of the Academy of Human Resource Development and of the International Management Development Association; and the principal consultant with ECCO Consulting. He received his Ed.D. from Columbia University.

KENNETH L. MURRELL is professor of management and management information services at the University of West Florida. He also teaches in the new doctoral program in organizational change at Pepperdine University, is working with the new Ph.D. program in organization development at Benedictine University, and is an adviser to the new Antioch graduate program in whole systems design. He is a management consultant with extensive international experience in improving organizational effectiveness. He earned his doctorate in business administration at George Washington University.

H. LYNN NEWMAN is the director of the Center for Innovation and Change at the California School of Professional Psychology. She has been in private practice as an organization development consultant for over fifteen years, focusing on executive coaching, team effectiveness, and large-scale organizational change efforts. She received her Ph.D. from the University of Southern California.

DEBRA A. NOUMAIR is an associate professor of psychology and education in the Department of Organization and Leadership at Teachers College, Columbia University, and on the faculty of leadership development programs sponsored by the Executive Education Department, Columbia University Business School. She is a fellow of the A. K. Rice Institute and a member of the American Psychological Association, the Academy of Management, and the Society for Industrial Organizational Psychologists. A licensed psychologist, Noumair maintains a private practice of organizational consultation and executive coaching. She received her Ph.D. from Teachers College, Columbia University.

JUDY O'NEIL is president of Partners for the Learning Organization, which specializes in action technologies; an assistant professor and coordinator of the master's of science in organizational management program at Eastern Connecticut State University; and on the adjunct faculty at Teachers College. She is the coeditor of *Action Learning: Successful Strategies for Individual, Team, and Organizational Development* (1999) and of *ASTD What Works Online: Action Learning: Real Work, Real Learning* (2000). She holds an Ed.D. from Teachers College, Columbia University.

WILLIAM A. PASMORE is a consultant to CEOs of Fortune 500 companies. He has over twenty-five years of experience in assisting corporations with strategy implementation, organizational redesign, management of change, executive development, and senior team effectiveness. He was a member of the Weatherhead School of Management faculty of Case Western Reserve University for twenty years and has authored and edited numerous books and articles, including *Research in Organizational Change and Development,* an annual series that he edits with Richard Woodman. He earned his doctoral degree in administrative science at Purdue University.

HALLIE PRESKILL is professor of organizational learning and instructional technologies at the University of New Mexico, Albuquerque, where she teaches graduate-level courses in program evaluation, organizational learning, and training. She is coauthor of *Evaluative Inquiry for Learning in Organizations* (1999) and *Evaluation Strategies for Communication and Reporting* (1996) and coeditor of *Human Resource Development Review* (1997). She received her Ph.D. from the University of Illinois at Urbana-Champaign.

STEVEN G. ROGELBERG is an associate professor of psychology at Bowling Green State University and the director of the Institute for Psychological Research and Application. He has published over twenty-five articles and book chapters addressing issues such as organizational research methods, team effectiveness, and employee morale and attitudes. He also is the editor of the *Handbook of Research Methods in Industrial and Organizational Psychology.* He holds a Ph.D. from the University of Connecticut.

NANCY T. TIPPINS, an industrial/organizational psychologist with over twenty-five years of experience as an internal consultant, is president of the Selection Practice Group of Personnel Research Associates. Throughout her career, she has used information technology to support organization development activities ranging from opinion surveys to succession planning, multisource feedback, and leadership development. She received her Ph.D. from the Georgia Institute of Technology.

ALAN G. WALKER is manager of personnel research for First Tennessee National Corporation. He has developed, implemented, and managed First Tennessee's upward, multisource, and employee opinion survey programs and has maintained an active applied research program. The results of these research efforts include a recently published five-year study on upward feedback in *Personnel Psychology* with Jim Smither as well as numerous presentations at professional conferences such as the Society for Industrial and Organizational Psychology. He received his master's degree in industrial/organizational psychology from Western Kentucky University.

KAREN E. WATKINS is professor of human resource and organizational development and the director of the School of Leadership and Lifelong Learning. Her research focus has been human resource and organizational development. Watkins is the author or coauthor of over seventy articles and chapters and six books. She holds a Ph.D. from the University of Texas at Austin in educational administration.

RICHARD W. WOODMAN is the Fouraker Professor of Business and professor of management at Texas A&M University. He has been program chair and division chair for the organization development and change division of the Academy of Management. He has been or is currently on the editorial review boards of a number of journals. In addition, he is coeditor of the annual series Research in Organizational Change and Development. His coauthored textbook, *Organizational Behavior* (2001), is in its ninth edition. He received his Ph.D. from Purdue University.

Organization Development

PART 1

Quantitative and Qualitative Approaches to Organization Development

Introduction and Overview of Organization Development as a Data-Driven Approach for Organizational Change

Janine Waclawski
Allan H. Church

Unlike medicine, accounting, law, police work, national politics, and many other disciplines, professions, and vocational callings that one might choose to pursue, all of which have a clear, consistent, and focused sense of purpose, the field of organization development (OD) is somewhat unique in its inherent and fundamental lack of clarity about itself. OD is a field that is both constantly evolving and yet constantly struggling with a dilemma regarding its fundamental nature and unique contribution as a collection of organizational scientists and practitioners. Although OD practitioners have been thinking, writing, and debating about the underlying nature of the field for decades (Church, Hurley, & Burke, 1992; Friedlander, 1976, Goodstein, 1984; Greiner, 1980; Sanzgiri & Gottlieb, 1992; Weisbord, 1982), the field itself has yet to come to agreement on its basic boundaries or parameters. Moreover, various practitioner surveys conducted in the 1990s (Church, Burke, & Van Eynde, 1994; Fagenson & Burke, 1990; McMahan & Woodman,

1992) have suggested that the field is no closer to finding the answer to these important questions than it was twenty years ago.

It should come as no surprise, then, that one of the most poignant criticisms leveled at OD since its inception is that there are almost as many definitions of the field as there are OD practitioners (Church, Waclawski, & Siegal, 1996; Jamieson, Bach Kallick, & Kur, 1984; Rothwell, Sullivan, & McLean, 1995). The field of OD has been characterized in the literature over the years by such divergent notions as a data-based process driven by survey feedback (Nadler, 1977), a sociotechnical approach focused on job tasks and characteristics (Hackman & Oldham, 1980), an interpersonal process approach to facilitating group dynamics (Schein, 1969), and even a religious movement driven by zealots out to democratize organizations (Harvey, 1974). To put it mildly, there is some disagreement in the field as to what is and is not OD (Church, 2000a).

This lack of a unified definition of or approach to the central nature of OD is due in large part to the diversity of backgrounds of those who engage in OD practice—from forestry, to law, to history, to the social sciences. Because one of the values of the field is inclusivity, relatively little attention has been paid historically to maintaining boundaries around the practice or labeling of OD. A cursory review of some of the professional associations with which OD practitioners affiliate (see Table 1.1), for example, highlights the breadth of membership even among somewhat like-minded groups.

Moreover, it has been argued by some that literally anyone can hang a shingle outside and be a self-proclaimed OD practitioner (Church, Waclawski, & Siegal, 1996). Thus, for some, OD represents anything and everything that might be offered. Moreover, because there are only a handful of OD doctoral programs in the United States, there is a real sense among many in the field (Allen et al., 1993; Church & Burke, 1995; Golembiewski, 1989; Van Eynde & Coruzzi, 1993) that the lack of common education, training, and experience is continuing to damage and erode its overall credibility as a profession.

Clearly, given the fractured state of the field and the nature of the many divergent perceptions regarding OD, there is a need in the literature and with respect to training future practitioners for

Table 1.1. Professional Associations with Major OD Representation.

Professional Organization	Mission and Objectives	Information About Membership
Organization Development Institute	"To promote a better understanding of and disseminate information about Organization Development and to build the field of OD into a highly respected profession."	500 members, 90 of them registered organization development consultants (RODCs) Split between practitioners and academics No requirement for general membership The only organization to institute a credential membership option of RODC with a test of knowledge, prior experience and letters of recommendations.
Organization Development Network	"The Organization Development Network is a values-based community which supports its members in their work in human organization and systems development, and offers leadership and scholarship to the profession."	4,000 members Practitioner majority No formal membership criteria required to join Largest single body of OD practitioners
Society for Industrial and Organizational Psychology	"To promote human welfare through the various applications of psychology to all types of organizations providing goods and services, such as manufacturing concerns, commercial enterprises, labor unions or trade associations, and public agencies."	6,000 members Split between practitioners and academics Specific educational requirements for membership No formal interest groups Approximately 15–25 percent of membership engage in OD-related activities

Table 1.1. Professional Associations with Major OD Representation, Cont'd

Professional Organization	Mission and Objectives	Information About Membership
Academy of Human Resource Development	"To encourage systematic study of human resource development theories, processes, and practices; to disseminate information about HRD, to encourage the application of HRD research findings, and to provide opportunities for social interaction among individuals with scholarly and professional interests in HRD from multiple disciplines and from across the globe."	850 members Academic majority (85 percent versus 15 percent) Emphasis on learning and performance improvement No interest groups but significant proportion of content overlap with OD theory and research
Academy of Management	"The purpose of the Academy is to foster the general advancement of research, learning, teaching and practice in the management field and to encourage the extension and unification of management knowledge."	10,000 members Academic majority (93 percent versus 7 percent) Emphasis on organization behavior and theory Several relevant interest groups including Organization Development and Change (2,000 members) and Managerial Consuling (1,000 members) members
American Society for Training and Development	"To provide leadership to individuals, organizations, and society to achieve work-related competence, performance, and fulfillment; a world-wide leader in workplace learning and performance."	70,000 members Practitioner majority Emphasis on workplace learning and performance No formal membership criteria required to join Several relevant interest groups including Organization Development; HRD Consultancy; Performance and Quality Improvement; Management Development; Learning Organizations

Source: Official association Web pages, documentation, contact with administrative offices and senior leadership, and assorted member survey efforts.

a conceptualization and framework that pulls together the fundamental aspects of OD into a single, unified approach to working with organizations. This chapter presents such an integrative framework for OD. It is intended to encompass the entire spectrum of OD work, from the macro to the micro and the hard data to the soft. Following an overview of some of the differences and similarities among key definitions of the field proffered throughout the past several decades, we explore what we believe are the fundamental guiding principles for OD (including, among other points, the singular importance of interpersonal or human data) and how these are manifested in contemporary practice.

Definitions of OD

Fundamentally, OD is the implementation of a process of planned (as opposed to unplanned) change for the purpose of organizational improvement (as opposed to a focus solely on performance). It is rooted in the social and behavioral sciences and draws its influences from a wide variety of content areas, including social psychology, group dynamics, industrial/organizational (I/O) psychology, participative management theory, organizational behavior, sociology, and even psychotherapy. This diverse background has been cited as both a strength and a weakness of OD. Its strength lies in the breadth and diversity that such openness affords. For the most part, all one needs to do to join a national network of OD professionals is to agree to abide by a set of stated principles and values; no specific tests of skills or knowledge are required. It is unlikely, for example, that a more restrictive or narrowly focused profession could yield practitioners specializing in one-on-one coaching using multisource feedback and large-scale interventions with five hundred or more executives in the same room at the same time. Such openness to new perspectives, approaches, and experiences as being equally representative of OD work, however, is seen by many as a weakness of the field as well. The lack of set boundaries contributes significantly to the perception among potential clients, colleagues, and card-carrying OD practitioners themselves of the field as a scattered and inherently lost profession that lacks a core ideology or set of fundamental assumptions.

Table 1.2 provides an overview of some of the more coherent and comprehensive definitions of the field offered over the past few decade. Although we are somewhat reticent to offer yet another definition, in the interest of integration and advancing the field forward, we believe the best and most current definition of OD is as follows:

Table 1.2. Some Definitions of OD.

Source	Definition
Burke (1982)	"Planned process of change in an organization's culture through the utilization of behavioral science technologies, research, and theory" (p. 10)
French & Bell (1978)	"A long-range effort to improve an organization's problem solving and renewal processes, particularly through a more effective and collaborative management of an organization culture . . . with the assistance of a change agent, or catalyst, and the use of the theory and technology of applied behavioral science, including action research" (p. 14)
Margulies & Raia (1972)	"A value-based process of self-assessment and planned change, involving specific strategies and technology, aimed at improving the overall effectiveness of an organizational system" (p. 24)
Porras & Robertson (1992)	"Planned, behavioral science-based interventions in work settings for the purpose of improving organizational functioning and individual development" (p. 721)
Jamieson, Bach Kallick, & Kur (1984)	"Long-term, planned changes in the culture, technology, and management of a total organization or at least a significant part of the total organization" (p. 4)
Warrick (1984)	"Planned, long-range systems and primarily behavioral science strategy for understanding, developing, and changing organizations to improve their present and future effectiveness and health" (p. 916)

Organization development is a planned process of promoting positive humanistically oriented large-system change and improvement in organizations through the use of social science theory, action research, and behaviorally based data collection and feedback techniques.

Regardless of the definition that one subscribes to, however, it should be apparent when reviewing these definitions that although they differ on several important dimensions—for example, some focus on the importance of technology in the change process, whereas others explicitly mention top management support, and still others reference values explicitly—they share common components as well. Given the nature of these definitions and our collective consulting experience in and exposure to others in the field over the past decade, it is our view that OD should be conceptualized as representing three essential components.

First and perhaps foremost, OD is fundamentally a data-driven process; diagnosis and intervention are based on some form of behaviorally relevant data (such as observations, assessments, and surveys) collected through a process known as *action research.* Second, the OD model represents a *total systems approach* to organizational change in which this change is a formal and planned response to targeted organization-wide issues, problems, and challenges. Finally, although this component is controversial and by no means universally accepted as yet (Church, Burke, & Van Eynde, 1994), we strongly believe that values represent a third key component to the field. OD is (or should be) a *normative and humanistic values-based approach* to organizational improvement. In short, from our perspective, OD work should be focused on and conducted for the good of the individual, as well as the good of the organization. Although balancing issues of effectiveness and profitability are certainly important for economic success and survival, we would argue that an OD approach does not prioritize these concerns over the human perspective. This emphasis represents our firm belief, as well as of most of the other practitioners writing in this book, and is without a doubt one of the key differentiators of the field of OD from other types of organizational consultants in the field today (Church, Waclawski, & Siegal, 1996; Margulies & Raia, 1990).

Next, we describe each these basic conceptual areas that we feel represent and characterize the field as a whole. Although these points have been made elsewhere in the context of using multisource feedback for organization development (Church, Waclawski, & Burke, 2001), because they apply to the entire field, it is important to describe them in this broader context as well.

OD as a Data-Driven Process Using Action Research

One of the most basic notions behind OD is that change and improvement are conducted through a data-based process known as action research. Kurt Lewin, who first conceptualized action research (1946) and has often been credited as saying that "there can be no action without research and no research without action," was truly one of the first scientist-practitioners in the social sciences and a major contributor to much of the thinking underlying OD theory and practice (Burke, 1982; French & Bell, 1990).

In OD work, action research entails systematically gathering data of whatever form, quantitative or qualitative, on the nature of a particular problem or situation, analyzing the data to find central themes and patterns, feeding back a summary and analysis of the data in some participative form, and then taking action based on what the analysis of the data and resulting diagnosis of the situation suggest (Church, Waclawski, & Burke, 2001). Given this framework, it is easy to see how both the classic and more contemporary OD tools and techniques described in this book meet the criterion of being data-driven OD, because they collect and apply information for various problem-solving and improvement purposes. Organization surveys, multisource feedback, focus groups and interviews, personality assessments, process observations and consultation, action learning, appreciative inquiry, and large-scale interventions all fall squarely within this framework. They follow the progression of steps outlined in the basic action research approach from data collection, through diagnosis, to taking action for improvement.

The process by which data are used to drive change is a relatively simple one. Lewin, a social psychologist who specialized in studying group dynamics, asserted that individual and organizational transformation is best described as a three-stage process (see Figure 1.1).

Figure 1.1. Classic Change Model.

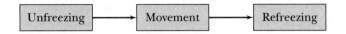

In the first stage, *unfreezing,* the goal is to create motivation or a readiness for change (Church, Waclawski, & Burke, 2001). In most cases in OD practice, this translates to surfacing dissatisfaction with the current state and identifying a better or more desirable alternative, which is commonly referred to in OD terms as the *ideal* or *desired future state* (see Beckhard & Harris, 1987). An analogy from everyday life is dieting. Most people go on a diet because they are unhappy with their weight. It is this dissatisfaction with the current situation, coupled with a vision of a better future state of weighing less and therefore being healthier and looking better, that motivates them to change their eating behavior.

The second stage in Lewin's model, *movement,* consists of making changes and engaging in new behaviors to help make the desired future state a reality. In short, once the need for change has been realized, steps toward achieving a new and better state must be taken. In the dieting example, this would represent the point at which the dieter makes a change in behavior—a reduction in caloric intake and an increase in exercise levels. In OD, the movement stage typically translates into focusing one's change efforts at three different levels: individual, group, and organizational.

The third stage, *refreezing,* requires establishing a system or process that will solidify (or refreeze) the new desired state. In the dieting example, this would mean making what people call a permanent lifestyle change, such that the new eating and exercise regimen becomes a permanent and normal part of everyday life. In OD, an example of the refreezing stage would be instilling a new reward and recognition program as a result of an organizational culture survey to reinforce a new and desired set of leadership behaviors. In reality, however, given the rapid pace of change experienced by most organizations today, refreezing occurs all too infrequently (Church, 2000b) if at all, and even when it does, it is not likely to last for very long before some other chaotic event affects the organization.

OD as a Total Systems Approach to Change

OD is fundamentally grounded in a social systems approach (Katz & Kahn, 1978). From this perspective, the organization is conceptualized as a system or series of interdependent subsystems and individual components, such as people, technology, or processes, that operate as a collective entity in response to changes in and pressures from the external environment, such as competitors, customers, or government regulations.

An example from biology is that of a single cell existing within a larger organism. In this context, the organization is the cell, and the larger organism is the global business environment. The cell, although self-contained with its own series of inputs and outputs, depends on the larger organism to survive. The larger organism, in turn, is dependent on the functioning of the unique cells comprising it because these cells collectively transform and produce materials that are vital to the organism's existence. As part of its function, the cell inputs certain materials from the larger organism, transforms them into other states, and then exports them back into the organism for use by other cells. Thus, the individual cell and the larger organism form a symbiotic relationship; each is dependent on the other for survival and growth.

By applying systems theory, an organization is seen as operating in much the same way. It takes in inputs from the outside world, such as raw materials, intellectual capital, human resources, or money for goods and service; acts on them to transform them into new products or services; and then exports them back into the business environment for distribution and dispersal (see Figure 1.2).

From this perspective, large-scale OD and change efforts are seen as occurring within an organizational system and are generally initiated in response to changes in the business or external environment in which the organization operates (Burke &

Figure 1.2. Systems Approach Model.

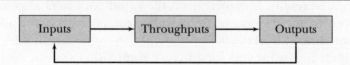

Litwin, 1992). Given this framework, it is apparent that an OD model is somewhat different from other consulting approaches because most OD interventions used are aimed at changing the entire system, as opposed to a specific portion or segment of the organization.

OD as a Normative Process

The third concept, and in many ways the truly unique element, driving OD theory and practice is the notion that OD is or at least should be a values-driven, humanistically oriented, normative process for change. OD is about helping people have better lives at work. Taken by some as an ethical mandate against the perceived evils of organizations, some OD practitioners focus their efforts on initiatives aimed at improving the state of human dignity, democracy, honesty, integrity, and empowerment in organizations (Burke, 1982; Friedlander, 1976; Margulies & Raia, 1990). Although these "OD missionaries," as they have been called (Harvey, 1974), are probably not the norm, they do represent a truly unique aspect to change management. Moreover, when certain executives and organizations are heralded for their innovative people-oriented practices or cultures (Roddick, 1994), the OD field is quick to focus on such triumphs of the human spirit at work.

Unfortunately, one of the results of this emphasis on instilling meaning and dignity in the workplace (particularly when taken out of context) has been the perception of OD as being too soft or "touchy-feely" in focus (Church & Burke, 1995). Interestingly enough, such perceptions both attract certain types of practitioners and clients while putting off others. Although the extent to which these values are truly enacted in practice remains a major question for the field, particularly given the financial realities of a consulting marketplace where expertise has been devalued and few can afford to stand for professional ideals or integrity (Church & Waclawski, 1998), it is nonetheless important to recognize, appreciate, and even reinforce such values. Values drive a profession and make it unique (Weisbord, 1982). Clearly, given the moral corruption that exists in some of today's political, social, and organizational systems, it is heartening to know that some group of professionals somewhere stands for a higher purpose.

Although the question regarding which values do or should drive the field of OD has been a topic of debate for decades (Burke, 1982; Friedlander, 1976; Gellermann, Frankel, & Ladenson, 1990; Goodstein, 1984; Greiner, 1980; Hurley, Church, Burke, & Van Eynde, 1992; Margulies & Raia, 1990), we believe strongly that OD does indeed represent a normative approach to organizational change. Just as the fields of I/O psychology and human resource development (HRD) are grounded in improving the conditions of people's lives and promoting human welfare and learning in organizations, so too is the field of OD. Although we know from research (Church, Burke, & Van Eynde, 1994) that not all OD practitioners act according to such ideals, there is a strong bias, and we believe an ethical imperative, in OD work toward promoting human development and positive growth (Waclawski, Church, & Burke, 1995). In sum, OD is driven by a value-based, systemic mind-set using action research methods for organizational improvement. Although these three elements represent the basic theoretical approach taken to OD work, they do not specifically reflect the role of data in the diagnosis and intervention process itself.

The Role of Data in the Consulting Process

One of the best-known approaches to OD practice is the seven-phase consulting model (Kolb & Frohman, 1970; Nadler, 1977). Based in Lewin's action research framework, this model consists of seven distinct phases that apply to every change initiative or engagement: *entry, contracting, data collection, data analysis, data feedback, intervention, and evaluation* (see Table 1.3).

In general, the seven-phase model has a wide range of applications in a variety of consulting situations and is especially important for OD practitioners for three reasons: (1) it reinforces the centrality of data in the process of organization development and change, (2) shows how and when data should be used to inform OD practice, and (3) is based on a systems approach to organizations.

Phase 1, entry, represents the first meeting between the OD practitioner and client. This is often the practitioner's first exposure to the current client system (Katz & Kahn, 1978) and is critical in terms of building what we might call a facilitative (as opposed

Table 1.3. Seven-Phase Consulting Model.

Phase 1. Entry: Initial meeting between client and consultant. .

The client and consultant meet to explore issues and the possibility of an OD effort. The client assesses if the consultant is trustworthy, experienced, and competent. The consultant assesses if the client is ready for change and has the resources and power to support change.

Phase 2. Contracting: Reach agreement on what each party will do.

This includes determining mutual expectations, expected time frame, schedule of activities, cost of activities, and ground rules for proceeding.

Phase 3. Data collection: Gather information about the organization.

Interviews, questionnaires, company documents and performance records, focus groups, and other methods are used.

Phase 4. Data analysis: Summarize information and draw conclusions.

From the data, the client and consultant determine next steps once the diagnosis is understood and accepted.

Phase 5. Data feedback: Present summary and conclusions to client.

The consultant presents the summary and preliminary interpretation, followed by a general discussion to clarify information. Next, the consultant and client arrive at a final diagnosis that accurately describes the organization. Together they generate plans for responding to the issues.

Phase 6. Intervention: Take action.

The selected interventions should be a direct reflection and response to the diagnosis.

Phase 7. Evaluation: Determine success or failure.

Change efforts are evaluated to see if the desired change has occurred.

---

to an expert) relationship. Typically, during this initial meeting, both the client and the OD consultant are assessing one another to determine whether they will be able to collaborate on the pending change initiative. This process includes the potential client's attempts to determine the competency and experience levels of the OD practitioner, as well as the practitioner's initial assessment of the presenting problem (that is, the symptom) and its underlying causes (the real problem), which will need to be examined through some form of data collection. As the potential client looks for signs of rapport with the practitioner, the practitioner looks for signs of the potential client's true level of motivation for and commitment to the potential change effort. The fact is that if a client has neither the intention nor the resources to implement a significant change effort, there is little reason from an OD perspective to pursue the situation in this context. In short, the quality of the interaction here determines whether the OD effort will occur at all. If positive relations are not established, the relationship and thus the change effort will go no further or stall in midprocess.

Contracting, phase 2, consists of setting the expectations, roles, and anticipated outcomes for the change effort (Block, 1981; Burke, 1994). From an OD perspective, the preferred mode here is to rely on open and honest communication rather than on a more formalized legal contracting process, though the latter is often requested in today's litigious and increasingly vendor-driven (Church & Waclawski, 1998) business environment. For example, if a client is interested in undertaking a series of one-on-one interviews to help diagnose the functioning of the senior leadership team of the organization, he or she may call in an external or internal OD practitioner to do this work. During entry and contracting, the consultant and client will not only discuss the work to be done and the practitioner's qualifications for doing this work, but they will also explore interpersonal issues (such as whether the two can communicate and therefore work with one another) and what can and cannot be realistically accomplished as a result of the diagnostic interviews and feedback process.

Once entry and contracting have been successfully completed, the internal or external OD consultant will need to collect data about the organization in order to gain a better understanding of the problems to be solved or the underlying issues at hand. To this end, phases 3 through 5 of the consulting model concern the collection, analysis, and feedback of data. These data can be either quantitative (multisource feedback, survey instruments, personality assessments, or performance measures) or qualitative (observations, interviews and focus groups, or process measures) in nature, or some combination of both. The consultant at this point would begin collecting and analyzing the major themes in interview data (see Chapter Five for more on this technique). By gathering perceptual, attitudinal, and perhaps behaviorally based critical incident data through one-on-one discussions, the practitioner is positioning himself or herself to develop a detailed understanding about the nature of the team's functioning. Moreover, by directing the discussions toward a focus on the nature of the team dynamics now, where members want these to be, and what barriers, real or perceived, might exist, the consultant is not only building awareness of the challenges but also simultaneously creating energy for change on the part of team members. This energy, caused by attending to the perceptual gap between the existing and future states, is one of the basic means for initiating behavior change in the Lewinian approach.

Once data have been collected and analyzed, phase 6 can begin: specific interventions based on the diagnostic summary performed using the interview results can be interactively discussed and selected for subsequent action. The important point to remember here is that regardless of which interventions are chosen, their determination should be based on an interpretation of the issues inherent in the data itself (and not simply because it is the trendiest, most expensive, or most flashy OD, I/O, or HRD technique available), and jointly selected by the consultant and client. This leads to commitment on the part of the client and ultimately contributes to the success of the entire change process.

Finally, an evaluation of the success of the OD effort should always be undertaken. Often this requires collecting additional data regarding the impact of the intervention in the light of the deliverables that were agreed on in the contracting phase, as well as brainstorming about process improvements for future OD efforts (see Chapter Fourteen for more on this subject). Clearly this is easier said than done. One of the truly unfortunate situations in many OD efforts over the past thirty years, and one that has damaged the reputation of the field somewhat as well, has been the lack of significant attention to evaluating the success or failure of an OD process. As many researchers and OD scholars have noted (Golembiewski & Sun, 1990; Porras & Robertson, 1992; Woodman & Wayne, 1985), there is a real need in the field for the consistent application of evaluation strategies to the entire consulting cycle. Although some firms believe in the value-driven approach enough to forgo this element, it is not a helpful or a recommended approach to practice.

Overall, the internal and external practice of OD work is a truly data-driven approach to helping organizations identify specific problems and issues and plan for improvement. The next point to consider is the role and function of OD within organizations as this relates to the areas in which practitioners (and particularly internal practitioners) can have and do have an impact within the larger system.

The OD Function in Organizations

Although much of the trade literature and case studies regarding the practice of OD focus on the skills, challenges, and role of external consultants (Burke, 1994; Block, 1981)—and indeed for many this lifestyle represents the perceptually more glamorous choice (Van Eynde, Church, & Burke, 1994)—the fact is that at least half of all practitioners in the OD, HRD, and even I/O psychology arenas work internally in corporations, universities, and nonprofit organizations. Unfortunately, this role and consequently the contribution of this half is underemphasized, underrepresented, and in some cases underappreciated in the field (Church, 2000b; McMahan & Woodman, 1992). Although a detailed discussion of these issues is beyond the scope of this chapter, it is important to highlight a few central themes regarding the nature of internal practice and the OD function itself that have emerged from research and experience.

Despite some popular claims that organizational change occurs from the bottom up (Schaffer & Thompson, 1992), research with the Fortune 500 Industrials and the Fortune 100 fastest-growing firms has shown that the primary client in most internal OD efforts is senior management (Church & McMahan, 1996;

McMahan & Woodman, 1992). Perhaps this is not surprising given that senior leadership support is almost always cited as a necessity for any effective intervention or systemic initiative. Nevertheless, this reinforces the notion that internal OD practitioners must be skilled at working within the political and cultural landscape of the organization if they are to effect change from within (Church, 2000b).

Despite an apparent resurgent interest in the field, the state of the OD function in the mid-1990s was less than optimal. Survey results noted that only 34 percent and 26 percent of the Fortune fastest-growing firms and industrials, respectively, had "well-established" functions, with the rest of the responses scatted among such categories as struggling (respectively, 20 percent and 18 percent), worried (7 percent and 5 percent), or even nonexistent (9 percent and 3 percent). Furthermore, in some organizations, the term *OD* has such negative connotations (as being ineffective or too "touchy feely") that alternative terms such as *organizational effectiveness* have been created (Church & McMahan, 1996; Golembiewski, 1989). In other organizations, this manifests itself as more of an issue of the location of OD within other groups, such as HRD, personnel research, or even the occasional organizational learning function. At Microsoft, for example, some of the more strategic-level OD efforts are conducted through the executive and management development function (Church, Waclawski, McHenry, & McKenna, 1998). Although it is likely given the improvement in the global economy in the past few years that internal OD functions have started to become more prominent once again (and particularly in response to the changing nature of work and emerging trends in training and retention issues among younger workers), it remains an unfortunate reality that many organizations either place little emphasis on or do not have internal OD function at their disposal at all.

Despite these issues and concerns, it is important to recognize that most of the legwork of organizational change and improvement is driven by these internal practitioners. As a field, we need to begin to recognize these individuals more (and, conversely, not chastise them for having "sold out" to big business). This means more partnerships (rather than circumnavigation) and more shared learnings and skills across the internal-external boundary. From the internal side, this also means focusing more on collaborating with externals as opposed to focusing on issues of turf, and less application of the vendor mind-set to the way external work is contracted and used (Church & Waclawski, 1998) before the unique contribution of the entire field has been eroded or supplanted by other consulting models. In short, we need to leverage our strengths as a field of internal and external practitioners to help promote OD and improve the state of organizations.

A New Framework for OD

Given the variety of issues and complexities regarding the field, there is a need to provide a single source, as well as an overarching framework or model, regarding the contemporary practice of OD. The chapters in this book provide a comprehensive review of the state of the art of OD practice and applications. The chapters in Part One provide a larger framework that bridges the gap between the variety of the specific methods and interventions and the sources of data available on how these drive organizational change. Figure 1.3 provides just such a framework.

Figure 1.3. Framework for a Data-Driven OD.

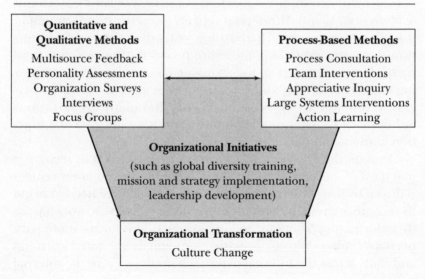

Quantitative and Qualitative Methods

Multisource Feedback
Personality Assessments
Organization Surveys
Interviews
Focus Groups

Process-Based Methods

Process Consultation
Team Interventions
Appreciative Inquiry
Large Systems Interventions
Action Learning

Organizational Initiatives

(such as global diversity training, mission and strategy implementation, leadership development)

Organizational Transformation

Culture Change

Although the framework is relatively self-explanatory, several points should be made about it. First, data represent the central set of inputs (in systems terms) into the overall process. *Data* here refers to quantitative, qualitative, or process-based inputs that reflect the different interventions and methodologies detailed in this book (see Chapters Two through Five and Seven through Ten). Because many practitioners rely on more than one form of data, and in many instances a diagnosis using one method might lead to further examination or an intervention based on another, an arrow indicates the reciprocal nature of their relationship. The outcomes of these data-driven methodologies drive the large organizational initiatives, which represent the movement stage in the change process. These initiatives include broad issues such as leadership development, global diversity training, and mission and strategy implementation. Moreover, some of the complexities involved in working with these initiatives as an OD practitioner include the challenges of using information technology effectively, developing an awareness of diverse cultures and practices in doing OD around the world, and the ethics and values OD practitioners need to embody (see Chapters Twelve, Thirteen, and Fifteen).

These interventions, when pursued in a focused and highly integrated manner, will ultimately help transform the organization and result in improvement and change. In addition, the role of evaluation and linkage research (see Chapters Six and Fourteen) is crucial for establishing the impact and credibility of OD as a field. Although we are not advocating an outcomes-only approach here, given the societal importance placed on metrics and numbers—our vital signs, as some have argued (Hronec, 1993)—it is time for the field to accept fully its roots in a data-driven approach and understand the value inherent in measuring what we do and how we do it.

Conclusion

How is the OD perspective truly different from other approaches to using data to inform organizational effectiveness and decision-making processes? The answer lies in the way the data are used and the level of formality that is attributed to them.

Historically, OD practitioners have used data as a means for opening a dialogue with their client (or client system) about difficult individual, team, and organizational issues. While other groups of practitioners have recently started to recognize the importance of ensuring that action (such as behavior change or organizational change) occurs as a result of the data feedback provided, OD has been focused on the action part all along. Despite this emphasis, the solitary nature of many OD practitioners, the inconsistencies in formal academic and experiential training across the majority of practitioners (surveys indicate that only a third of those practicing have some doctoral training and another third have a master's degree), and the lack of high-quality published OD research detailing methods, processes, and outcomes (particularly when compared to other disciplines such as I/O psychology, social psychology, and HRD) have resulted in an approach to working with data that is considerably different from that of formally trained scientist-practitioner professionals.

In our experience, most OD practitioners rely on a more informal approach to collecting and working with data. This often translates to less specific attention to such empirical issues as item construction, instrument layout and design, establishing criterion validity, and performing confirmatory factor analyses. It is not that these issues are unimportant to practitioners (though clearly some OD practitioners would not know what these terms even mean), but rather that in the mind of the OD practitioner, data are used as fodder for the consulting relationship and as a vehicle or means to problem solving and creating change in OD. Data typically are not collected solely or even primarily for the purpose of performance assessment (as is the case in much I/O work). The principal use of data in OD is to inform the consulting process and provide a means for delving deeper into a situation or tracking progress and improvement over time. Generally, the data are not the primary intervention but rather the means by which issues are uncovered, energy is created, and change is initiated.

As practitioners operating in the realms of OD, I/O psychology, and HRD, we strongly advocate a more central role for data in the consulting process. Indeed, the data-driven methods detailed in this book should be included in every OD, I/O, or HRD practitioner's tool kit.

Our numbers-driven world makes facility with these data and data-based decision making a necessity. In our experience, organizations are far less receptive to non-data-based approaches to OD today than they were ten years ago. Proven methods that lead to financial as well as humanistic gains are now a requirement. The days when a consultant's charisma and intuition were enough to get by on are gone. Clients today are more knowledgeable, sophisticated, experienced, and demanding than ever before. Thus, contemporary OD practitioners must be well versed in a wide variety of areas, possess a myriad of skills, and embrace the use of data in their work. We believe that practitioners who do not embrace this approach do so at their own peril.

References

Allen, K., Crossman, D., Lane, L., Power, G., & Svendsen, D. S. (1993). The future of OD: Conversations with "living legends." *OD Practitioner, 25*(1), 28–32.

Beckhard, R., & Harris, R. T. (1987). *Organizational transitions: Managing complex change* (2nd ed.). Reading, MA: Addison-Wesley.

Block, P. (1981). *Flawless consulting: A guide to getting your expertise used.* San Francisco: Jossey-Bass/Pfeiffer.

Burke, W. W. (1982). *Organization development: Principles and practices.* Glenview, IL: Scott, Foresman.

Burke, W. W. (1994). *Organization development: A process of learning and changing* (2nd ed.). Reading, MA: Addison-Wesley.

Burke, W. W., & Litwin, G. H. (1992). A causal model of organizational performance and change. *Journal of Management, 18,* 523–545.

Church, A. H. (2000a, April 13). *The future of OD: Relevant or not?* Presentation to the Best Practices in Leading Change Conference, Bowling Green State University, Bowling Green, Ohio.

Church, A. H. (2000b, Winter). Managing change from the inside out. *Performance in Practice,* pp. 13–14.

Church, A. H., & Burke, W. W. (1995). Practitioner attitudes about the field of organization development. In W. A. Pasmore & R. W. Woodman (Eds.), *Research in organizational change and development* (Vol. 8, pp. 1–46). Greenwich, CT: JAI Press.

Church, A. H., Burke, W. W., & Van Eynde, D. F. (1994). Values, motives, and interventions of organization development practitioners. *Group and Organization Management, 19,* 5–50.

Church, A. H., Hurley, R. F., & Burke, W. W. (1992). Evolution or revolution in the values of organization development? Commentary on the state of the field. *Journal of Organizational Change Management,* 5(4), 6–23.

Church, A. H., & McMahan, G. C. (1996). The practice of organization and human resource development in America's fastest growing firms. *Leadership and Organization Development Journal, 17*(2), 17–33.

Church, A. H., & Waclawski, J. (1998). The vendor mind-set: The devolution from organizational consultant to street peddler. *Consulting Psychology Journal: Practice and Research, 5*(2), 87–100.

Church, A. H., Waclawski, J., & Burke, W. W. (2001). Multisource feedback for organization development and change. In D. W. Bracken, C. W. Timmreck, & A. H. Church (Eds.), *The handbook of multisource feedback: The comprehensive resource for designing and implementing MSF processes* (pp. 301–317). San Francisco: Jossey-Bass.

Church, A. H., Waclawski, J., McHenry, J., & McKenna, D. (1998). Organization development in high-performing companies: An in-depth look at the role of OD in Microsoft. *Organization Development Journal, 16*(3), 51–64.

Church, A. H., Waclawski, J., & Siegal, W. (1996). Will the real OD practitioner please stand up? A call for change in the field. *Organization Development Journal, 14*(2), 5–14.

Fagenson, E. A., & Burke, W. W. (1990). The activities of organization development practitioners at the turn of the decade of the 1990s: A study of their predictions. *Group and Organization Studies, 15,* 366–380.

French, W. L., & Bell, C. H., Jr. (1978). *Organization development: Behavioral science interventions for organization improvement* (2nd ed.). Upper Saddle River, NJ: Prentice Hall.

French, W. L., & Bell, C. H., Jr. (1990). *Organization development: Behavioral science interventions for organization improvement* (4th ed.). Upper Saddle River, NJ: Prentice Hall.

Friedlander, F. (1976). OD reaches adolescence: An exploration of its underlying values. *Journal of Applied Behavioral Science, 12,* 7–21.

Gellermann, W., Frankel, M. S., & Ladenson, R. F. (1990). *Values and ethics in organization and human systems development: Responding to dilemmas in professional life.* San Francisco: Jossey-Bass.

Golembiewski, R. T. (1989). *Organization development: Ideas and issues.* New Brunswick, NJ: Transaction.

Golembiewski, R. T., & Sun, B. C. (1990). Positive findings bias in QWL studies: Rigor and outcomes in a large sample. *Journal of Management, 16,* 665–674.

Greiner, L. (1980). OD values and the "bottom line." In W. W. Burke & L. D. Goodstein (Eds.), *Trends and issues in organization development* (pp. 319–332). San Diego, CA: University Associates.

Hackman, J. R., & Oldhan, G. R. (1980). *Work redesign.* Reading, MA: Addison-Wesley.

Harvey, J. B. (1974). Organization development as a religious movement. *Training and Development Journal, 28,* 24–27.

Hurley, R. F., Church, A. H., Burke, W. W., & Van Eynde, D. F. (1992). Tension, change, and values in OD. *OD Practitioner, 24*(1), 1–5.

Jamieson, D. W., Bach Kallick, D., & Kur, C. E. (1984). Organization development. In L. Nadler (Ed.), *The handbook of human resource development* (pp. 29.1–29.16). New York: Wiley.

Katz, D., & Kahn, R. L. (1978). *The social psychology of organizations* (2nd ed.) New York: Wiley.

Kolb, D., & Frohman, A. (1970). An organization development approach to consulting. *Sloan Management Review, 12*(1), 51–65.

Lewin, K. (1946). Action research and minority problems. *Journal of Social Issues, 2,* 34–46.

Margulies, N., & Raia, A. (1972). *Organization development: Values, process, and technology.* New York: McGraw-Hill.

Margulies, N., & Raia, A. (1990). The significance of core values on the theory and practice of organization development. In F. Massarik (Ed.), *Advances in organization development* (Vol. 1, pp. 27–41). Norwood, NJ: Ablex.

McMahan, G. C., & Woodman, R. W. (1992). The current practice of organization development within the firm: A survey of large industrial corporations. *Group and Organization Management, 17,* 117–134.

Nadler, D. A. (1977). *Feedback and organization development: Using data-based methods.* Reading, MA: Addison-Wesley.

Porras, J. I., & Robertson, P. J. (1992). Organizational development: Theory, practice, and research. In M. D. Dunnette & L. M. Hough (Eds.), *Handbook of industrial and organizational psychology* (2nd ed., Vol. 3, pp. 719–822). Palo Alto, CA: Consulting Psychologists Press.

Roddick, A. (1994). *Body and soul: Profits with principles—the amazing success story of Anita Roddick.* New York: Crown.

Rothwell, W. J., Sullivan, R., & McLean, G. N. (Eds.). (1995). *Practicing organization development: A guide for consultants.* San Francisco: Jossey-Bass.

Schaffer, R. H., & Thompson, H. A. (1992). Successful change programs begin with results. *Harvard Business Review, 70*(1), 80–89.

Schein, E. H. (1969). *Process consultation.* Reading, MA: Addison-Wesley.

Van Eynde, D. F., & Coruzzi, C. (1993). ODN future search: A word from our senior practitioners. *OD Practitioner, 25*(1), 8–16.

Warrick, D. D. (1984). Organization development. In W. R. Tracey (Ed.), *Human resources management and development handbook* (pp. 915–925). New York: American Management Association.

Weisbord, M. R. (1982). The cat in the hat breaks through: Reflections on OD's past, present, and future. In D. D. Warrick (Ed.), *Contemporary organization development: Current thinking and applications* (pp. 2–11). Glenview, IL: Scott, Foresman.

Woodman, R. W., & Wayne, S. J. (1985). An investigation of positive findings bias in evaluation of organization development interventions. *Academy of Management Journal, 28,* 889–913.

CHAPTER 2

Multisource Feedback for Organization Development and Change

Allan H. Church
Alan G. Walker
Joel Brockner

The field of organization development (OD) has often been described by both its members and critics as comprising a body of interventions and models with no connective tissue—that is, no overarching theory, framework, or set of guiding principles. This could not be further from the truth. In fact, at its core, the practice of doing OD is driven by three fundamental dimensions: (1) action research, that is, collecting, analyzing, and using information to create energy for change; (2) understanding the organization from a systemic perspective and therefore in relation to its context; and (3) a normative values-based framework in which individual development and growth, as well as organizational improvement and health, are of paramount concern. Taken as a whole, these three elements represent the fundamental tenets of OD, and inherent in all of them is the role of data.

Collecting behaviorally based data about how individuals, groups or teams, or an entire management population act on a day-to-day basis is central to understanding, diagnosing, energizing (through feedback), and ultimately improving that organizational system. Clearly, without knowing how people behave in an organization, it is difficult, if not impossible, to diagnose a problem and target a potential solution correctly. Data in some form represent a central element of any significant change effort. Ideally, data should feed both the diagnostic, or front-end, process and the evaluative, or back-end, component. Thus, it should come as no surprise that certain data-driven methodologies, such as multisource feedback (MSF) and organizational surveys, represent key techniques for driving organization development and change efforts and should be included in the tool kit of every OD, and every industrial/organizational (I/O) and human resource development (HRD), practitioner.

MSF is one of the potentially most powerful methodologies, and yet it is least associated with OD work in many people's minds. It is rarely cited as a core methodology in contemporary OD textbooks (Cummings & Worley, 1997; French & Bell, 1990) in spite of the fact that it is a central component to many large-scale organizational change efforts (Church, Waclawski, & Burke, 2001; Waldman, Atwater, & Antonioni, 1998). Moreover, the contemporary practice of MSF is based on a long-standing OD tradition of using data-driven methods for change (Nadler, 1977).

The Basics of Multisource Feedback for OD

Generally, MSF is the process of (1) collecting information (typically behaviorally based ratings or descriptive written comments of some sort, and often collected confidentially) on a focal individual manager, leader, or executive from multiple sources (often including, but not limited to, direct reports, peers, team members, supervisors, mentors, clients, customers, and suppliers); (2) synthesizing that information in a summary or report; (3) providing feedback to the focal individual (whether formal or informal, programmatic or one-on-one, facilitated or without support using a "desk-drop") regarding his or her strengths and areas for improvement; and (4) using that information to drive behavior change.

Also known as *multirater feedback, multisource assessment, 360-degree feedback,* and *full-circle feedback,* MSF enjoyed enormous popularity during the 1990s as the intervention of choice for many organizations and consulting firms (Bracken, 1994; Church, 1995; O'Reilly, 1994; Tornow, 1993). In fact, because of its popularity, some practitioners have started asking tough questions about overly zealous adoption of MSF (Church & Waclawski, 1998; Waldman, Atwater, &Antonioni, 1998) and the extent to which it lives up to its promises (Church & Bracken, 1997; Kluger & DeNisi 1996). Although a complete treatment of the complexities inherent in implementing an MSF process is beyond the scope of this chapter (see Bracken, Timmreck, & Church, 2001), given its widespread application in today's business environment, it is important to understand a few central points about MSF as used in an OD and change context versus other types of applications, such as MSF for performance appraisal and personnel decision making.

First and foremost, the use of MSF for OD efforts depends almost entirely on the social-psychological notion that providing individuals with highly personal, meaningful, and behaviorally specific feedback will lead to increased levels of self-awareness with respect to their own actions and the consequences of those actions on others, and a felt need for behavior change and improvement (Church, 1994; Church & Bracken, 1997; Church & Waclawski, 1998; London & Smither, 1995; Tornow, 1993). Figure 2.1 provides a conceptual overview of how MSF ratings are used to promote understanding and change.

Although using MSF as a process for enhancing self-awareness has received attention in the research literature only in the past ten years (Atwater & Yammarino, 1992; Church, 1997; Furnham & Stringfield, 1994; Van Velsor, Taylor, & Leslie, 1993), and hence is part of the reason that some practitioners do not associate MSF with OD, it is in fact a fundamental method of OD work that dates back to the origins of the field in the 1960s (Church et al., 2001; Hedge, Borman, & Birkeland, 2001; Nadler, 1977). Moreover, recent research (Walker & Smither, 1999) has provided evidence that given the right delivery mechanism, feedback does lead to behavior change and improvement.

The second point about MSF for OD is centered on the concept of individual development (as opposed to assessment or appraisal). Given the humanistic values framework of the field of OD (Burke, 1987; Church, Burke, & Van Eynde, 1994; Gellerman, Frankel, & Ladenson, 1990; Gottlieb, 1998), the vast majority of MSF applications under the OD rubric are likely to be purely developmental versus personnel decision making in intent (for more

Figure 2.1. The Multisource Process for Behavioral Change.

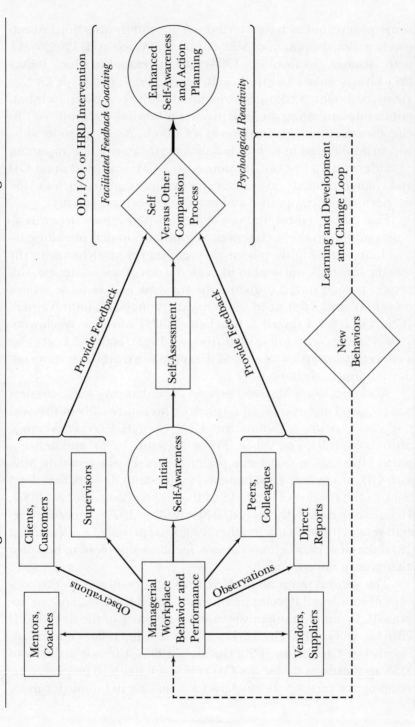

Source: Adapted from Church (1994) and Church and Waclawski (1998).

on this issue, see Dalessio, 1998; London, 2001). Rarely would an OD practitioner have an interest in collecting individual feedback for appraisal or performance management purposes. Instead, the OD approach to MSF is focused on maximizing the developmental nature of the measure used. This translates to a preference for using specific and actionable behaviorally based instrumentation for the feedback process; ensuring that meaningful and concrete linkages exist between the measure itself and the core competencies, leadership principles, fundamental values, or strategic objectives of the organization as a whole; and using a facilitative coaching process to ensure that individuals understand and ultimately make use of the MSF results. Thus, by implication, most MSF processes used for large-scale change initiatives are likely to use highly customized rather than standardized measures. An off-the-shelf product is far less likely (though not impossible) to fit this level of systemic integration, even if the feedback effort is aimed only at improving a single work group or management team. Given the systemic nature of OD, any related MSF effort should reflect this same integrated and developmental mind-set.

Finally, MSF for OD fundamentally represents a systemic process. Although it may seem counterintuitive to some practitioners to equate feedback on individual behavior with large-scale, systemwide organizational improvement, such as the culture or management practices of a global firm of 150,000 employees, it is important to remember that change occurs one step (and one leader or manager) at a time (Waclawski, 1996). Even if entire functions or divisions are sold or downsized, each manager remaining with the organization must learn to adapt and change his or her behavior in the evolving social system. Thus, although MSF is at its core an individual assessment and development process, its purpose and direction as an OD intervention truly represent the bigger picture. The central question for an MSF intervention then becomes, "At which level of impact am I operating?"

Levels of MSF for OD and Change

MSF can drive OD and improvement efforts through three central processes, each operating at different levels of the organization.

The Systemic Level

Those who have worked with or in organizations for any length of time probably agree with the age-old adage that what gets measured gets done. In other words, by simply measuring an outcome or performance indicator, organizations are focusing their attention and energy on whatever it is that is being measured. Realizing that resources are finite, employees inherently understand that outcomes that lie at or near the pinnacle of organizational importance are the ones that are formally measured and tracked. Thus, when organizations officially measure some element of work, they are sending a clear message about what is important to individual and organizational survival and success. By applying significant organizational resources of time, money, and people to implement an MSF process, such an effort can send a powerful message to those individuals involved in the process, as well as their direct reports, peers, supervisors, and customers regarding the importance of behavior feedback. This is true whether an MSF process is fully institutionalized, newly implemented following a change in leadership or strategic direction, or an ailing process that is being reinvigorated. At the most basic level, simply having a formal and acknowledged MSF process in place communicates and reinforces the significance of the measurement process itself, as well as the content of the items being measured.

Unfortunately, as with many other organizational initiatives, communication alone is not enough. In order for MSF to be an effective tool for organizational change, three key factors must be present. First, the feedback measures themselves—the behaviors being rated by coworkers—must be based on leadership and management competencies that have been identified as being critical to organizational success and clearly linked to the corporate vision, values, mission, and strategy. Second, the MSF process must be in alignment with other ongoing key human resource processes, such as staffing and selection, training and development, performance management and evaluation, succession planning, and reward systems. Third, the items used in the instrument must be truly actionable—that is, behaviorally based. In short, implementing an MSF process can send a powerful message regarding the desired ideal or future state of the organization, but it is critical that the right message be sent, using the right means.

Building MSF from a Customized Competency Model

MSF instruments should be based on a well-developed competency model that has been customized for each specific organization's context as opposed to an off-the-shelf product. Although there are many fine (valid, reliable, norm-referenced) off-the-shelf MSF instruments on the market that can help individuals assess their personal strengths and areas for improvement, most of these measures are too generic to be useful in a focused OD effort. By design, standardized measures tend to miss the unique cultural and behavioral components—the terminology, values, contexts, and behavioral content areas—that are critical for driving an OD-related systemic shift in the culture or leadership style of an entire organization. They may do a good job of measuring important general managerial dimensions, such as decision-making style, whether communication is open or closed, and whether employees are empowered, but they inevitably lack the cultural and behavioral specificity that is key to an organization-wide development and change effort. (For a detailed discussion of instrument selection, see Van Velsor & Leslie, 2001.)

For example, if keeping associates in a law firm well informed on projects and answering their voice-mails quickly is a significant problem, results from a standard feedback question such as "fosters good communication" will be far less meaningful and relevant than those from customized items such as "shares information and ideas with the full project team" and "responds to associates' phone calls in a timely fashion." The challenge is to develop a set of relevant and meaningful items for use in the MSF process.

Although standard feedback tools certainly have their place in the development arena, when using MSF for OD purposes, it is critical that the content of the measure be fully linked to a larger framework that is relevant, meaningful, and important to people, that is, the mission, vision, values, competencies, basic beliefs, principles, or strategic objectives of the organization. Although measuring any competency or behavior sends a powerful message, if the right message is not sent, the cultural change effort will be severely compromised, if not entirely unsuccessful. (For more on competency development, see Green, 1999, or Schippmann, 1999.)

Aligning MSF with Key Human Resource Processes

The second important element in making MSF effective at the systemic level concerns its relationship with other key human resource (HR) processes. If MSF is clearly linked to the ongoing HR systems and cycles, it is far more likely to have a significant impact. If MSF is seen as a stand-alone or one-off effort, it is far less likely to make a lasting difference or be sustainable. In short, it is either an integral part of the larger system or it is not.

Making these linkages can be accomplished more readily when the entire organization is moving or changing in the same direction. For example, if an organization develops a new customized competency model that identifies critical success factors for executives, that same competency model can be used to design or reframe a host of integrated tools and processes such as MSF, selection, promotion, culture surveys, performance management, and training and development. With a consistent framework in place, MSF can serve as one of many spokes connected by a central hub based on the core competency model. This competency hub provides a means for focusing the content of the various HR systems while also reinforcing a more consistent language and set of criteria for informing HR processes. Although the MSF is still being used for developmental purposes (we are not advocating the use of MSF for decision making in this context), its inclusion in the larger HR framework will help managers and employees make the right connections and see the relevancy and interconnectedness of each of the individual HR components.

Such integration also allows MSF data (when summarized) to be used as a competency-based criterion measure at the organizational level to evaluate the effectiveness of various changes, interventions, and initiatives. For example, MSF data could be used to examine the impact of a new competency-based selection system—for example, to see if the initial skill levels are different for those newly hired under the old and revised systems. Similarly, if MSF is used to evaluate the effectiveness of a training and development effort, MSF ratings from program participants can be compared over time with ratings of individuals who did not complete the training.

A related benefit of these types of competency-based summaries is the ability to use them to identify key areas for interventions as well as monitor improvement. Our experience has been that organizations that use aggregated MSF data to drive targeted change initiatives to improve key competencies will show results over time. Moreover, by tracking longitudinal data (assuming the item content does not change), it is also possible to identify potentially dangerous declines in other competency areas due to changes in leadership, systems, or culture that may have once been managerial strengths.

If MSF is well integrated, it can provide a means for measuring, reinforcing, and tracking change throughout the entire system as people focus on the behaviors and competencies that are truly important.

Making the Items Behaviorally Based

The third key element to using MSF as a systemic tool for organizational change is ensuring that the items themselves are behaviorally based. More specifically, if the instrument is intended to communicate what is important, the content must reflect specific behavioral examples of how the underlying competency being measured would actually be observed on the job.

For example, feedback from direct reports and peers was used following the SmithKline Beecham (SB) merger to communicate the new five core values to employees and to help crystallize important behavioral practices required for the success of the new Simply Better culture (Burke & Jackson, 1991). Thus, rather than just measuring generalized managerial effectiveness or leadership qualities, targeted and linked behavioral practices that taught as they measured were employed at SB following the merger. This OD bias toward a behavioral item ideology is in sharp contrast to other common feedback approaches that require coworkers to rate attitudes, traits, or attributes (such as "fairness" or "honesty") that often must be inferred. Although certain types of trait-based information such as personality preferences can be helpful in an executive coaching context, and particularly when paired with MSF results (see Chapter Three), many of these types of measures are neither developmental nor actionable on their own. Moreover, some communicate only how a manager is perceived by others, not the behaviors through which this perception is accomplished.

This behavioral emphasis also has other benefits. MSF data can be summarized and used to identify organizational strengths and weaknesses on key competencies. If the items are behavioral as opposed to attitudinal in nature, it is fairly straightforward to identify what managers are and are not doing. For example, in contrast to the typical attitudinal item, "How satisfied are you with your job?" which provides little guidance for the practitioner or HR manager, "My manager treats me with respect," a behavioral question, offers a clear indication of the situation. Moreover, when summarized across an entire executive population, these data can serve as a powerful means for assessing the need for other types of change initiatives.

MSF is an effective means of driving organizational change at the systemic level through its role as a communication, measurement, and linkage device. It is important to realize, however, that using MSF for these purposes requires significant resources, dedication, and cultural integration to be maximally effective. These are issues that are best addressed in the initial stages of contracting (see Chapter One).

The Meso Level

Just as MSF is an effective process for change at the systemic level, the same concepts can be applied to the middle or meso levels of an organization: teams, work groups, functions, departments, lines of services, manufacturing plants, regions, and other related business units. These subsystems (Katz & Kahn, 1978) of the larger whole represent the very core of the organization—the parts that carry out the work. Because summarized data at these levels are far more specific, the importance and role of MSF as a diagnostic tool increases dramatically. In other words, whereas a simple summary of organization-wide MSF results can provide a useful means for tracking a cultural shift, when the data are collectively examined for a specific department, function, or business unit, the relevance of key findings, such as the highest- and lowest-rated items or re-lationships among different questions, becomes crucial to under-standing the unique dynamics of that specific group of leaders or managers. The application of data summaries (also known as data rollups or cuts) to explore relationships and trends in this meso layer is an important component to the OD approach, although relatively few practitioners think of using existing MSF data for these types of analysis (Church, 1999). Of course, how the data are actually used after they are summarized to drive action plan-ning and team improvement is clearly the most critical aspect.

In general, there two ways in which MSF can be used to help improve the functioning of groups, teams, and departments: (1) taking a largely diagnostic and facilitative approach and (2) em-pirically linking the data to other existing measures in the organi-zation and developing a set of predictive models (such as key driver analysis) for that group.

MSF for Team Diagnosis and Facilitation

Perhaps the most common approach to using MSF at the meso level is for the purpose of diagnosis and facilitated action planning. This approach generally requires that a strong diagnostic or content-relevant MSF tool (for example, one focused on team climate) be used to collect data from all the individuals in the group on their own perceptions and the collective perceptions of peers, cowork-ers, or even team leaders. Sometimes ratings from other interde-pendent groups, such as internal suppliers or even customers, might be included as inputs as well. These data are then analyzed at the group and individual levels to provide a composite picture of the shared group experience. Using a simple report that pro-vides a comparative analysis among self and various other layered perspectives (this is where MSF goes beyond a standard survey ef-fort), the OD practitioner facilitates a working feedback session where the results are given back to the entire group membership using an action research approach (see Chapter One).

Although first popularized in Nadler's classic OD book on data-driven feedback for change (1977), the notion of providing peo-ple with specific information about how they interact and behave with one another dates back to the early works of Lewin (1946,

1958), Likert (1967), and Mann (1957), among others. The application of MSF to a team, function, or work group setting is simply a natural extension of this original idea.

When applied as a diagnostic tool in this manner, MSF data can be extremely useful for determining aspects of effective and ineffective group functioning. Moreover, when the feedback is provided to the group members on these issues in a safe and open environment, significant energy is created for change. At this point, it is up to the OD practitioner to use his or her knowledge of group dynamics (see Chapter Eight) and uniquely OD-based process consultation skills (see Chapter Seven) to help catalyze the energy from the group into concrete plans for action and a means for tracking improvement over time.

Although collecting targeted information from group members is the preferred approach, summaries of existing MSF data gathered on related content areas or for other purposes such as leadership development sometimes can serve as a proxy input for this group diagnostic process. Similar to the outcome of a targeted OD-driven organizational survey effort (see Chapter Four and Church & Waclawski, 2001), data rollups can provide an important means for summarizing key issues among various groups or teams. As long as the items are behaviorally based, accurate demographic and group or department information exists at the individual level to generate specific types of summary analyses and the practitioner has the requisite skills to prepare and interpret these analyses, existing MSF data can be leveraged to generate powerful results.

Moreover, because behaviorally based MSF items are almost always targeted at a specific focal individual, it is far more difficult for recipients to discount the relevance and collective agreement on who or what was being rated, which is a common defensive tactic used to avoid ownership of survey results. In addition, other contextual factors, such as recent layoffs, a pending merger or acquisition, dissatisfaction with the benefits plan, or a change in the chief executive officer are unlikely to have the same attitudinal impact on individual managerial ratings that they would on a broader set of general satisfaction and culture survey items. In this way, MSF summary data may be more defensible and therefore potentially more powerful than standard survey findings.

Whether based on a targeted assessment or a rollup of individual data, the specificity of the results at the group level provides key insights into how the individuals in that unit operate.

Using MSF to Model Key Relationships

The second approach to applying MSF at the meso level of analysis is fundamentally more analytical in nature; it uses applied statistical analysis to understand, model, and predict key relationships and drivers of performance. If the feedback-based facilitation model represents the softer side, this approach represents the harder side of OD (see also Chapter Six). Referred to in the survey industry as *linkage research,* this approach can be complex, but when all the data elements have been aligned properly, the resulting story that can be told is invaluable to the organization and its leadership.

Typically. this approach requires a solid knowledge of multivariate statistics (an area in which many OD practitioners unfortunately are lacking) and access to one or more objective measures of performance collected at a similar level of analysis—individual, team, store, department, region, or division, for example. Some of these measures or indicators might include turnover, profitability, net sales, patents, customer service ratings, meritorious awards and recognition, loyalty, and even market share, depending on the nature of the organization and the types of and levels of information gathered. In addition, in some situations, other types of internal measures, such as organizational survey results, functional competency assessments, or even performance appraisal ratings, might also be available for analysis. For example, a recent MSF effort with a national retail supermarket chain used a customized managerial performance model with behavioral data from over five hundred store managers, matching climate survey data from employees at each store and objective measures of performance, including net sales and product shrinkage (Church, 2001).

By linking the results of an MSF effort at the functional, team, or business unit level with these types of existing internal and external performance indicators, the OD practitioner is in a unique position to identify significant and meaningful relationships between behavioral ratings on the MSF instrument and key organizational measures. Although this approach can be too sophisticated and analytical in some situations, particularly if the organization is new to feedback or does not have a good understanding of its own performance metrics, the linkage approach is nonetheless one of the most meaningful and powerful means for using MSF in an OD context. Moreover, this methodology is almost a requirement for the evaluation of the true impact of any OD or related intervention (see Chapters Six and Fourteen). Given the relative dearth of statistical skills among many contemporary OD professionals, this is an area where the teaming of I/O psychologists with HRD and OD practitioners could prove particularly valuable.

MSF for meso- or group-level change and development efforts requires a unique set of skills for OD practitioners, ranging from process consultation (if the results are to be worked within a group context in an action planning setting) to applied statistics (if the data are to be linked for empirical analysis and modeling). Whatever method is chosen, MSF can play an important role in helping managers and employees understand the consequences of their behaviors.

The Individual Level

Although macro- and meso-level approaches are important for understanding, directing, and reinforcing change throughout the larger organizational context, in the end people make the difference. At its most basic level, MSF is an individualized means for driving a collective and systemic organizational change effort one manager at a time. In short, large-scale culture change across an organization of 120,000 employees can be defined as the collective outcome of individual behavior change by managers, employees, and executives. Perhaps the most fundamental aspect of MSF for organizational change and development is the psychological and interpersonal processes by which individuals come to understand, accept, and ultimately use individual feedback for their personal growth and development.

Although a detailed presentation of the entire process of behavior change is beyond the scope of this chapter (see Bracken et al., 2001; London, 1997), there are several important points regarding the use of MSF from an OD context that are appropriate to describe in detail here. All of these concern the nature of the feedback process and its role in enhancing self-awareness, raising expectations, and providing targeted behavioral direction for improvement.

The Psychological Process of Receiving Feedback

As depicted in Figure 2.1, MSF for individual and organization development is based on the psychological notion that data-based feedback, quantitative or qualitative, provides a set of powerful stimuli to the individual that must be cognitively and emotionally addressed. The collective and cumulative impressions of direct reports, clients, peers and supervisors, and others activate self-perceptions and self-referent mechanisms and can be used to compare perceived strengths and weaknesses against this new standard (Carver & Scheier, 1981). People feel the implicit need for a self-regulated response—that is, a desire to reduce discrepancies between how they are actually perceived by others and how they would like to be perceived. When the collective set of coworker ratings converges and is distinctly dissimilar to self-perception, there is a cognitive and emotional push to change one's behavior to meet these new standards in a form of self-regulatory corrective action. This comparison process serves to enhance both self-reflection or self-directed attention and other-directedness, which together drive the next level of response (Ashford & Tsui, 1991; London, 1997). This is where the nature of the approach taken to delivering the feedback results—or in OD terms, the intervention—plays a critical role in the outcome of an MSF effort.

As with many other complex psychological dynamics and, in particular, issues of procedural justice and fairness (Brockner & Wisenefeld, 1996), there is both a process determinant (Were the procedures used to plan and implement the MSF effort fair, valid, meaningful, and appropriate?), and an outcome determinant (Were the ratings received as positive or negative?) to individuals' response to feedback. The nature of the interaction between process and outcome at the point of intervention (that is, feedback delivery) provides either the catalyst or the barrier to effective internalization and subsequent change as a result of the entire process. In short, this is one of the few areas in which both researchers and practitioners agree; it is the combination of how and why the data were collected (process), with what the feedback says (outcome), and how it was delivered (intervention) that ultimately determines the effectiveness of the entire MSF effort.

Let us examine this process in more detail. If we start with the notion that MSF is provided to managers to assist in identifying strengths and areas for improvement and to enhance self-awareness, there are three key psychological responses or stages to feedback that the individual must be coached through in order for the process to be successful: understanding, acceptance, and commitment (see Figure 2.2).

First, the manager needs to have a clear understanding and belief in the purpose of the MSF process, the means by which the data were collected and tabulated from raters, and the relevance and implied validity of the instrumentation itself. Clearly, if there are issues regarding the fairness of the methodology, a lack of per-

Figure 2.2. Psychological Stages of MSF Receptivity.

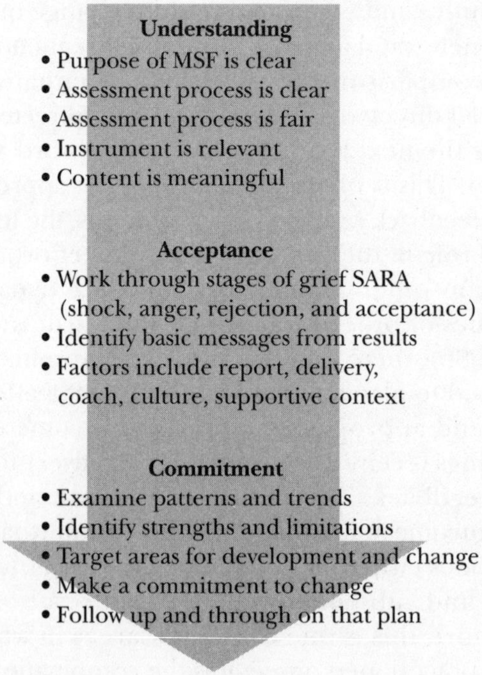

Understanding
- Purpose of MSF is clear
- Assessment process is clear
- Assessment process is fair
- Instrument is relevant
- Content is meaningful

Acceptance
- Work through stages of grief SARA
  (shock, anger, rejection, and acceptance)
- Identify basic messages from results
- Factors include report, delivery,
  coach, culture, supportive context

Commitment
- Examine patterns and trends
- Identify strengths and limitations
- Target areas for development and change
- Make a commitment to change
- Follow up and through on that plan

ceived importance of the items on the measure, questions about who was selected to provide ratings and why, or concerns regarding the quality and integrity of the data analysis and reporting process, it will be very difficult for the focal manager to understand and accept the MSF results provided. Thus, passing through the understanding stage requires the provision of important information regarding such mundane but meaningful contextual elements as why the specific behavioral items were chosen, how the data were collected and tabulated, who chose the raters and why, and the purpose of the feedback effort and who has access to the information. Although providing this information should be commonsense and represent good MSF practice, often practitioners may overlook attending to these critical issues. Not facilitating understanding of the process itself, however, almost guarantees that the feedback recipients will not be able to move beyond their initial suspicious reactions, however justified.

Once an individual is comfortable with the quality and integrity of the system, he or she can be directed to the first-level analysis of the data itself. This is the *acceptance* stage of the psychological process. At this junction, however, a whole new series of fears and anxieties needs to be addressed through one-on-one coaching or facilitated group response in a context of support and encouragement (London, 1997). Even when this process is done in a highly sensitive way, it is likely that managers and executives receiving MSF (particularly for the first time) will become defensive, withdrawn, challenging, or even hostile. The role of the OD practitioner at this stage (again using his or her process consultation skills) is to help the manager work through this initial defensiveness. Often this progression is described by OD professionals in terms of the classic Kübler-Ross (1969) model of the four stages of grieving: shock, anger, rejection, and acceptance (SARA, with some practitioners adding *H* for hope). Although some people are naturally intuitive and self-aware and can therefore easily glean their own meaningful themes from the feedback, the vast majority are less skilled in this area and require experienced assistance to help clarify the major issues. Strong one-on-one coaching skills can play an important role in this regard (see Chapter Three for some detailed examples and Waclawski & Church, 1999, for a model of data-driven coaching).

Using MSF for Executive Coaching

Aside from reactance issues, the quality and user-friendliness of the report itself, and the nature of the setting—for example, an informal off-site conference center or a meeting in one's own office— are also important factors to acceptance. Another key element is the quality of the coach. This includes his or her ability to create rapport and the level of dynamic fit achieved between the personal style of the coach and the organizational culture in which he or she is assisting managers. It is for these reasons that many organizations rely on and pay well for a host of external professionals who have had great experience in working with and delivering feedback to executives in many settings. In our experience, OD practitioners and counseling psychologists often have a unique set of process and facilitation skills that add particular value to this element of feedback delivery.

The final role of the coach is to help the manager or executive absorb the data provided and, most important, commit to personal change and improvement. This is the *commitment* phase of the psychological process because it emphasizes the action that is required for MSF to have an impact. Action planning and follow-through, among the most common concerns in many OD, I/O, and HRD interventions, are critical yet often underappreciated elements in practice (Church & Waclawski, 2001). Clearly, if individuals are not committed to improvement following a personalized and presumably relevant MSF experience, it is unlikely that any behavioral change will result. Certainly, the feedback delivery and coaching process must be sensitive to the needs of individuals and their context, but given the importance of use at the individual level, it must also hold people accountable for their actions. Termed by some as the Achilles heel of MSF (London, Smither, & Adsit, 1997), accountability means ensuring true commitment (as opposed to lipservice) to behavior change once the manager or executive leaves the protective environment of the developmental setting. This is one of the greatest coaching challenges overall and goes to the heart of an effective systemic OD effort.

The process of delivering MSF is complex, but it is crucial to the effective use of results by individuals and thus systemic organizational change. Given the impact of the factors involved, OD practitioners pursuing MSF initiatives should be sure to attend to the nature of the delivery mechanism (process, that is, understanding), the quality of the interpretive effort (outcome, that is, acceptance), and how delivery and action planning are facilitated. The Practice Tips are helpful for giving and receiving feedback (Waclawski, 2000).

Practice Tips

1. Provide specifics, not generalities, when giving feedback.
2. Provide feedback as soon as possible after the observed behavior.
3. Check that the recipient understands and agrees with the feedback.
4. When giving feedback, focus on observed behaviors and not personality, avoid making inferences, and provide examples of the observed behavior.
5. Provide suggestions for improvement and change, and give support and resources for these changes.
6. Provide follow-up feedback to reinforce changes and to discuss changes that have not occurred.
7. Reward changes in behavior.
8. When receiving feedback, listen carefully and avoid being defensive. Think of the feedback as a learning opportunity.
9. Paraphrase what you hear to check for understanding, and ask for clarification and examples from the person providing the feedback.
10. Compare this feedback to other feedback you have received to identify patterns and themes.
11. Discuss action plans to create meaningful change.
12. Seek follow-up feedback on whether changes have occurred.

Case Examples of Multisource Feedback

Using MSF for OD is not as simple as ordering ten packets of standard instruments from some assessment firm. MSF is a complex process, and when it is applied to organizational change efforts, the challenges increase in magnitude. In this final section, we briefly describe two cases in which an MSF process was applied to a complex OD and change situation. The first case describes MSF as a means for integrating different cultural elements following merger and acquisition (M&A) activity, and the second provides an example of how MSF was used to drive culture change in an organization mired in bureaucracy and facing external pressure to adapt or face extinction.

Using MSF in a Merger and Acquisition Context

A financial organization was recently in the process of rapidly acquiring many smaller firms as part of an overall growth strategy aimed at increasing national presence. As with most other M&A activity, a key OD-related challenge was integrating and aligning many separate cultures, missions, strategies, and visions (as represented by each acquired company) with the larger acquiring organization. Based on a number of iterative rounds of interviews and focus groups (see Chapter Five) with senior executives and high performers, a customized MSF tool and process was developed that effectively delineated the organization's vision, mission, strategy, and key competencies needed for success in these M&A efforts. The new measure also helped the organization capture and communicate its unique culture, which emphasized employee empowerment and an employees-first philosophy. Perhaps most important, because the items developed were behaviorally based, the MSF articulated to raters and ratees in behavioral terms what exactly managers were expected to do.

Instituting a sound MSF process was only the first major step in the change effort. Management-based feedback delivery and coaching programs were developed that focused on acceptance and action planning, which were used to drive behavioral change. The organization also offered additional training and development efforts to address specific competency deficiencies in the newly created overall model.

In the end, the MSF process helped the organization communicate and over subsequent MSF administrations reinforce the critical behaviors needed for the acquired companies to be effectively integrated into its culture. Managers of the acquired companies reported back that the MSF process ultimately helped them to figure out what was expected of them in their new roles. In addition, the feedback effort helped them better understand the culture of the acquiring organization, as well as its vision, mission, and strategy. Although many other factors contributed to the final outcome, this organization made the list of the best Fortune 100 companies to work for several years later.

Using MSF for Culture Change

This example concerns a publicly funded and extremely well-respected broadcasting organization in which MSF played a significant role in a large-scale culture change effort. Although the organization had experienced considerable stability in its industry historically, by the early 1990s increased competition in the external environment (both locally and globally) due to changes in regulations and communication technology had resulted in increased competition for viewers and reduced shares in a market that earlier was practically exclusive. Perhaps the most immediate challenge to the organization's survival, however, was the need to secure continued financial support from the government as well as greater commercial revenue to supplement the fees from viewers and listeners. At this point, senior leadership realized that a new culture was needed that focused on the efficiency of process as much as on the quality of the programming content created.

In order to address these concerns, a new vision and corporate strategy were established in conjunction with senior management, line, and staff personnel that would carry the company forward. After an initial release of corporate material aimed at communicating the new vision and strategy to employees failed to generate sufficient energy for change, it was decided that a more impactful approach was needed, one that would truly engage and motivate employees around these messages. To this end, a corporate-wide diagnostic culture survey was developed and implemented based on the new vision and strategy and in conjunction with the Burke-Litwin (1992) model of organizational performance and change (see Chapter Four and Church & Waclawski, 2001). The results of the survey process were used for a variety of targeted follow-up OD interventions.

One of these interventions was the development of a customized MSF process for senior and middle management. Linked to the same new behaviors in support of the vision and strategy from the survey, the feedback effort was designed to promote a new leadership and management mind-set among a group of lifetime employees who previously had little experience with being accountable for how they managed people. The first participants in the process were the top 250 managers, who received feedback from their supervisors, peers, and direct reports in conjunction with function and department-level survey results.

Results from the follow-up culture survey a year later indicated that significant improvements had been made in certain areas, including clarity of the new mission and strategy, visibility of senior leadership, greater focus among middle managers on working collaboratively in teams, and to some extent employee motivation. Improvements in managerial behaviors were linked directly to participation in the MSF process. Although change in this type of organization is neither quick nor easy, the use of multiple levels of data-based interventions, including surveys, MSF, senior leadership coaching, and improved information systems, resulted in improvements in certain areas of the culture overall.

Conclusion

In general, the OD approach to designing, implementing, and using MSF processes in organizations is somewhat different from the more traditional assessment-based approach. Nonetheless, many of the same fundamental challenges and assumptions regarding feedback measurement, delivery, individual receptivity, and the action planning process are consistent with what we know about MSF from practice and research. To this end, based on our experiences working with many different organizations and across many industries, we have developed Practice Tips to consider when implementing MSF for OD purposes.

Practice Tips

1. Ensure senior management support of the MSF effort. Require that executives experience MSF themselves firsthand, which will reinforce their acceptance and support of others in the organization.

2. Base the MSF instrument on a customized competency model. This model should incorporate or reflect the desired key competencies, strategy, vision, mission, values, principles, and culture of the organization. This helps ensure relevancy, meaningfulness, and face validity.

3. Involve managers and leaders in the development process. Ensuring participation from as many key individuals as possible in the development of both the competency model and the subsequent MSF instrument will help increase understanding, acceptance, and commitment of the effort, as well as the feedback. Avoid having a black box process.

4. Ensure that MSF items are behaviorally based. Items should be observable to raters (as opposed to attributes or attitudes) and relevant, and provide enough guidance for change. Behaviorally based items communicate to employees how managers are expected to behave.

5. Provide room for write-in or verbatim comments. Whenever possible (from either a cost or logistics perspective), include a section on the MSF instrument where raters can provide comments in their own words. This provides focal managers with additional insights, context, and in some cases feedback behaviors and issues that are not being formally assessed but are nonetheless important to people.

6. Pilot-test the MSF instrument. Before using a customized measure, pilot-test it with a large and diverse group of individuals. This provides an opportunity to fine-tune items (as well as reports and training) to make them as meaningful and relevant as possible.

7. Provide clear communication regarding the process. Messages and information should be honest, thorough, and timely in order to enhance receptivity. They should address the purpose of the MSF effort, its relation to the larger organizational context or change effort, confidentiality of the results, and how results will be delivered. If done well, this will help prevent unpleasant surprises, alleviate inevitable suspicions, and ensure a more open and honest rating and feedback experience.

Practice Tips, cont'd.

8. Allow managers to choose their own raters. Although some feedback practitioners disagree with this approach, this is the preferred method for identifying raters from an OD perspective. It ensures that the focal manager will perceive value in the ratings obtained and allows him or her to maintain a sense of control and ownership. When concerns that extensive positive selection bias might be present (that managers will select only people who will give them good ratings), the best alternative is to have managers develop the list and then share it with the supervisor, who can then add to (but not subtract from) the initial list.

9. Provide developmental commitment, support, and resources. The organization should demonstrate the importance and significance of the change effort using MSF by offering formal developmental training, coaching, mentoring, and any other resources required to make change happen. This includes training efforts specifically designed to address managers' developmental opportunities as identified by their MSF data.

10. Promote integration. Design the system and modify existing processes so that all relevant HR products and services are integrated into the hub of the competency model. This helps to ensure that the MSF and all other HR activities are in alignment and working together for the overall development and change effort.

If we have learned one thing from our work in this area over the years, it is that culture change does not happen overnight and indeed is a multiyear processes. MSF provides a powerful means of communicating, driving, and reinforcing change throughout an entire organizational system. Despite the wealth of practice guides for conducting MSF in various contexts and settings (see Bracken et al., 2001), however, many organizations continue to believe that simply doing "some of that 360-stuff" is enough to improve their leadership and management effectiveness. We hope it is apparent that this is a misconception.

We believe that organizations should pursue MSF applications only after fully understanding the pros and cons of engaging in this type of data-driven method. Fundamentally, an OD approach to pursuing multisource feedback represents an effort that is developmental in purpose, strategic in scope, customized in content, grounded in behavior, linked to initiatives and systems, delivered in a facilitative coaching context, positioned as a means of enhancing managerial self-awareness, and most of all, anchored in taking action from the data. Any other form of MSF is not OD.

References

Ashford, S. J., & Tsui, A. S. (1991). Self-regulation for managerial effectiveness: The role of active feedback seeking. *Academy of Management Journal, 34,* 251–280.

Atwater, L. E., & Yammarino, F. J. (1992). Does self-other agreement on leadership perceptions moderate the validity of leadership and performance predictions? *Personnel Psychology, 45,* 141–164.

Bracken, D. W. (1994). Straight talk about multirater feedback. *Training and Development, 48,* 44–51.

Bracken, D. W., Timmreck, C. W., & Church, A. H. (Eds.). (2001). *The handbook of multisource feedback.* San Francisco: Jossey-Bass.

Brockner, J., & Wisenefeld, B. M. (1996). An integrative framework for explaining reactions to decisions: Interactive effects on outcomes and procedures. *Psychological Bulletin, 120*(2), 189–208.

Burke, W. W. (1987). *Organization development: A normative view.* Reading, MA: Addison-Wesley.

Burke, W. W., & Jackson, P. (1991). Making the SmithKline Beecham merger work. *Human Resource Management, 30,* 69–87.

Burke, W. W., & Litwin, G. H. (1992). A causal model of organizational performance and change. *Journal of Management, 18,* 523–545.

Carver, C. S., & Scheier, M. F. (1981). *Attention and self-regulation: A control theory approach to human behavior.* New York: Springer-Verlag.

Church, A. H. (1994). Managerial self-awareness in high performing individuals in organizations. *Dissertation Abstracts International, 55–05B,* 2028. (University Microfilms no. AAI9427924).

Church, A. H. (1995). First-rate multirater feedback. *Training and Development, 49,* 42–43.

Church, A. H. (1997). Managerial self-awareness in high-performing individuals in organizations. *Journal of Applied Psychology, 82,* 281–292.

Church, A. H. (1999, Spring). Large scale applications of small scale data. *Performance in Practice,* 7–8.

Church, A. H. (2001). Modeling the impact of managerial behavior in a store environment. In O. A. Aliage (Ed.), *Academy of Human Resource*

Development 2001 Conference Proceedings, Vol. 2, pp. 583–590. Baton Rouge, LA: Academy of Human Resource Development.

Church, A. H., & Bracken, D. W. (1997). Advancing the state of the art of 360-degree feedback: Guest Editors' comments on the research and practice of multirater assessment methods. *Group and Organization Management, 22,* 149–161.

Church, A. H., Burke, W. W., & Van Eynde, D. F. (1994). Values, motives, and interventions of organization development practitioners. *Group and Organization Management, 19,* 5–50.

Church, A. H., & Waclawski, J. (1998). Making multirater feedback systems work. *Quality Progress, 31,* 81–89.

Church, A. H., & Waclawski, J. (2001). *Designing and using organizational surveys: A seven-step process.* San Francisco: Jossey-Bass.

Church, A. H., Waclawski, J., & Burke, W. W. (2001). Multisource feedback for organization development and change. In D. W. Bracken, C. W. Timmreck, & A. H. Church (Eds.), *The handbook of multisource feedback* (pp. 301–317). San Francisco: Jossey-Bass.

Cummings, T., & Worley, C. (1997). *Organization development and change* (6th ed.). St. Paul, MN: West.

Dalessio, A. T. (1998). Using multisource feedback for employee development and personnel decisions. In J. W. Smither (Ed.), *Performance appraisal: State of the art in practice* (pp. 278–330). San Francisco: Jossey-Bass.

French, W. L., & Bell, C. H., Jr. (1990). *Organization development: Behavioral science interventions for organization improvement* (4th ed.). Upper Saddle River, NJ: Prentice Hall.

Furnham, A., & Stringfield, P. (1994). Congruence of self and subordinate ratings of managerial practices as a correlate of supervisor evaluation. *Journal of Occupational and Organizational Psychology, 67,* 57–67.

Gellerman, W., Frankel, M. S., & Ladenson, R. (1990). *Values and ethics in organization and human systems development: Responding to dilemmas in professional life.* San Francisco: Jossey-Bass.

Gottlieb, J. Z. (1998). Understanding the role of organization development practitioners. In R. W. Woodman & W. A. Pasmore (Eds.), *Research in organization change and development* (Vol. 11, pp. 117–158). Greenwich, CT: JAI Press.

Green, P. C. (1999). *Building robust competencies: Linking human resource systems to organizational strategies.* San Francisco: Jossey-Bass.

Hedge, J. W., Borman, W. C., & Birkeland, S. A. (2001). History and development of multisource feedback as a methodology. In D. W. Bracken, C. W. Timmreck, & A. H. Church (Eds.), *The handbook of multisource feedback* (pp. 15–32). San Francisco: Jossey-Bass.

Katz, D., & Kahn, R. L. (1978). *The social psychology of organizations* (2nd ed.) New York: Wiley.

Kluger, A. N., & DeNisi, A. (1996). The effects of feedback interventions on performance: A historical review, a meta-analysis, and a preliminary feedback intervention theory. *Psychological Bulletin, 119,* 254–284.

Kübler-Ross, E. (1969). *On death and dying.* Old Tappan, NJ: Macmillan.

Lewin, K. (1946). Action research and minority problems. *Journal of Social Issues, 2,* 34–46.

Lewin, K. (1958). Group decision and social change. In E. E. Maccoby, T. M. Newcomb, & E. L. Hartley (Eds.), *Readings in social psychology* (pp. 197–211). Austin, TX: Holt, Rinehart and Winston.

Likert, R. (1967). *The human organization: Its management and value.* New York: McGraw-Hill.

London, M. (1997). *Job feedback: Giving, seeking and using feedback for performance improvement.* Mahwah, NJ: Erlbaum.

London, M. (2001). The great debate: Should multisource feedback be used for administration or development only? In D. W. Bracken, C. W. Timmreck, & A. H. Church (Eds.), *The handbook of multisource feedback* (pp. 368–385). San Francisco: Jossey-Bass.

London, M., & Smither, J. W. (1995). Can multisource feedback change self-awareness and behavior? Theoretical applications and directions for research. *Personnel Psychology, 48,* 803–840.

London, M., Smither, J. W., & Adsit, D. J. (1997). Accountability: The Achilles' heel of multisource feedback. *Group and Organization Management, 22,* 162–184.

Mann, F. C. (1957). Studying and creating change: A means to understanding social organization. *Research in Industrial Human Relations, 17,* 146–167.

Nadler, D. A. (1977). *Feedback and organization development: Using data-based methods.* Reading, MA: Addison-Wesley.

O'Reilly, B. (1994). 360° feedback can change your life. *Fortune, 130,* 93–100.

Schippmann, J. S. (1999). *Strategic job modeling: Working at the core of integrated human resources.* Mahwah, NJ: Erlbaum.

Tornow, W. W. (1993). Editor's note: Introduction to special issue on 360-degree feedback. *Human Resource Management, 32,* 211–219.

Van Velsor, E., & Leslie, J. B. (2001). Selecting a multisource feedback instrument. In D. W. Bracken, C. W. Timmreck, & A. H. Church (Eds.), *The handbook of multisource feedback* (pp. 63–78). San Francisco: Jossey-Bass.

Van Velsor, E., Taylor, S., & Leslie, J. B. (1993). An examination of the relationships among self-perception accuracy, self-awareness, gender, and leader effectiveness. *Human Resource Management, 32,* 249–263.

Waclawski, J. (1996). Using organization survey results to improve organizational performance. *Managing Service Quality, 6,* 53–57.

Waclawski, J. (2000). The real world: It is better to receive than to give. Practice tips for giving and receiving feedback. *Industrial-Organizational Psychologist, 38,* 91–97.

Waclawski, J., & Church, A. H. (1999, Summer). Four easy steps to performance coaching. *Performance in Practice,* 4–5.

Waldman, D. A., Atwater, L. E., & Antonioni, D. (1998). Has 360-degree feedback gone amok? *Academy of Management Executive, 12,* 86–94.

Walker, A. G., & Smither, J. W. (1999). A five-year study of upward feedback: What managers do with their results matters. *Personnel Psychology, 52,* 393–423.

CHAPTER 3

The Role of Personality Assessment in Organization Development

W. Warner Burke
Debra A. Noumair

In our work as organization development (OD) practitioners, we deal with client personalities much of the time, but the work itself does not focus on personality. Personality is always there, however, usually more in the background than in the foreground. Thus, it is imperative that we as OD practitioners be highly cognizant of the role and function of individual personality in organizations. What we address in this chapter is not only individual personality in organizational settings but more particularly how personality is relevant to and interrelated with OD and how practitioners can make use of personality assessment for OD purposes.

Personality Assessment: What Do We Mean?

Personality can be assessed in a variety of ways. Clinicians rely on tests. but they depend just as much, if not more, on personal history. As a physician does a clinical workup, a therapist similarly traces an individual's life experience and family relationships to determine patterns of behavior that reflect personality.

For our purposes in this chapter, we rely primarily on paper-and-pencil (or Web enabled if available) questionnaires for personality assessment. Individuals answer a number of questions about aspects of behavior, beliefs, attitudes, and values. This form of assessment results in an array of scores on a selected group of dimensions of personality that are then compared with a set of norms that help individuals to determine how they compare with others. This comparison reflects how close to or far from the norms, that is, the so-called average dimensions of personality, the individual falls. Most of these questionnaires are based on self-ratings only, but some include both self and other ratings.

For the OD work described in this chapter, we have tended to rely on assessment instruments that relate to leadership because the experiences described were primarily with senior managers and executives. Moreover, our use of these instruments is to enhance OD and change work, not to assess people for selection or promotion purposes (see also Chapter Two).

What follows is a brief description of the personality instruments commonly used in OD work and ones that we have used often. We have been selective in the personality instruments chosen to describe here. There are many instruments of high quality such as the Guilford Zimmerman, the California Psychological Inventory, and the 16 PF (personality factors), to name but a few. Our choices here provide the best fit for coaching clients who are executives, senior managers, or others in positions of leadership. There are also many other questionnaires that assess, or purport to assess, leadership. Our choices here meet at least two criteria for us: they are well researched, and we feel most comfortable with these selections as we attempt to help our clients learn and develop.

Myers-Briggs Type Indicator

The MBTI is not a perfect assessment tool (there are questions regarding validity and the factors involved; see, for example, McCrae & Costa, 1989), but it is one of our favorites because clients find it easy to understand, reasonably accurate as far as they are concerned, and fun and interesting. Also as psychologists, we are partial to the MBTI because of its grounding in Jungian theory and the instrument's unique evolution.

In addition to being rooted in Jung's thinking, the MBTI dimensions lend additional credibility with their relationships to the historical four temperaments of Hippocrates, Adickes, Kretschmer, Spranger, and Adler. Moreover, there is considerable overlap of the MBTI dimensions with what is known today as the big five factors of personality (neuroticism, extraversion, openness, agreeableness, and conscientiousness).

Jung believed strongly in individual differences and that people differ according to four primary pairs of preferences, as he called them, or along four continua of personality dimensions:

- Extraversion-Introversion, or the extent to which people differ regarding sociability and being energized when with others versus the introvertive side, which is characterized by territoriality, protecting oneself, and being energized when alone.
- Intuition-Sensing, or the extent to which people rely more on intuitiveness and hunches for taking in information from the external world versus relying on concrete, factual information that is based more on what one sees, hears, touches, and smells than on some hunch or belief.
- Thinking-Feeling, or the extent to which people differ about how they process information once it is taken in. Some think long and hard about matters using logic, analysis, and objectivity versus those who "feel" the information and make decisions based less on logic and objectivity and more on human relations, values, and internal personal standards
- Judging-Perceiving, or the extent to which people differ about their desire for order in life and closure on things versus a desire for living life as it comes and keeping options open.

An individual's results on the MBTI are eight preference scores—for example, when compared with others, how strongly one prefers extraversion compared with introversion or how strongly one prefers intuition compared with sensing. These preferences are then combined into sixteen possible types, so an individual's outcome on the test results in four letters (I for introvert, N for intuition, and so on). The result is a four-letter description of these characteristics (for example, ENTJ or ISFP).

Fundamental Interpersonal Relations Orientation-Behavior

The Fundamental Interpersonal Relations Orientation-Behavior (FIRO-B; Schutz, 1990) is a personality instrument that measures two aspects of relationships: how one typically behaves with others and how one wants others to behave toward him or her. Similar to the MBTI, clients typically enjoy this instrument because it provides a simple framework for understanding interpersonal relationships, there are no right or wrong answers, it can be self-scored in a short time, and it can provide the missing piece of a puzzle when analyzing complex interpersonal relationships. The FIRO-B can be used by both individuals and groups to foster self-awareness or highlight patterns of interpersonal behavior among members of a designated group (see also Chapter Eight).

The FIRO-B measures interpersonal needs in three areas:

- *Inclusion,* which concerns forming new relations and associations with people, bringing people together, reaching out, and determining the extent of contact and involvement that a person seeks
- *Control,* which focuses on decision making, influence, and persuasion between people and determines the extent of power or dominance that a person seeks
- *Openness,* which addresses emotional ties and the extent of warm connections between people and determines the degree of closeness that a person seeks

The FIRO-B measures two dimensions for each need: the *expressed* dimension, which indicates how much one prefers to initiate a behavior, and the *wanted* dimension, which indicates what one wants from others and how one wants others to behave toward him or her. An essential characteristic of the expressed dimension is that it refers to observable behavior that one likes to demonstrate; for the wanted dimension, an essential characteristic is that it refers to how much one wants to receive the particular behavior from others, whether or not one's desires are made explicit.

Separate scores in each of the six cells are meaningful because they indicate one's low, medium, and high scores and what one's most compelling and least compelling interpersonal needs are.

Combining the scores can also be an important source of information because the scores on all three needs interact and influence each other. For example, a person who is high on both expressed and wanted inclusion, low on expressed control, and high on wanted control may be mistaken for wanting to control a group rather than wanting to be part of it. One example from our consulting work comes from an executive development program we conducted at the National Aeronautics and Space Administration (NASA), in which a group of participants would not engage in any group task and yet enthusiastically anticipated their one-on-one coaching sessions. The results of the FIRO-B for this group revealed that every individual in the group scored low on wanted inclusion; thus, their disengagement from the group task was the result of being very selective about the amount of interaction they wanted with others. Most apparent was that group work did not add value to the program for them; they were comfortable and productive when working with very few others. Thus, their preferred mode of interpersonal contact with their coach was one-on-one rather than in a group.

The FIRO-B is a valuable tool for a variety of OD interventions. We have used it in combination with other personality measures in multisource feedback programs, as one of several tools to assess organizational culture, and also to build organizational culture; to facilitate conflict resolution by understanding interpersonal needs of both parties; and to facilitate team building.

NEO Personality Inventory

The NEO Personality Inventory (NEO-PI) is a measure of personality that links characteristics of one's personality to the big five factors of personality derived from extensive research and practice (Costa & McCrae, 1991, 1992). The NEO-PI has 240 items and can be administered to just the self, or self and others. The NEO-PI consists of five domain scales and thirty facet scales that collectively provide a comprehensive picture of one's personality. The domain scales and accompanying facets follow:

- *Neuroticism*—a preoccupation with negative affects, such as depression, anxiety, and anger. The facets are anxiety, angry hostility, depression, self-consciousness, impulsiveness, and vulnerability.

- *Extraversion*—a tendency to be sociable, productive, energized, and outgoing. The facets are warmth, gregariousness, assertiveness, anxiety, excitement seeking, and positive emotions. (This factor is similar to the one on the MBTI.)
- *Openness*—characterized by creativity, intelligence, curiosity, and aesthetic sensitivity. The facets are fantasy, aesthetics, feelings, actions, ideas, and values. (This factor is not the same as the FIRO-B dimension.)
- *Agreeableness*—a predisposition toward being sympathetic, cooperative, trustworthy, and kind. The facets are trust, straightforwardness, altruism, compliance, modesty, and tender-mindedness.
- *Conscientiousness*—a tendency to be organized, reliable, planful, and responsible. The facets are competence, order, dutifulness, achievement striving, self-discipline, and deliberation.

Among practitioners, the NEO-PI is considered a user-friendly instrument because it provides a comprehensive picture of personality in terms that are easily understood; however, a word of caution is necessary when using this instrument as part of leadership development programs. It is essential that there be adequate time during the introduction to provide context for the development and purposes of the NEO-PI. The neuroticism domain, for example, easily puts off individuals who are not facile with psychological language or comfortable with psychological labels. Combining the NEO-PI, MBTI, and FIRO-B, or some subcombination of them, allows the differences among the instruments to provide for a more balanced picture of personality.

Leadership Assessment Inventory

The eighteen items that comprise the Leadership Assessment Inventory (LAI) have their origin in the notion that people in leadership and management positions may relate to their work and the people with whom they work in at least two different ways. Burns (1978) used the terms *transformational leadership* and *transactional leadership* to describe these different ways of behaving, thinking, and feeling. Just a year earlier, Zaleznik (1977) had made a similar distinction. Instead of *transformational,* Zaleznik used simply *leader,* and instead of *transactional leader,* he used *manager.* Later, Burke (1986) elaborated on these distinctions with his definition of *empowerment.*

Transformational types, or leaders, are primarily concerned with change; they are future oriented and mission focused. Transactional types, or managers, are more concerned with existing matters, see their relationship with followers as an exchange (that is, as providing contingent rewards for fulfilling expectations previously agreed to), and seek to maintain stability rather than initiate change.

The LAI therefore assesses the degree of preference one has or is perceived to have by others for leadership compared with management. The questionnaire comprises eighteen pairs of statements. For each pair, the respondent is asked to indicate which of the statements is more descriptive by dividing 5 points between the two choices using only a whole number. In other words, the LAI is based on a forced-choice format, similar to the one used in the MBTI. (For early research work on the LAI regarding reliability, factor analysis, and validity, see Sashkin & Burke, 1990, and Van Eron & Burke, 1992.) More recently, research has used the LAI to assess global leadership among executives (Church & Waclawski, 1999), as well as the consulting style of OD practitioners (Church, Waclawski, & Burke, 1996).

Due to significantly higher use of the LAI in recent years, five factors have emerged that form the current five subdivisions of leadership for the questionnaire. In addition to an overall preference score on the leader-manager distinction, respondents receive preference scores based on these subdivisions:

- Determining direction (five items)—for example, "As a leader I have a primary mission of change [leader response]—or maintaining stability [manager response]."
- Influencing followers (five items)—for example, "When I give followers assignments, I am effective at engendering enthusiasm [leader response]—or being clear [manager response]."
- Establishing purpose (three items)—for example, "My requests of followers are typically more than they expect [leader response]—or only what is required [manager response]."

- Inspiring followers (three items)—for example, "To me, leadership should be inspirational [leader response]—or practical [manager response]."
- Making things happen (two items)—for example, "As a leader I must cause events [leader response]—or facilitate events [manager response]."

When the LAI is used in a multisource context, the majority of respondents rate themselves higher on the leadership preference than others rate them. The multisource process can therefore help considerably in providing an individual with realistic feedback regarding leadership and management (see also Chapter Two). Also, when coaching individuals after they have received feedback on behavioral practices, in addition to the LAI, linkages can be made between leadership and management preference and certain ratings on leader or manager practices. For example, it is often possible to show an individual consistencies across ratings: "Even though you rated yourself on the leader preference more than the manager choice, you can see that your direct reports rated you more toward than manager preference and the following management practices ratings bear this out."

A major point, then, is that the LAI provides a broad leader-manager context and highlights a person's beliefs and attitudes that can help the individual to understand better why he or she may have received ratings on behavioral practices that may have otherwise been puzzling. This is especially true when the practices from a multisource process have implied but not necessarily obvious leader or manager behaviors.

Campbell Leadership Inventory

The Campbell Leadership Inventory (CLI; Campbell, 1991) is another instrument designed to assess leadership. It differs from the LAI by focusing on the link between personality traits and effective leadership behavior rather than on attitudes and preferences for leadership and management. Given the complexity and multifaceted nature of leadership, it is important to view it through multiple lenses. Thus, using several leadership instruments in combination with each other provides multiple sources of feedback and facilitates development of a leadership story. We have found that using the combination of the LAI and the CLI provides a rich, detailed picture in which an individual's personality traits, behavior, attitudes, and preferences can be related to leadership effectiveness and predictive of leadership preferences.

Leadership is defined in the CLI as "actions which focus resources to create desirable opportunities" (Campbell, 1991, p. 3). Key terms in the definition are *actions, resources,* and *desirable opportunities* and refer to what a leader actually does behaviorally, the object of a leader's attention, and the result that leaders can expect from their actions. This framework underlies the construction of the CLI and provides the basis for the three components: tasks, orientations, and adjectives.

The CLI defines the tasks of leadership as vision, management, empowerment, politics, feedback, entrepreneurship, and personal style. These tasks provide a link between the CLI and the LAI because the tasks are related to the dimensions of the LAI. Vision, politics, and entrepreneurship are viewed as transformational, and management and empowerment are viewed as transactional. Feedback and personal style are viewed as both transformational and transactional. Linking these instruments is especially helpful when developing a multidimensional profile of an individual's leadership is warranted.

A major benefit of the CLI is that it provides both self and others' ratings, and reports include a gap awareness indicator in which discrepancies between self and other are noted. Although self-ratings are important data points for consideration, observer ratings usually carry more weight. Gaps between self and other in which others' ratings are greater than self-ratings indicate unusual modesty, whereas gaps between self and others' ratings in which self-ratings are greater than others' ratings indicate a tendency to overlook or not recognize errors. Overall, the gap awareness indicator serves as a gross measure of self-awareness and as a framework to assess areas of strength and areas for improvement.

Although the underlying assumption of the CLI is that the more a person is highly rated, the more effective leader he or she is considered to be, even good leaders are not expected to exhibit high ratings on all the scales. Furthermore, the ratings are mutually interactive; that is, some highs can compensate for some lows.

One outcome is that the CLI offers individuals an opportunity to understand their leadership profile as a combination of their strengths as well as areas for future development.

Examples of Uses of Personality Assessments

One of the most common uses of a personality instrument in OD is team building. The MBTI and FIRO-B have been used in this manner for many years. Our first example is a brief description of a team-building intervention using the MBTI. Next, we briefly describe an assessment center intervention at NASA, followed by an in-depth coverage of an executive coaching case in which personality assessment was involved, and finally we discuss a comprehensive OD effort that also included personality assessment.

Team Building

Team building with an organizational unit can take many forms, ranging from a series of facilitated sessions where the consultant helps with meeting effectiveness over time to an intensive, three-day, off-site meeting where long-standing, if not recalcitrant, problems are tackled and worked to some resolution. This is a brief description of an extended team-building effort with a newly formed team that had a need to come together quickly and act as one for the overall good of the newly merged global corporation.

In July 1989, SmithKline Beckman, a large pharmaceutical company based in Philadelphia, and the Beecham Group of the United Kingdom and based in London merged and immediately became one of the early global pharmaceutical firms: SmithKline Beecham. The following January, Warner Burke was hired as an external consultant to help with the organizational merger, a transformational change, and to provide team-building facilitation for the newly formed top team. The CEO, Bob Bauman, wanted to establish a model at the top for how he believed the entire corporation should operate culturally: pulling together as one.

Burke began the team-building effort with the usual procedure of individual interviews with each member of the top team: the executive management committee (EMC). The interviews asked "EMC members' opinions on how well they thought the merger was going, whether they were working as a team (some six months into the merger), and what they would change if they could change anything. The goal was to find out how far apart members really were and why" (Bauman, Jackson, & Lawrence, 1997, p. 145). Although gentle persuasion was required, Burke also got the EMC members to agree to answer the MBTI. At the subsequent two-day off-site meeting with the EMC consisting of twelve members, the first day was devoted to feedback-interview and MBTI results and discussion of how they could come more together as individual members of a group and work more together as a team. Regarding the outcome of this day, the clients can speak for themselves:

The test data helped identify individual behaviors and how these influenced the team. Members learned that personally they were far more intuitive than they cared to admit and great at generating ideas but poor at following them through. It was as if once they had spoken an idea, they considered it done and then moved on to the next challenge. The implications for the organization were far-reaching: no sooner would employees be given one task than another would come hurtling toward them. Warner's explanation of the test findings created a forum that was non-threatening and non-evaluative as EMC members tried to gain insight into the collective impact of their individual behavior. That was when they realized the real value of the simple team-building tool. The test data was incidental to its true purpose: providing a legitimate opportunity to talk through their differences.

The EMC gained two important insights from the results. (1) Given the chance, they would try to tackle everything at once. (2) There would have to be a more definitive decision-making process to ensure that each proposal was completely thought through. To work more effectively as a team, they would have to work harder at setting priorities and be more focused and consciously disciplined about their demands on employees. As a simple first step, members agreed that future EMC meeting agendas would be limited to ten items (compared with the present average of eighteen), permitting greater focus and more discussion time.

As the discussion continued, EMC members grew more relaxed. Tension seemed to dissipate as strangers took their first steps toward becoming friends. By the end of that day Bob knew he had the core team he needed to move forward, and EMC members had a clearer idea of how they could all work together. When they met for dinner that evening, everyone agreed that the day had been a success [Bauman et al., 1997, pp. 159–160].

Specific to the MBTI, eleven EMC members had a Thinking preference, ten were Intuitive rather than sensing (one of the exceptions was the chief financial officer, thank goodness!), and ten were Judging rather than Perceiving. They were more reasonably balanced regarding Extraversion-Introversion. The summary provided by Bauman et al. (1977) was a reflection of these more specific details. Following this off-site session, the MBTI began to be used in many more places in the corporation; essentially, a cascading effect occurred, and the language of the MBTI became a fundamental aspect of the SmithKline Beecham culture.

About a year later at another off-site meeting of the EMC, spouses were invited. Burke conducted two MBTI sessions at this meeting, one exclusively for the spouses and then one for both of the groups together. Based on MBTI patterns of each couple, he predicted how each couple would spend a vacation together—who would read a book or take solitary walks, who would plan the vacation well in advance and who would rebel, and so forth. It was clear by then that the MBTI had permeated not only the corporation but families as well.

Assessment Center at NASA

Whereas the case of team building was primarily group focused, this example emphasizes the individual. With respect to background, during the Carter presidency a new executive level in government was established, the Senior Executive Service (SES), which had associated with it such corporate borrowings as bonus and incentive pay plans. The SES today is well established in the U.S. federal government.

During the mid-1990s, NASA initiated a series of programs that were similar to assessment center activities at corporations like AT&T. NASA's Candidate Development Program (CDP) was designed to help NASA managers who had been nominated for future SES positions become prepared for these higher-level assignments as soon as possible rather than to be promoted and then have to learn on the run. The CDP consisted of two major components: (1) several different stretching job assignments for about six months each to help the candidate learn more about NASA as a total system (these assignments were typically ones that forced the candidate out of his or her comfort zone of work experience and business as usual) and (2) an assessment center of five days held at an off-site residential location. Six staff members, all psychologists, were assigned to the assessment center part of the CDP process. The elements of the off-site program consisted of typical assessment center activities: individual and group exercises designed to elicit required leadership behavior (the staff of psychologists observed five or six participants who were assigned to each one of them) and a battery of psychological tests. The tests used for the CDP were the MBTI, NEO-PI, FIRO-B, CLI, and the LAI. Another important element of the assessment center was a multisource feedback process based on forty SES practices that had already been designed and implemented especially for NASA (see also Chapter Two). The six staff psychologists were therefore able to combine personality with behavioral practice ratings.

On the final day of the CDP program, each participant met with a staff psychologist for ninety minutes. This one-on-one session consisted of feedback from the psychologist and joint action planning for how the participant could use the feedback to become better prepared for SES in NASA. The feedback provided was in three categories: observations the psychologist had made of the participant's behavior in small group exercises, scores on the personality and leadership assessment instruments, and outcomes from the multisource process based on the forty senior executive practices that had been tailored for and used in executive programs over the previous decade within NASA.

Although this was not an OD effort, this example nevertheless illustrates how an intervention based on personality assessment can serve both career aspirations of the individual and developmental goals of the organization.

An Executive Coaching Case

While some OD efforts include 360-degree or multisource feedback and coaching (for more on this application, see Chapter Two and Church, Waclawski, & Burke, 2001), the case presented here began as an individual intervention rather than as part of a leadership development program or OD effort. However in order for coaching to be authorized by the organization, the coach was required to develop a contract that addressed the outcome of assessment (MSF, MBTI, FIRO-B, and CLI) and both the client's and his boss's view of organizational needs. To the extent possible, the results were intended to target "boss-change" objectives, be measurable, and be able to be accomplished within a limited time frame. The contract needed to meet the approval of the boss, the client, a human resource representative, and the director of executive resources. The process of negotiating across boundaries of these stakeholders highlighted the interaction between the individual and the organization and the multidimensional impact of executive coaching on both individuals and the system in which they work.

Jack was referred for executive coaching because he received feedback from his boss that his behavior in interpersonal relationships was unacceptable; he was viewed as condescending, arrogant, shooting from the hip, and argumentative. Although Jack was aware of how his boss viewed him, initially he was somewhat skeptical and doubted that her view of him had much to do with him; he believed that the problems emerged because she was promoted from being his peer to being his boss. Shifting from peer to boss resulted in a loss of friendship for both of them; neither felt that they could maintain this kind of relationship across the boss-subordinate boundary. The loss triggered negative responses in both of them. Jack's critique of his boss heightened; in fact, he often made snide comments and acted more aggressively than he otherwise might. His boss used personal information about Jack's history to explain his limitations on the job and often highlighted the power and status differences between herself and Jack. Although both felt betrayed by the other, Jack was convinced that her perception carried more weight in the organization, and as the subordinate, he was powerless to affect it. Although he was willing to "give coaching a try" because a number of colleagues at his company had coaches, he was not eager to buy in to the process. Jack's reticence to engage the task of being coached eroded fairly quickly however (to his surprise, as well as to that of the coach) when the assessment process grabbed his attention and he began to develop a more complex and nuanced understanding of himself.

It seemed that the hard data made an impact on Jack in part because of its apparent objectivity; he was able to work with the information because it was not tainted by his boss's biased view of him. His position reverted back, however, when he reviewed the scores on the MSF instrument. Once again, the dramatic difference between his boss's perception of him and his direct reports' and peers' perception of him raised the question for him about the credibility of his boss's evaluation. The coaching process paralleled a wide-ranging shifting pendulum as Jack's concern about the veracity of his boss's feedback occurred on an intermittent basis. Jack would move from convincing himself and his coach that he was at least 50 percent responsible for contributing to the difficulties his boss described and demonstrating a commitment to developing a contract to work on his development to an extreme position on the other side in which the problem was entirely his boss and not him. At these times, he often stated that if a friend of his described this work situation to him, he would advise him to resign. These conversations were characterized by dramatic verbal expression and body language indicating that Jack felt as if he had been asleep at the wheel. How could he have not known how bad the situation was? What kept him from knowing the extent to which he was at risk in his position? Why did he perceive coaching as possibly adversarial rather than as a tool for accomplishing individual and organizational tasks, and moreover, for facilitating alignment between himself and the system in which he was working?

A review of the assessment results provides some clues for understanding Jack and the context in which he was operating. On the MBTI, Jack's type is ENTP (Extraverted, Intuitive, Thinking, and Perceiving), and in terms of strength of preference, E, N, and T are very clear, and P is clear. On the FIRO-B, Jack scores high on expressed inclusion, control, and openness. He also scores high on wanted inclusion and openness, but he scores *low* on wanted control. Results of the CLI reveal self-ratings that are very high on all five orientations and others' ratings that are very high on leadership and affability and high on energy, dependability, and resilience.

A summary of the results from the MSF instrument indicated that the largest discrepancies in perception existed between Jack and his boss. Moreover, these gaps were most dramatic among practices that were more people oriented than the more business-oriented practices. For example, Jack was rated more consistently by self and others on domain scales "Strategist—Drives Global

Competitiveness" and "Change Agent—Drives Change and Innovation," whereas the largest gaps between him and his boss existed
on the domain scales "Learner—Builds Personal Effectiveness" and
"Developer—Develops Our People." Jack and his direct reports
also assessed climate, and in general their perceptions were in
alignment. The only gaps that were noteworthy were that Jack
rated recognition and involvement higher than his direct reports
did, and his direct reports rated cross-organizational relationships
higher than jack did. The following written statements summarize
the feedback: "Jack needs to develop more awareness of how his
behavior is perceived by others. He needs to look for ways to work
with people who have a different viewpoint, to work better with
others, to develop better listening skills and to learn subject matters in depth before offering his point of view." On the positive
side, "Jack is bright, articulate, and demonstrates a great deal of initiative. He is visionary and able to handle difficult tasks and get the
job done. He has a good analytical mind, is quick thinking, has a
good sense of humor, and the ability to lighten a stressful situation."

A summary of the results of the personality assessment, the
multisource feedback including written comments, and interviews
with Jack and his boss indicated that Jack has a strong personality
characterized by an intense need for interpersonal contact, connection, and control. He focuses on the big picture and uses facts
and logic to make decisions. He works best in environments that
permit autonomy and the freedom to pursue projects that require
innovation, strategic thinking, and complex challenges. Barriers
to his success include his competitiveness and lack of appreciation
for input from others, his resistance to following standard procedures, and his inattention to relevant facts and details that he views
as impeding his actions. Although the MBTI and the FIRO-B suggest that he is extremely involved with other people, his relationships are not necessarily viewed as a resource. Instead, Jack often
feels burdened by his needs and finds it difficult to acknowledge
and validate the importance of others' contributions to his life.
One of his greatest resources is his leadership ability, as indicated
by high scores on all five orientations of the CLI. Jack has the ability to take initiative and create a sense of urgency in others. He can
make a compelling case for what he wants to do, and he can engage others to follow him. However, it is the ongoing nurturance

of followers that he avoids; his need for control combined with his preference to get lost in ideas and systems can cause him to roll over people without realizing his impact on them.

Ultimately, Jack will have to deploy his considerable intellectual and personality resources in order to overcome his lack of attention to people and systems. In order to achieve alignment between his goals and the organization's goals, he will need to understand how the development of better relationships is directly related to accomplishing the complex challenges that await him and his company.

A Case of Organization Development

This case example illustrates the use of psychological assessment as part of a much larger organization-wide initiative: an OD effort. The consultation begins with the merger of two financial services organizations in a large metropolitan area of the United States. Although the two companies were similar in many ways (same form of commerce, similar in size regarding number of employees and annual revenues, and operating in essentially the same markets), their respective organizational cultures were highly dissimilar. To make the merger succeed, much work with the people and information systems sides of the business was required.

Early consultation involved three primary initiatives. The first was a strategic planning effort that was launched to help the newly merged organization deploy its different internal resources effectively in order to increase market share. Second, an organizational survey of all employees was designed and administered to assess the state of morale some six months into the merger; check on employees' understanding and perception of the financial organization's strategy, the newly emerging merged culture, leadership, organizational structure and systems, and other areas; and establish an internal benchmark for future survey data comparisons so that trends and degree of progress could be determined (see also Chapter Four). Third, the two previous companies' mission statements were discarded, and a new one for the merged organization was drafted by an internal task force that represented a cross-section of the enterprise. Through a highly involving process of well over one hundred employees, this task force eventually produced a mission statement that generated significant commitment throughout the organization.

Results from the initial organizational survey showed that most employees at all levels were positive about the merger and their top leaders, understood and were clear regarding the company's business strategy, and believed in and strongly supported the new mission statement. But they were not very clear at this stage about the organization's culture, its managerial structure, and processes of accountability; critical of a number of systems elements such as information technology, budget, and rewards, especially compensation; and were rather negative about leadership (below the top four or five senior executives) and management throughout the organization.

In response to these survey results, several action steps were taken. The information system was strengthened with new software and computers as well as new management, the reward system was improved, some structural changes were made, and a major initiative was launched to improve leadership and management, beginning with the top 125 executives and managers. A program lasting two and a half days and concentrating on leadership was designed and conducted with approximately twenty-five individuals attending at a time. Some six months later, a three-day program was conducted that concentrated on management. Elements of the initial leadership program included sessions on the nature and qualities of leadership, leading change, and group dynamics, but the core of the program was individual feedback. Elements of the second program included sessions on such topics as program and project management, but again a strong emphasis was on individual feedback.

Feedback for the leadership program was based on a combination of personality assessment and behaviorally based feedback. The MBTI was relied on for personality assessment, and the LAI, a mix of personality aspects and behavior, was used to highlight the distinctions between leader and manager. Because the decision was made to have two programs, one focusing on leadership and the other on management, it seemed appropriate to use the LAI as a way of helping the executives and managers understand the distinctions conceptually and for themselves personally. Feedback was therefore based on individuals' ratings of themselves on the MBTI (self-ratings only); ratings on the LAI by themselves, their bosses, and the individuals' direct reports; and ratings on thirty-six behaviorally based leadership practices by themselves, their bosses, their direct reports, and their peers.

These leadership practices were especially and expressly written for the client organization. Instead of using some off-the-shelf and generic set of practices, these thirty-six were extracted from the financial services organization's mission statement. Why go through this rather elaborate procedure? In addition to the training program's being designed to provide all participants with a greater understanding of leadership and of themselves as leaders through the feedback process, this initiative was also designed to leverage change in the organization's culture (see Chapter Two). The client's desire was to move the culture more toward the value system that was reflected in the organization's mission statement. With the help of yet another task force from the organization, values embedded in the mission statement were extracted or surfaced to see if these individuals representing a cross-section of the company believed the trial values to be representative of the desired culture. Eventually, six values were chosen. The consultant then drafted some eighty leadership practice statements and asked task force members to agree on a final set, which turned out to be six practices behaviorally reflecting each value, for a total of thirty-six. The multisource process was then conducted with the thirty-six practices.

The core of the brief leadership program was feedback. Two different one-on-one coaching sessions were held: one early in the program to ensure that the participants understood the feedback and a more intensive one at the end to integrate all the feedback and plan action steps for individual change in leading others.

The MBTI and the LAI were used as context and background for understanding the multisource feedback on the thirty-six leadership practices. For example, on the leadership practice "provides clear direction regarding performance goals," participants scoring high on the intuitive dimension were more likely to be rated low on this practice by others. Intuitive types, in other words, are not as clear and specific in their communication as sensing types tend to be. The coaching process therefore was an attempt to deepen the understanding of one's feedback, integrate the various parts, and plan action for change.

Finally, at about the same time that the leadership got underway, the second organization-wide survey was conducted—a time 2 measure that used about 90 percent of the questions from time 1. On 125 questions, time 2 results showed that except for two items, which remained about the same, all the other ratings were higher.

Conclusion

Personality assessment can help with increasing individual self-awareness and support an OD effort as well. We hope that the case studies from actual OD interventions with individuals, teams, and whole systems that we have explored will stimulate OD researchers and practitioners to make linkages between individual and group personalities, behavior, and organizational life.

Practice Tips

1. It is important to remember Lewin's simple yet profound formula: $B = f(P, E)$, "B is a function of P and E"—that is, to diagnose behavior (B), one must understand both the individual's personality (P) and how the person perceives his or her environment (E). In a coaching situation, we must work to understand the individual's personality we are attempting to help and the context, particularly the workplace situation, within which the person is functioning.

2. No single personality assessment is sufficient to understand thoroughly an individual's personality. Individual personality is too complex for one questionnaire to do the job (although the NEO-PI does a reasonably comprehensive job, it is not thorough enough for assessing personality for leadership purposes), and a single assessment instrument is not perfect, after all, when it comes to reliability and validity. We must therefore rely on two or more instruments and look for patterns, overlap, and convergence to be more effective with our understanding. Choices regarding instruments need to be closely related to our OD objectives.

3. When using personality assessment as part of an OD effort, we must be patient and careful with the client. Personality assessment is personal. In the case of SmithKline Beecham's use of the MBTI,

Practice Tips, cont'd.

there was reluctance at the mere suggestion. Patiently describing the MBTI, its strengths and limitations, and responding to any and all questions was required. Moreover, what must be explained is how such assessment links to organization development goals and larger purposes. In the SmithKline Beecham example, it was linked to and in support of team building and to infuse a new language and ethos into the desired new culture of the merged corporation.

4. Consider using personality assessment as a means of determining root causes of behavior patterns, and develop action plans designed to address the drivers, rather than the symptoms, of the problem. Results of personality assessment can serve as a catalyst for a deeper conversation with a client in which an understanding of reinforcing attitudes and behaviors can be determined. A composite of personality instruments allows for a complex picture of the individual to emerge by making explicit what the interaction of behavior, thought, and emotion is and how it drives particular personality patterns within an individual.

   In the case of Jack, the understanding that developed as a result of personality assessment was in sharp contrast to how Jack initially described himself. The results of personality assessment revealed that Jack was not as disengaged from others as he initially presented; instead, he was driven by a strong need for interpersonal contact and intense relations with others. In this case, personality assessment was an effective tool to surface his derailers more quickly and hence develop an action plan aimed at the root cause of his behavior patterns.

5. Maintain a working hypothesis that when assessing personality of individuals and organizations, collecting data across situations facilitates a diagnosis. The level of understanding presented in the case of Jack is especially helpful when it is clear that an individual's specific pattern of behavior is self-defeating across situations, and as a result, he or she is at risk for not accomplishing business objectives and thus may be marginalized in the company. By determining an individual's valence, that is, a predisposition to act in certain ways across contexts, awareness can help the client to gain control of self-defeating behavior and allow for cognitive awareness to interrupt characteristic, knee-jerk reactions. Moreover, the individual will be less likely to explain the behavior as solely a function of the environment.

Practice Tips, cont'd.

6. Consider personality assessment as an intervention that can influence organizations at multiple levels. By using individual personality assessment in service of OD objectives, Jack's personality could be understood in the light of the company's, and more specifically, his department's, personality. Jack was referred for coaching as part of an overall OD intervention that was aimed at multiple levels of the organization. While other strategies were employed with the total system, the aim of coaching was to develop and implement an action plan that would take into account both the organization's goals and his goals. By focusing first on assisting Jack to understand his personality, the later work highlighted the interaction of his personality with that of his boss. The next step involved linking dyadic interactions between Jack and his boss to others in their department, as well as to the means by which work was accomplished. This resulted in a change in both vision and structure of the department.

References

Bauman, R. P., Jackson, P., & Lawrence, J. T. (1997). *From promise to performance.* Boston: Harvard Business School Press.

Burke, W. W. (1986). Leadership as empowering others. In S. Srivastva (Ed.), *Executive power: How executives influence people and organizations* (pp. 51–77). San Francisco: Jossey-Bass.

Burns, J. M. (1978). *Leadership.* New York: HarperCollins.

Campbell, D. P. (1991). *Manual for the Campbell Leadership Index.* Minneapolis, MN: National Computer Systems.

Church, A. H., & Waclawski, J. (1999). The impact of leadership style on global management practices. *Journal of Applied Social Psychology, 29*(7), 1416–1443.

Church, A. H., Waclawski, J., & Burke, W. W. (1996). OD practitioners as facilitators of change: An analysis of survey results. *Group and Organization Management, 21,* 22–66.

Church, A. H., Waclawski, J., & Burke, W. W. (2001). Multisource feedback for organization development and change. In D. W. Bracken, C. W. Timmreck, & A. H. Church (Eds.), *The handbook of multisource feedback* (pp. 301–317). San Francisco: Jossey-Bass.

Costa, P. T., & McCrae, R. R. (1991). *Revised NEO Personality Inventory (NEO PI-R)*. Odessa, FL: Psychological Assessment Resources.

Costa, P. T., & McCrae, R. R. (1992). *Revised NEO Personality Inventory (NEO PI-R): Professional manual*. Odessa, FL: Psychological Assessment Resources.

McCrae, R. R., & Costa, P. T. (1989). Reinterpreting the Myers-Briggs Type Indicator from the perspective of the Five-Factor Model of Personality. *Journal of Personality, 57,* 17–40.

Sashkin, M., & Burke, W. W. (1990). Understanding and assessing organizational leadership. In K. E. Clark & M. B. Clark (Eds.), *Measures of leadership* (pp. 297–325). West Orange, NJ: Leadership Library of America.

Schutz, W. (1990). *FIRO-B*. Palo Alto, CA: Consulting Psychologists Press.

Van Eron, A. M., & Burke, W. W. (1992). The transformational/transactional leadership model: A study of critical components. In K. E. Clark, M. B. Clark, & D. P. Campbell (Eds.), *Impact of leadership* (pp. 149–167). Greensboro, NC: Center for Creative Leadership.

Zaleznik, A. (1977). Managers and leaders: Are they different? *Harvard Business Review, 55*(3), 67–78.

CHAPTER 4

Surveys as a Tool for Organization Development and Change

Salvatore V. Falletta
Wendy Combs

The organizational survey is one of the most prevalent and long-standing data-driven methods for organization development (OD) and change. Surveys are common instruments used for many different purposes in organizational settings, among them to assess employee opinions and attitudes, evaluate programs and interventions, and conduct organizational research. Survey use in OD, however, is an entirely different process. More specifically, the survey itself is only part of the larger change effort. When this type of data collection methodology is applied to OD efforts, there are generally four underlying tenets: it is (1) grounded in systems theory and organizational behavior research, (2) model driven, (3) action research oriented, and (4) focused on strategic action planning and large-scale change. If a survey effort does not result in outcomes that yield widespread change throughout the organization, it cannot be characterized as an OD approach.

Four Tenets of Surveys for OD

The first way in which surveys used for OD purposes are distinct from other types of surveys is the extent to which the former are rooted in systems theory and empirical research on organizational behavior (Nadler, 1977). From an OD perspective, the organization is seen as a vital, living, interdependent entity that is a part of and reacts to its external surroundings. To this end, open systems theory characterizes an organization as a system that is dependent on its environment for input (for example, resources and raw materials), throughputs, and the consumption of organizational outputs (such as products and services) (Katz & Kahn, 1966). Systems theory recognizes both external and internal influences on the organization (see Chapter One). External factors that influence the organization include world financial conditions, global competition for products and services, and political and governmental regulations (Burke, 1994). Internal factors that influence the organization are the organization's senior leadership, functional design, culture and climate, human resource systems, and the quality of middle management, to name just a few. Applied research on the relationships and dynamics among these and other internal factors has led to specific models of organizational functioning and performance (Burke & Litwin, 1992; Nadler & Tushman, 1992; Tichy, 1983). Moreover, many of these factors and relationships have been determined through applied behavioral research to effect, or predict, specific organizational outcomes such as improved performance (Waclawski, 1996; Wiley, 1996). This is often done through linkage research where perceptual data from various surveys and feedback instruments are matched to hard performance measures (see also Chapters Two and Six).

The second way in which surveys for OD purposes differ from more traditional surveys is that they are model driven; that is, they are based on a specific model or conceptual framework that depicts how an organization functions. Model-driven survey efforts have recently become more popular in industrial/organizational (I/O) and related survey applications (Kraut & Saari, 1999), but they have long been the mainstay for conducting surveys within the context of OD.

From an OD perspective, a model is an abstract representation of the organization that depicts key factors within the system, their relationships to one another, and their overall effects on organizational outcomes. Some models describe the world in terms of leadership, culture, and employee motivation, while others focus more on issues of alignment, people and processes, or adaptability and organizational learning. Whatever their content, these models enable OD practitioners to gather and interpret information about the organization systematically. When used for OD purposes, these models are both a guide to the design of the survey content itself and an interpretation of the resulting diagnostic information obtained (Church & Waclawski, 1998, 2001). Aside from this contribution, however, it is important to recognize that the survey itself is only one piece of the larger change effort, which is typically also driven by the same organizational model. Thus, in an OD context, a survey might be used to assess the current state, as well as identify potential levers for change and perhaps measure improvement over time. It is not, however, meant to be the entire OD effort. The survey itself, after all, is only a tool for collecting information. What is actually done with that information is what defines the OD effort.

The third differentiator is that surveys done for OD are action research oriented. Action research is the systematic process of collecting data based on a specific goal or organizational problem (see Chapter One and French & Bell, 1995). The process involves repeated cycles of diagnosis, feedback, and action planning and change. The notion of diagnosis involves gathering and analyzing specific data and information to assess an organization's current level of functioning (Beer & Spector, 1993; Cummings & Worley, 1993). Diagnosis of the system or subsystem is necessary to understand fully the nature of the underlying problem, which may be symptomatic of something larger (Nadler, 1977). Hence, systematic diagnosis, as opposed to narrow and symptomatic diagnosis, involves examination of the total organizational system (Tichy, 1983). Following diagnosis, the results are fed back to the client or major stakeholders, that is, the decision makers, for the purpose of planning action. Although action planning and "action doing" are considered an integral part of the action research cycle, they are rarely carried out effectively and hence are considered crucial to the success of a survey used as part of an OD effort. Following implementation of the OD change intervention, the cycle begins anew.

The fourth and final difference between traditional surveys and surveys for OD is that the latter are considered an instrument for action planning and change. The action planning process involves identifying the most important issues for the organization to address, generating ideas and solutions to address these issues, selecting appropriate OD interventions for change, deciding on the best approach to implementation, actually making the change happen, and then tracking the results over time (Church & Waclawski, 1998, 2001; Hinrichs, 1996). It is not enough for the OD practitioner to report the results of a survey and leave the action planning to the client. For lasting change to occur across the entire system, all levels of the organization—corporate, business units, work groups, and individual line managers—must be held accountable for developing and implementing action plans and monitoring improvement. As part of this process, it is crucial that OD practitioners use their intimate understanding of the total organizational system to facilitate meaningful action planning, action doing, and follow-up with key stakeholders.

Using Models to Drive OD Survey Practice

Although numerous models for diagnosing organizations exist, three specific models that we recommend for OD-driven surveys are the Nadler-Tushman Congruence Model for Organization Analysis (1980, 1992), Tichy's Technical, Political, Cultural Framework (1983), and the Burke-Litwin Model of Organization Change (1992). (For a review of additional models, refer to Howard, 1994, and Harrison & Shirom, 1999.)

Each of these models differs with respect to the factors, or constructs, that are considered to be essential components of organizational functioning. Since no one model is inherently better than another, the choice of model on the part of the OD practitioner should be based on comfort, familiarity, and expertise with the model; fit within the given context and culture; the appropriateness given the issues being addressed; and the types of outcomes and interventions that the model generates.

Beginning with the Nadler and Tushman model (1980, 1992), the major premise here is, as the name implies, the notion of congruence. Nadler and Tushman define congruence as the degree to which needs, demands, goals, objectives, or structures of one construct of the model (for example, the system inputs) are consistent or fit with the needs, demands, goals, objectives, or structures of another construct of the model (such as the outputs). Figure 4.1 provides a graphical representation of this framework.

Figure 4.1. Nadler-Tushman Congruence Model.

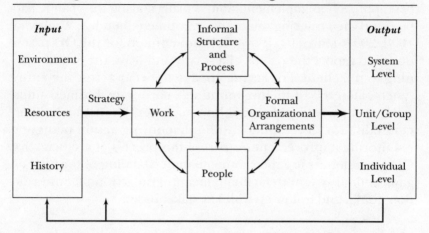

Source: Nadler & Tushman, 1992, p. 54. Reprinted by permission of Jossey-Bass, Inc., a subsidiary of John Wiley & Sons, Inc.

In diagnosing an organization through the use of this model, paired comparisons of constructs in the model are performed. For example, by comparing the people construct with the work construct, the OD practitioner would question how individual employee needs are met through work tasks and whether employees possess the skills and abilities to meet these task demands. In comparing the formal organizational arrangements with the informal organization, the OD practitioner would analyze whether the goals, rewards, and structures of the informal organization were consistent with those of the formal organization. Six pairs of these comparisons between the constructs in the system are typically performed (Nadler & Tushman, 1992). By analyzing the congruence of parts of the system, an organization can be characterized as exhibiting relatively high or low system congruence. Nadler and Tushman believe that incongruence between any of the system constructs will have a negative impact on organizational functioning and effectiveness.

Tichy (1983), in comparison, offers a far more streamlined approach for assessing organizational functioning in his model of strategic change. Although Tichy's framework is fundamentally similar to the Nadler and Tushman notion of congruence, there

Figure 4.2. Tichy's Strategic Rope Model.

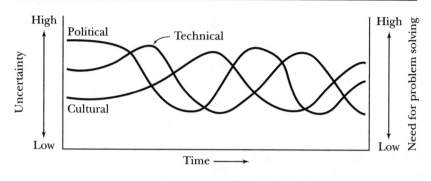

Source: Tichy, 1983, p. 12. Reprinted by permission of John Wiley & Sons, Inc.

are only three primary variables to consider: the technical (production methods, resources, organizational design, management systems), the political (power, decision making, senior leadership, union relations), and the cultural (normative glue, values, beliefs, history, communication) dynamics of the organization. Figure 4.2 provides a graphic depiction of this approach.

Using the metaphor of a strategic rope, diagnosis with the Tichy model centers on determining whether the three strands are unraveled entirely, weakened, or well woven (that is, integrated) together. Thus, the primary difference in this approach is that Tichy's model contains only one output variable: organizational effectiveness. Nonetheless, his model is often preferred by managers and executives (and many OD practitioners as well) because of its simplicity, ease of application, and the universal nature of the elements in the model.

The third and final OD framework is the Burke-Litwin model of organizational change and performance (Burke & Litwin, 1992). Figure 4.3 describes the basic components and their underlying relationships inherent in this approach.

Although many of the variables are familiar, one key difference in this approach is that Burke and Litwin distinguish *transactional* from *transformational* dynamics within the organization. This premise is rooted in leadership theory (Bass, 1997; Zaleznik, 1977), specifically in the difference between leaders (those charged with

Figure 4.3. Burke-Litwin Model.

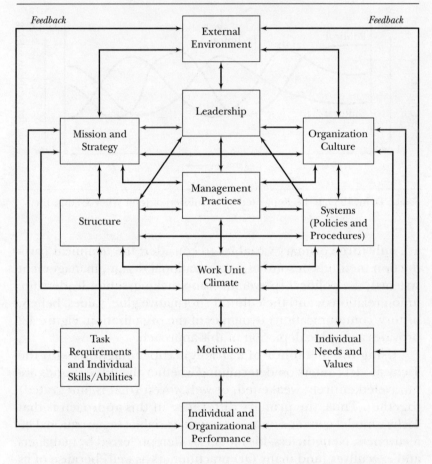

envisioning, guiding, inspiring, and transforming the organization) and managers (those charged with implementing the day-to-day routine transactional aspects of work). To this end, the transformational factors in the model include the external environment, mission and strategy, leadership, and culture and its impact on performance. These variables represent the top half of the model, where the most leverage for large-scale change resides.

Unlike the first two models, Burke and Litwin do not place an emphasis on diagnosing system congruence or alignment. Instead, they emphasize the importance of the interrelationships (or drivers) among the variables in the model and how these predict behavior and affect change (for an applied survey-driven example of this framework, see Burke, Coruzzi, & Church, 1996). In addition, performance in this model is conceptualized at both the individual and organizational levels—hence, the motivation, needs, and values, and task requirements boxes in the lower portion of the model in Figure 4.3. Organizational performance is a critical yet multidimensional construct. Performance can be measured in terms of revenue, productivity, quality, error reduction, employee turnover, and other factors, some of which are hard data (actual indicators of performance) rather than perceptual data. More often than not, performance outcomes are measured through survey items assessing individuals' perceptions of organizational performance. Ideally, the OD practitioner should strive to link survey data to direct performance indicators.

Designing Surveys for OD Purposes

Given that the content of surveys used for OD purposes typically is customized, although based on a consistent model and even some core items, it is important that any practitioner intending to use a survey for these purposes to be facile at the entire item development and construction process. (For a detailed discussion of the many steps involved in the construction of a survey instrument, see Church & Waclawski, 1998, 2001; Edwards, Thomas, Rosenfeld, & Booth-Kewley, 1997; Kraut, 1996; Rea & Parker, 1997.)

At a very general level, the customized content of surveys used for OD efforts is largely derived from two sources: the organizational model of choice (selected by the OD practitioner) and information from the client organization.

Selecting an OD Model

OD consulting models vary with respect to their level of specificity and applicability in different organizations and settings. Therefore, practitioners must be careful to select the right framework for clients. Sometimes this means using a model or survey framework that is simpler than the one he or she may be accustomed to working with, especially if the client organization has never conducted a survey before or has concerns about being able to work with a complex diagnostic framework.

As the old OD saying goes, one must "take the client where the client is." Savvy practitioners must be able to assess the client organization in terms of both its readiness for change and the level of comfort in using data-driven change methods. This is essential in that surveys done for OD purposes (especially "BIG OD" purposes, involving large-scale systemwide change—see Chapter Eight) are often driven by organizational members who are not usually (if at all) familiar with survey methods: senior management.

Moreover, the content of these surveys must be sufficiently strategic. That is, the issues or content included in a survey for OD are not the same as those included in an employee satisfaction survey. Without exception, surveys done for OD purposes need to include content that is in large part focused on transformational factors, such as the mission and strategy of the organization, the impact of the changing business environment, or global competition, as opposed to transactional or tactical factors, such as employees' satisfaction with their vision benefits and the extent to which work group members recognize one another for a job well done. After all, this is what chief executive officers and senior management (the ultimate drivers of change in any organization) are interested in and, perhaps more important, the level at which they operate and make decisions that affect the direction of the entire company.

In this capacity, the use of an OD consulting model as a framework for the survey is an invaluable tool, as many of these models place strong emphasis on transformational factors of organizational functioning. Furthermore, most include the essential elements of any good OD model: a means for assessing critical organizational inputs, throughputs, and outputs (see also Chapter One). This is quite different from the traditional I/O approach to surveying in which the organization survey would be based on a framework derived from extensive psychological theory and research or targeted at a specific problem, such as a highly focused survey on work-life balance. Moreover, whereas I/O surveys are more likely to be thoroughly tested and validated instruments, OD surveys are more likely to have been built using less rigorous psychometric standards. This is not to say that surveys constructed for OD purposes are poorly put together (particularly because many I/O practitioners in organizations are involved), merely that the process by which OD tools are designed is often quite different from that of traditional I/O surveys. This brings us to our second point: getting input from the organization.

Input from the Organization

In order to bring about fundamental change in an organization, the commitment of its members is an essential ingredient. From the OD perspective, the best way to gain commitment is through involving leadership and the rank and file in the OD effort.

When developing a survey for OD purposes, this often means doing some preliminary work to collect data about the organization and to build rapport with and get buy-in from key organizational members (Church & Waclawski, 1998, 2001). Both of these objectives can be accomplished (or at least facilitated) by the conduct of interviews and focus groups with senior leadership and other stakeholders (see Chapter Five).

Data collection before the survey through the use of interviews and focus groups is important because results from these efforts can be used to present a picture of the organization to senior leadership to help them identify and agree on areas in need of change, and therefore areas on which to focus the OD survey effort. Although the client (often the chief executive officer and his or her top team) may have many ideas about what needs to be fixed in the organization, there is rarely agreement among top team members on these areas.

For example, the CEO may think that the source of the organization's problem is its culture, whereas the chief financial officer is convinced that the organizational structure that is flawed. Moreover, these opinions about what is wrong may be inaccurate. Perhaps it is neither the culture nor the structure that is at fault, but the fact that organizational members are unclear about the organization's mission and strategy.

In fact, often what the OD consultant is brought into the organization to fix is not what he or she actually ends up helping with. In OD terminology, this initial interpretation of the problem by the client is known as the *presenting problem* (the problem that the client presents to the OD consultant to solve). In many instances, the presenting problem is not the actual problem, and the only way to determine this is through diagnosis (see Chapter Seven). Therefore, it is always advisable to conduct a preliminary diagnosis before launching an OD survey effort in order to get a general sense of the actual, not the presenting, problem in the organization.

Finally, the results of the preliminary diagnosis are typically presented back to senior leadership and others before the design and launch of the survey, organized according to the diagnostic model that will be used to drive the survey content (for example, by the various boxes of the Burke-Litwin model). This is helpful in getting the client to become familiar and comfortable with thinking about the organization in terms of the model. This also gives the OD practitioner a head start because it will make the design, conduct, and dissemination of the survey that much easier.

In the end, preliminary data collection is crucial to the success of an OD survey for five reasons:

1. It is a useful mechanism for building rapport.
2. It helps the OD practitioner learn about the people and organization he or she will be working with.
3. It is invaluable in getting senior leadership to come to agreement on major issues facing the organization and, as a consequence, act on them in a unified fashion going forward.
4. The ensuing survey content will be driven in large part by the combination of the organization model and the preliminary diagnosis.
5. In OD surveys, the survey is also a tool for communicating areas in need of focus. Therefore, using the diagnosis to drive the content of the survey will help the organization avert the potential problem of communicating the wrong messages about what needs to change (see Chapter Two).

The Survey as a Catalyst for Change

The importance of building rapport and commitment and gaining a shared understanding of the fundamental issues the organization is facing cannot be overstated; surveys when conducted for

OD are really being used as catalysts for change rather than for the purpose of data collection alone. More specifically, the end result of any OD survey effort is fundamental organizational change, not merely the dissemination of the survey results (as is often the case with surveys used for more traditional purposes). Therefore, it is essential that the OD practitioner spend time at the beginning of the survey effort building relationships with and gaining the support and commitment of organizational members. This is vital to being able to mobilize an organization to create change.

In addition, key organizational processes (rewards systems, information technology systems, organizational structure, leadership, and management behaviors) will be affected by the results of an OD survey effort; these elements of the organization will need to change. In some cases, the changes will be quite profound; they may entail changing the organization's compensation and reward systems to support new desired management behaviors or the implementation of a new organizational structure, for example. Changes of this magnitude cannot happen without involving the most senior leaders in the organization, because they alone have the power and authority needed to make and implement them. Therefore, their involvement in leading change must be unwavering, unified, and visible before the launch of the survey.

Putting the Survey Together

Once the results of the preliminary analysis have been gathered, analyzed, presented to, and owned by senior leadership, developing the content of the OD survey can begin. Again, this will be organized according to the consultant's model of choice. For example, an OD survey that is based on the Burke-Litwin model (Burke & Litwin, 1992) would be organized in twelve sections, each corresponding to the main factors: external environment, mission and strategy, leadership, culture, structure, management practices, systems, work group climate, skills and job match, motivation, individual needs and values, and individual and organizational performance. The survey items representing each of these factors would be developed based on the conceptualization of each construct and the specific needs of the client organization. Specifically, the skills and job match construct in the model is defined as the specific skills and abilities that people need to do their work and how well these skills match the requirements of their jobs (Burke & Litwin, 1992). Based on this conceptualization, the OD survey items corresponding to the skills and job match factor might include items such as these:

1. To what extent do you believe your skills appropriately fit the job you currently hold?
2. To what extent do you feel challenged in your job?
3. To what extent are the right people selected for assignment to projects in your organization?

In terms of the number of items per factor, three to five survey items is a good rule of thumb for adequately covering each model construct while minimizing item redundancy. Broader constructs such as leadership or culture may require more items to measure the phenomenon of interest adequately.

Given that the OD survey is being used to drive change within a particular organization (and not necessarily to provide an assessment or benchmark of how the organization compares with other organizations), the content of an OD survey typically contains both a set of core items, which have been used and tested in other organizations and are therefore more generic, and a set of customized items developed specifically for the client in question and generally based on results of the preliminary diagnosis.

The last step in the item development process is the selection of the item-response alternatives and scales. The 5-point Likert-type scale is the most common, but many scale alternatives are available (for good references on the subject, see Church and Waclawski, 2001).

Delivering the OD Survey

Just a few years ago, computer and Web-based technology was considered an alternative to the traditional paper-and-pencil survey (Kuhnert & McCauley, 1996). Today, Web-based technology provides an efficient vehicle for OD survey delivery (see Chapter Twelve). Moreover, recent research has found no significant difference in measurement equivalence between paper- and Web-based survey administration (Donovan, Drasgow, & Probst, 2000; Stanton, 1998). Therefore, these types of delivery methods can prove invaluable for OD survey practitioners (or any other survey practitioners, for that matter). Following are some of the advantages to using Web-based technology for survey delivery:

- Global reach—the ability to distribute surveys to a geographically dispersed population in real time
- Real-time monitoring—the ability to monitor response rates in real time
- Automatic data validation—the ability to alert the respondent to missing data and invalid responses
- Instant feedback and reporting—the ability to provide immediate on-line feedback and reporting to stakeholders
- Customization for specific audiences—the ability to skip ahead of irrelevant items based on previous responses
- Higher-quality open-ended responses due to typed, as opposed to handwritten, responses—the ability to edit comments prior to survey submission

Advances have also been made in information security and the means through which survey confidentiality is ensured. For example, many Web-based survey providers use data encryption, firewall security technology, and password protection to assure employees and organizations of data security.

Although Web-based surveys represent the preferred mode of delivery, paper-and-pencil surveys will continue to be used with populations without access to the Internet. Thus, both modes of delivery, either separately or together, are likely to continue in use.

Types of Analysis

The means by which an OD practitioner analyzes survey data are generally no different from those employed for the analysis of more traditional surveys. However, often the actual presentation of the survey data is different.

The Gestalt of OD Survey Analysis

Surveys for OD purposes in general place more effort and emphasis on the development of a highly developed executive summary that tells a story about the organization, including what is going well and what is not. This goes beyond the more typical survey summary presentation of high and low ratings and presents the OD practitioner's data-based diagnostic inferences.

This strategic emphasis on the executive summary component is logical since the OD practitioner's first presentation of the survey results will be to the CEO (usually one-on-one) and then with the CEO and the top team of executives as a group. During this presentation, which generally lasts anywhere from one to four hours, the OD practitioner spends the majority of time reintroducing the consulting or diagnostic model and subsequently walking the top team through this summary.

The summary is almost always presented in a narrative form and not as a series of bar and pie charts, although these will be included in the report as supplemental material. And although the OD survey report will certainly contain a full listing of factor summary scores and item averages for every survey question, these elements will not be the focus of the survey debriefing with the top team. Rather, the practitioner will present his or her diagnosis of the organization using the consulting model of choice and which happens to be based on the results of the survey organized according to that model. In essence, the practitioner is using the survey results to tell a compelling story to senior management about the current state of the organization (see Church & Waclawski, 2001). This is the power of the survey done for OD purposes: it is a vehicle for diagnosing and understanding the complex interrelationships among issues in the organization that affect its functioning at both the strategic and tactical levels.

The Nuts and Bolts of Survey Analysis

OD surveys can be analyzed using four techniques: item analysis, conceptual analysis, comparative analysis, and content analysis (Church & Waclawski, 1998, 2001). Item, conceptual, and comparative analyses are all used when working with quantitative survey data; content analysis (see Chapter Five) is used for qualitative data. (For a complete description, see Church & Waclawski, 2001.)

Item analysis generally involves describing data in terms of frequencies, means, standard deviations, ranges, and percentages and is the simplest type of analysis. This method is an important first step in identifying relative highs and lows in the data set. Because item analysis is applicable to individual survey items only (the unit of analysis is at the item level alone), the more complex relationships evident in the data are not uncovered without further analysis.

Conceptual analysis is more advanced and generally involves testing relationships among the different factors in the survey—those identified by the OD consulting model being used. In this type of analysis, descriptive statistics are also used to describe the relative highs and lows and the relationships among constructs. However, the analysis goes further in that inferential statistics are used to test relationships among the various elements of the model in relation to the survey data. One trend that is gaining popularity in all realms of survey practice is linking these conceptual-level data to other types of performance-related data (or hard measures; see Chapters Two and Six) collected by the organization, such as increased sales, net profits, or turnover (Waclawski, 1996; Wiley, 1996). If done with the appropriate level of rigor, this technique adds power, utility, and credibility to any survey process.

Comparative analysis involves comparing the survey results of one group or organization to another, comparing the results over time, or comparing the results of one company to another or to the industry (Church & Waclawski, 1998, 2001). These comparisons may involve item or construct comparisons, as well as demographic comparisons.

The fourth type of analysis is performed on open-ended or write-in survey questions—for example, "What is currently going well at Company XYZ?" *Content analysis* involves categorizing open-ended responses into major themes. These data are far more descriptive in nature and are a rich complement to quantitative data because they often help to add context.

In analyzing and interpreting the data through each of these techniques, the OD practitioner should be aware of the level of organizational behavior (macro versus micro level) that is being described. Data may represent the individual, group, or organizational level, and as a result, interpretations may be more valid at one level of the organization than another. For example, the survey results for the company as a whole are likely to obscure findings at the group or individual level. Because this is a typical effect when working with large data sets and accompanying averages, recommendations for change should be targeted at the appropriate level.

Hence, specific interventions should be planned at the functional manager or group level, and large-scale strategic change efforts should be aimed at the corporate level. Because the organization is a complex system, multilevel analyses and interpretations are required (Klein & Kozlowski, 2000).

Once analyses have been conducted, the results are typically reported back to the organization through a series of cascading workshops beginning with the CEO and senior team. The ultimate goal of these workshops is the transfer of data ownership from being the practitioners' data to being the clients' data, action planning, and ultimately action doing. (For a model discussion of the types of action planning strategies that OD practitioners often use, see Church & Waclawski, 2001.)

Reporting in an Age of Speed

Today's business environment requires rapid data analysis and reporting, and OD practitioners are under constant pressure to deliver timely and meaningful results to stakeholders. Rapid reporting also has a clear, positive effect on stakeholders and the overall change process: they are eager to hear the results, identify changes and interventions, and implement solutions in a rapid decision-making cycle. Although technological advancements such as real-time feedback and reporting are promising, data analysis, interpretation, and reporting activities are still relatively time-consuming activities. Nevertheless, there are several ways of planning for rapid turnover of results:

- Allocate extra resources to analysis, interpretation, and reporting activities.
- Specify anticipated analyses up-front in a data analyses plan.
- Prepare and approve customized reporting templates for different audiences in advance of data collection.

Reporting may include item analysis, conceptual analysis, comparative analysis, and content analysis. Customized reports should be available shortly after. The bottom line is that a considerable amount of forethought is required to deliver high-quality survey reporting in a timely manner.

Action Doing

Stakeholders may experience general anxiety over the survey results, and there may be a tendency to blame the messenger. This reluctance in accepting responsibility for the OD survey results is a barrier to transferring ownership of the data to stakeholders (Church & Waclawski, 1998, 2001). Even with a well-intentioned action planning process, organizations may fail to implement changes for a number of reasons:

- A clear mandate for change from organizational leaders may be lacking.
- Senior leaders may not have a line of sight into the survey results and hence may not acknowledge or legitimize action planning as critical to the company's success.
- Reward and incentive systems may not promote a results-oriented organizational culture, or these systems may reward other indicators of success, minimizing any incentive to attend to survey results.
- Formal mechanisms such as operations reviews for reporting and tracking performance may be lacking.

Because of these and other potential barriers to the change process, the action planning cycle is fairly structured. It involves the following steps:

1. Prioritizing organizational issues or gaps identified by the OD survey initiative
2. Identifying possible solutions or interventions across the organization
3. Selecting and committing to specific interventions at each level of the organization
4. Planning the implementation of each intervention
5. Following up with a new data-gathering cycle for further improvements

Only through this final step of the OD survey process will the effort lead to systemic change across the organization.

Case Study: Intel's Global OD Survey

Intel Corporation, a Fortune 100 company, used the Burke-Litwin Model of Organization Change as the basis for a company-wide OD survey effort. Intel supplies the computer and telecommunications industries with networking and communications products such as microprocessors, boards, systems, software, and servers. In 2000, the company had a worldwide workforce of over eighty-five thousand employees.

The Human Resources Research (HRR) group, part of Intel's corporate human resource organization, was chartered to design and implement an OD survey to diagnose current levels of organizational functioning. HRR chose to apply the Burke-Litwin model to design a valid and reliable OD survey, identify high-leverage factors affecting organizational outcomes, prescribe OD interventions for large-scale change, and develop a better model for Intel to use in subsequent survey administrations. The Burke-Litwin model was chosen because of its level of specificity and its theoretical and empirical grounding.

The Burke-Litwin model served as a framework for the development of the survey constructs and specific items. Warner Burke was personally contacted to obtain approval to use the survey instrument he had developed and used for research on the model in the past. Additional survey items were constructed to fully represent each of the survey constructs as applicable to Intel. The wording of many of the items was also changed to reflect business terminology commonly used at Intel. In total, the survey contained 112 items. More than 5 survey items were used for each construct because the design team planned to perform advanced statistical analysis to identify those items contributing the most measurement precision.

The OD survey was delivered primarily through the Internet, with a paper-based version made available to employees without Internet access. The Web-based survey technology tracked and reported employee responses in real time. Internet response rates (54.3 percent, with 7,530 responses) were higher than the paper-based response rates (42.4 percent, with 833 responses), and the overall response rate was considered adequate within the context of organizational behavior research (Roth & BeVier, 1998).

OD Survey Analysis

Item analysis, conceptual analysis, comparative analysis, and content analysis were performed simultaneously as soon as the data set was complete. As part of the item analysis, cross-tabulations were calculated for each item and for constructs by select demographic variables, such as organization and job type. The tabulations were reviewed and compared from one organization to the next to highlight any differences in the data at the organizational level. Each of the thirty-six business units received a customized report with descriptive statistics (for example, means, standard deviations, and sample sizes) for their organization in particular and the corporation as a whole. These customized reports were later used for action planning at the business group level. Comparative analysis of the data from group to group was limited to comparisons between individual groups and the summary results; for example, the descriptive statistics for the e-business organization were compared to the descriptive statistics for the corporation as a whole.

As part of the conceptual analysis, regression analysis was performed on the complete data set to assess the strength of relationships among survey constructs, that is, the extent of correlation between survey constructs. Significant and practically meaningful relationships among the constructs were evident. To refine the survey for future administration, structural equations modeling was planned and is currently being performed to build a better model for Intel's unique business culture. Through this process, certain items will be identified as contributing minimal added measurement value and will be deleted. The revised survey will likely include fewer constructs (seven to eight variables) and fewer survey items (fifty to sixty items). The purpose is to use only the constructs and items with high validity and reliability in the next iteration of the survey.

Content analysis was performed on the open-ended survey items. One open-ended item had been included on the survey for each of the twelve constructs, for a total of twelve open-ended items. The written, or rather, typed comments to the open-ended items yielded over fifteen hundred pages of responses requiring analysis. This data were reviewed and analyzed for major themes that were identified after the survey. This information was extremely useful in providing context around the results of the quantitative analysis within the overarching survey constructs.

The results of these analyses were presented to stakeholders at multiple levels of the corporation for action planning. These presentations and working sessions included an educational component to help stakeholders understand the purpose of the Burke-Litwin model, the survey results, and the usefulness of the theory underlying the model in terms of identifying actions for change.

Action Planning and Change

The survey results were immediately presented to the vice president of human resource and the senior executive staff, including Intel's CEO and board of directors. Following these formal presentations, the HRR group hosted a research symposium. The OD survey results were used as a primary data source for action planning at the corporate level.

Action planning at the corporate level primarily centered around four of the constructs in the Burke-Litwin model: leadership, structure, culture, and systems. While the management practices construct was relatively high, the leadership construct was slightly lower. Further examination of the items and open-ended responses related to the leadership construct suggested that new approaches to leadership development are needed to ensure Intel's continued success given the company's new vision and mission, growth in business diversification, and increasingly global workforce. As a result of the OD survey effort, a leadership development strategy is being designed to address executive training and development, succession management, and coaching. The organizational structure, culture, and systems constructs were also identified as priority areas for action at the corporate level, with specific initiatives under way to address each area.

The Burke-Litwin model was valuable in providing a framework for designing the OD survey, interpreting the resultant data, identifying the high leverage factors with the biggest impact on organizational functioning, and ultimately guiding the prescription of OD interventions for change. Of importance, the model illustrated the interrelation among the constructs in the model and the importance of targeting interventions at each of these areas to achieve the greatest overall impact on the system. The success and impact of the interventions that are being designed will be measured through subsequent administrations of the refined survey.

Conclusion

Surveys conducted for OD purposes differ from organizational surveys conducted for other purposes in several important respects. First and foremost, surveys when conducted for OD are used for the explicit purpose of creating large-scale organizational change (as opposed to other purposes for which one might conduct a survey). As a result, their design is typically based on a model of organizational functioning that is rooted in OD theory and practice. This means that the items contained in the survey are developed within the framework of an OD consulting model and are typically generated by or customized from the results of a preliminary diagnosis conducted within the framework of the same model. Results are then analyzed and presented to the organization with an emphasis on providing the client with a focused diagnostic picture of the organization as a whole that takes into consideration inputs, throughputs, and outputs. Finally, the OD survey process requires that action be taken at multiple levels of the organization as a result of the data-gathering process. In the end, if the survey does not result in taking action and creating change in the organization, then it was not truly an OD effort. Finally, by applying the action research framework, follow-up is built into the cycle with subsequent data-gathering efforts, revealing the extent and impact of actual change across the organization.

Practice Tips

1. Use an OD diagnostic or consulting model derived from theory and research to guide OD survey development.
2. Conduct a preliminary diagnosis of the organization (if feasible) using interviews and focus groups.
3. Use Web-based technology for survey delivery, monitoring, and reporting if appropriate; otherwise, use paper and pencil or optical scan forms.
4. Plan to analyze and interpret data in a rapid decision-making cycle.
5. Analyze the data using item, conceptual, comparative, and content analysis techniques; analyze and interpret the data with respect to the appropriate level (individual, group, or organization).
6. Build in time for key stakeholders to review the results before planning OD and change interventions.
7. Require executives and managers to build accountability into the action planning and action doing cycle from the start.
8. Track action planning activities across the company to leverage best practices and share lessons learned.

References

Bass, B. M. (1997). Does the transactional-transformational leadership paradigm transcend organizational and national boundaries? *American Psychologist, 52,* 130–139.

Beer, M., & Spector, B. (1993). Organizational diagnosis: Its role in organizational learning. *Journal of Counseling and Development, 71,* 642–650.

Burke, W. W. (1994). *Organization development: A process of learning and changing* (2nd ed.). Reading, MA: Addison-Wesley.

Burke, W. W., Coruzzi, C. A., & Church, A. H. (1996). The organizational survey as an intervention for change. In A. I. Kraut (Ed.), *Organizational surveys: Tools for assessment and change* (pp. 41–66). San Francisco: Jossey-Bass.

Burke, W. W., & Litwin, G. H. (1992). A causal model of organizational performance and change. *Journal of Management, 18,* 523–545.

Church, A. H., & Waclawski, J. (1998). *Designing and using organizational surveys.* Aldershot, England: Gower.

Church, A. H., & Waclawski, J. (2001). *Designing and using organizational surveys: A seven-step process.* San Francisco: Jossey-Bass.

Cummings, T. G., & Worley, C. G. (1993). *Organization development and change* (5th ed.). Minneapolis, MN: West.

Donovan, M. A., Drasgow, F., & Probst, T. (2000). Does computerizing paper-and-pencil job attitude scales make a difference? New IRT analyses offer insight. *Journal of Applied Psychology, 85,* 305–313.

Edwards, J. E., Thomas, M. D., Rosenfeld, P., & Booth-Kewley, S. (1997). *How to conduct organizational surveys: A step-by-step guide.* Thousand Oaks, CA: Sage.

French, W. L., & Bell, C. H., Jr. (1995). *Organization development: Behavioral science interventions for organization improvement* (5th ed.). Upper Saddle River, NJ: Prentice Hall.

Harrison, M. I., & Shirom, A. (1999). *Organizational diagnosis and assessment: Bridging theory and practice.* Thousand Oaks, CA: Sage.

Hinrichs, J. R. (1996). Feedback, action planning, and follow-through. In A. I. Kraut (Ed.), *Organizational surveys: Tools for assessment and change.* San Francisco: Jossey-Bass.

Howard, A. (Ed.). (1994). *Diagnosis for organizational change: Methods and models.* New York: Guilford Press.

Katz, D., & Kahn, R. L. (1966). *The social psychology of organizations.* New York: Wiley.

Klein, K. J., & Kozlowski, S.W.J. (Eds.). (2000). *Multilevel theory, research, and methods in organizations: Foundations, extensions, and new directions.* San Francisco: Jossey-Bass.

Kraut, A. I. (Ed.). (1996). *Organizational surveys: Tools for assessment and change.* San Francisco: Jossey-Bass.

Kraut, A. I., & Saari, L. M. (1999). Organization surveys coming of age for a new era. In A. I. Kraut & A. K. Korman (Eds.), *Evolving practices in human resource management: Responses to a changing world of work* (pp. 302–327). San Francisco: Jossey-Bass.

Kuhnert, K., & McCauley, D. P. (1996). Applying alternative survey methods. In A. I. Kraut (Ed.), *Organizational surveys: Tools for assessment and change* (pp. 233–254). San Francisco: Jossey-Bass.

Nadler, D. A. (1977). *Feedback and organization development: Using data-based methods.* Reading, MA: Addison-Wesley.

Nadler, D. A., & Tushman, M. L. (1980, Autumn). A model for diagnosing organizational behavior. *Organizational Dynamics,* 35–51.

Nadler, D. A., & Tushman, M. L. (1992). Designing organizations that have good fit: A framework for understanding new architectures. In D. A. Nadler, M. S. Gerstein, & R. B. Shaw (Eds.), *Organizational architecture: Designs for changing organizations* (pp. 39–59). San Francisco: Jossey-Bass.

Rea, L. M., & Parker, R. A. (1997). *Designing and conducting survey research: A comprehensive guide* (2nd ed.). San Francisco: Jossey-Bass.

Roth, P. L., & BeVier, C.A. (1998). Response rates in HRM/OB survey research: Norms and correlates, 1990–1994. *Journal of Management, 24,* 97–117.

Stanton, J. M. (1998). An empirical assessment of data collection using the Internet. *Personnel Psychology, 51,* 709–725.

Tichy, N. M. (1983). *Managing strategic change: Technical, political, and cultural dynamics.* New York: Wiley.

Waclawski, J. (1996). Using organization survey results to improve organizational performance. *Managing Service Quality 6,* 53–57.

Wiley, J. W. (1996). Linking survey results to customer satisfaction and business performance. In A. I. Kraut (Ed.), *Organizational surveys: Tools for assessment and change* (pp. 330–359). San Francisco: Jossey-Bass.

Zaleznik, A. (1977). Managers and leaders: Are they different? *Harvard Business Review, 55,* 67–78.

CHAPTER 5

Interviews and Focus Groups

Quintessential Organization Development Techniques

Janine Waclawski
Steven G. Rogelberg

Interviews and focus group data have a multitude of applications and are essential to organization development (OD) practitioners (Cummings & Worley, 1997; Fordyce & Weil, 2000). This chapter explores uses including but not limited to team building, organizational assessment, and developing multisource feedback and survey instruments for strategic change. In addition, we present best practices for conducting effective interviews and successfully facilitating focus groups within the context of OD work.

It is important to recognize that interviews and focus groups represent a qualitative and therefore somewhat subjective approach to data-driven OD. This is not meant to diminish the importance of these two staples of OD practice, but instead is meant as a point of differentiation. More specifically, the type of information collected from these methods is somewhat different from data obtained using some of the more quantitative methods discussed throughout this book, such as surveys and multisource feedback. This is an important distinction because this difference also affects the uses of these types of data.

Uses of Interviews in OD Work

Although interviews as a technique have well documented applications in many other areas of industrial/organizational (I/O) practice, such as job interviews and exit interviews, this chapter focuses on using interviews specifically for the purpose of OD. Interviews often receive short shrift in many OD texts, yet they are one of the principal data collection methods for OD work (Burke, 1994; Cummings & Worley, 1997; Fordyce & Weil, 2000) and are probably one of the most widely used techniques in all of OD (Cummings & Worley, 1997). Typically, interviews are used for two purposes in OD practice: to diagnose the functioning of teams or working groups, such as senior executive teams, steering committees, and task forces, and to gather exploratory data for other interventions and initiatives.

Using Interviews for Diagnosis

Arguably, the most prevalent use of interviews in OD is for diagnostic work. This entails conducting interviews with teams or intact work groups in order to solve problems or better understand the nature of a group's interaction style or dynamic. Used in this context, interviews represent one of the fundamental tools of OD practitioners. In fact, for many, this approach represents the fundamental characterization of what is truly an OD approach. When most people think of "doing OD," they think of conducting interviews with teams. Moreover, when used in this manner, interviews are considered to be a self-contained (Morgan, 1997) or stand-alone tool for research and diagnosis. In other words, no additional method of data collection is necessary.

OD practitioners often use interviews with senior management teams (Church & Waclawski, 1998, 2001) in order to help team members better understand previously unsurfaced issues they have around a certain topic or problem, such as poor communication, lack of intragroup cooperation, the inability to deal with conflict, or turf issues. In this context, the purpose of these interviews is not only to enhance understanding and raise awareness of existing conditions within the team but also to identify action items for improvement based on information that has been identified in the interview process. Moreover, and more important, from the OD perspective, interviews when used as the sole means of diagnosis in teams or groups are designed not only to gain a better understanding of the issues under consideration, but fundamentally to serve as a catalyst for change and improvement (see Chapter Eight for a discussion of team-based OD interventions). By providing a means for soliciting the thoughts, opinions, beliefs, and perceptions of team members, the interview represents a powerful tool for validating people's concerns and providing the interviewer with rich information that can be fed back to team members in their own words. In this way, data that are qualitative in nature can be used to create change and improve group functioning.

Using Interviews to Gather Exploratory Data

In OD, interviews are also often used to gather exploratory data, used for three primary purposes. First, these data are useful as preliminary input for informing and developing additional diagnostic tools. For example, interview results are often used to determine the appropriate content for the development of a culture change survey or the critical management behaviors that an organization needs to assess through a customized multisource feedback system (see Chapters Two and Four for descriptions of survey and MSF processes).

Second, exploratory interview data are often used to provide more detail regarding previously identified issues and concerns. In fact, it is not uncommon for OD practitioners to use the interview process to collect specific and targeted information on a problem or issue that has arisen, such as a prior survey, another consulting effort, or the client's own opinions or theories. In this instance, interviews are the method of choice primarily because of the detailed nature of the information that can be collected. Interviews as compared with more quantitative measures such as questionnaires provide the interviewer the opportunity to probe not only for additional information with respect to the nature, characteristics, or causes of a problem, but also for contextual and explanatory information that cannot be captured through other means. For example, interviews allow the OD practitioner the flexibility to ask why and how questions that rarely get explored in detail through traditional survey methods because of their structured format (an example is a 5-point Likert-type scale). As a result, the flexibility of the interview process is a major factor in using interviews for this type of OD work. Furthermore, interviews when done well establish rapport (Morgan, 1997) between the OD practitioner and the interviewee. This is vitally important to helping the practitioner build a relationship of trust and mutual respect that will serve as a foundation for much of the OD work that is likely to result from the interview diagnosis. This rapport may also serve to produce more honest and complete information than one could obtain from the administration of a more formal questionnaire. Finally, individual background and biographical information that may shed light on the presenting problem or issue can be explored in much greater detail in the one-on-one interview process (Kvale, 1996; Morgan, 1997).

The third use of interviews for exploratory data collection is for post-OD intervention evaluation. More specifically, interviews are often conducted at the conclusion of an OD intervention, such as a team-building effort, to evaluate the effectiveness of the work. Similarly, interviews are useful after a large-scale survey to evaluate the success of the survey effort and plan modifications and improvements to the process in the future.

All of these approaches help explain the popularity of interviews as an OD tool. They can be used in all phases of an OD effort, from the diagnosis of a problem through the intervention and including follow-up.

Four Steps to Using Interviews in OD

In general, there are four steps to conducting an effective interview: (1) preparing for and staging the interview, (2) conducting the interview, (3) analyzing the interview results, and (4) presenting the interview results and taking action. (There are many excellent sources on specific interviewing techniques. See Kvale, 1996; Miles & Huberman, 1994; Seidman, 1991; and Van Maanen, 1988.)

Step 1: Preparing for and Staging the Interview

Setting the stage for the interview is important (Kvale, 1996); it determines not only whether the interview will run smoothly but also has an enormous impact on the nature (whether the responses are honest and candid) and the amount of data collected (whether the interviewee is comfortable and talkative). In fact, some of the biggest obstacles to effective interviews in any context are related to lack of interviewer skill and preparation (Hyman, 1955). This includes the ever-popular concern about getting buy-in or commitment to change from the appropriate organizational stakeholders. In short, OD practitioners must do their homework in terms of preparing for the interview itself and contracting with the client organization to get support for the interview process.

In our experience, preparation for the interview consists primarily of selecting interview participants, developing an appropriate interview protocol, and making sure that the interviewee is comfortable and receptive to the interview process.

When conducting interviews for diagnostic purposes, we strongly recommend that the OD practitioner include the entire team in the interview process. In other words, an individual interview should be conducted with each team member. The duration of the interview will generally range from one to two hours in length depending on the nature of the problem or issue being discussed. When conducting interviews for exploratory purposes, either a census or sampling approach can be used. (A census involves interviewing everyone in a department or function; sampling involves interviewing a selected number of people.) Which approach is chosen depends on a host of factors, including the purpose of the data collection, the size of the group, and the costs. Sampling procedures for choosing interviewees should follow the guidelines normally associated with sampling guidelines established for other qualitative and quantitative research methods research (for more detail, see Babbie, 1973; Morgan, 1997; Schuman & Kalton, 1985). Although employees sometimes complain about participating in data collection efforts such as these, not selecting a particular employee or group of employees could present more serious issues, such as perceptions of unfairness, exclusion, biases, and lack of appropriate representation.

Regarding interview protocol preparation, the questions asked should reflect the issue or series of issues to be examined. When using interviews for team diagnoses, for example, questions are often designed to assess topics such as the extent to which team members cooperate with one another in accomplishing work, whether there is a shared vision for the future, and how well members get along with one another. Regardless of what questions are used in the interview protocol, one significant consideration is timing. It is important to make sure that the interviewee has enough time to answer each question completely and thoughtfully. (See Exhibit 5.1 for an example of interview questions for diagnostic purposes.)

Creating a positive environment that fosters receptivity is also important to the quality of the interview. For example, it is usually a good idea to sit where the interviewee can see your notes. This will ease the mind of the interviewee, who may be nervous about what you are recording and whether it is accurate. It also lets him or her know that you are open and have nothing to hide. This is important given the sensitive nature of some of the questions that are often asked in a diagnostic interview—for example, "What is not going well in your team, and how does your manager contribute to this situation?" "What should he or she stop doing?" "What should he or she do more of?" "Is he or she competent?" The important thing to keep in mind here is that the interviewee should be as comfortable as possible to facilitate the free flow of information, which ultimately affects the quality of the data that are obtained.

Exhibit 5.1. Sample Interview Questions.

1. Briefly tell me about yourself, your background, and your current work situation.
2. What is going well at PetroCorp? In your area?
3. What is not going well at PetroCorp? In your area?
4. Describe the current PetroCorp culture.
5. Describe the ideal PetroCorp culture.
6. How does the PetroCorp management committee operate as a team? Is it effective?
7. What changes have you seen since Pat Doe became CEO? Is she effective?
8. What changes would you like to see at PetroCorp?
9. If you were the CEO of PetroCorp, what would you do differently?

Step 2: Conducting the Interview

In order to set the proper tone and ground rules for the discussion, it is customary to begin the interview with an introduction of yourself and your background, and provide an explicit description of the purpose of the interview and the data analysis plan (Kvale, 1996). It is imperative that you never assume that the interviewee has been informed, fully or otherwise, as to the purpose of the interview and the plans for using the results. In fact, in many interviews we have conducted, the meeting with the interviewer marked the first instance in which the interviewee received a detailed explanation of the purpose of the interview. Furthermore, when using an interview for OD purposes, being honest and candid about the reason for the interview and what will happen to the results is of paramount importance. Moreover, an assurance of confidentiality is critical so that the interviewee feels that he or she can share freely without fear of having his or her individual comments identified. This is essential to the quality of the data collected and is a standard part of most OD efforts.

Finally, in order to ensure consistent conditions across interview sessions, it is best to read the questions as written and probe inadequate answers for clarification (Kvale, 1996). Always provide your contact information in case the interviewee has any questions or concerns, and before closing, be sure to discuss what the summary of findings will contain, as well as what it will not, and how the data will be used to help the organization. Once all of the interviews have been completed, it is a good idea to send a letter to all of the participants both to thank them for their participation and to inform them about next steps.

Step 3: Analyzing the Interview Results

There are two tools often used that OD practitioner often use to analyze interview results: force-field analysis and content analysis.

Force-field analysis (Lewin, 1951) is a fundamental tool for team and organization diagnosis in OD (Burke, 1982, French & Bell, 1990). It is also a very useful approach for analyzing interview results for diagnostic purposes (French & Bell, 1990). However, before we describe the technique itself, it is useful to understand some of the fundamental social-psychological assumptions on which it is built.

According to Lewin (1951), an individual's behavior (B) is a function (f) of his or her personality (P), operationalized as motivations, and the environment (E) within which he or she is operating (Burke, 1982)—hence, the equation $B = f(P, E)$. To understand individual and group behavior better, it is necessary to understand not only the motivations of the individuals involved but also the forces that are acting on them in their own environment.

Operating under these assumptions, the OD practitioner uses a force-field analysis to understand group process and performance better through an examination of individual and group motivations and actions, in the environment or context within which these actions occur. This approach is founded on the principle that a group is a social system operating within a field (its environment) and that in order to understand and predict the actions of the individuals who comprise the group as well as the group itself, one must consider the forces (environmental conditions) involved. These environmental forces can be positive or negative in nature; that is, they can enable (drive) or hinder (restrain) performance. Because it takes into account the impact of environmental or contextual factors, force-field analysis is a unique and fundamental component of the OD approach. Moreover, it is this systemic perspective that differentiates this method of analysis from others more familiar to I/O practitioners.

For example, when analyzing interview results (see Exhibit 5.2), OD practitioners often use this force-field analysis framework to categorize interviewee responses and to formulate a diagnosis of the group or team's functioning. This approach is very practical since the outcome typically suggests actions for improvement, such as barriers to performance that need to be removed and enabling forces that need to be maintained and strengthened.

The second technique for analyzing interview results is content analysis, which consists of analyzing interview results in order to identify and quantify major themes of responses and their frequency (see Exhibit 5.3). A major benefit of this approach is that it allows the practitioner to provide organization, structure, and some level of quantification to the verbal data collected through interviews and focus groups. This benefit cannot be understated, as it often lends greater credibility to the qualitative interview data in the eyes of clients who are accustomed to thinking of data solely as numbers.

**Exhibit 5.2. Sample Force-Field Analysis
Results of Team Performance.**

Enablers	Pressures	Barriers
We have a clear vision for the future.	⬅➡	We have weak organizational support for the innovation and process improvement needed to achieve our vision.
We have clear objectives linked to vision.	⬅➡	We operate not as a team but as independent agents.
We have the right people (skills and abilities) in place to achieve our vision.	⬅➡	Our current culture does not foster teamwork, which will be needed to achieve our vision
We have a strong and unified culture.	⬅➡	Our culture is highly politicized and thwarts growth and creativity.

When done correctly, content analysis is very systematic and follows a prescribed and sequential process (Church & Waclawski, 1998, 2001). Generally, it is done by the investigative team, which typically consists of the practitioner and his or her assistants (Krueger, 1994). The process itself is a series of steps beginning with the identification and validation of content themes, followed by training content coders about appropriate coding rules, and concluding with the categorization of comments by the themes identified and a tabulation of the number of similar responses (typically a frequency count) per theme (see Morris, 1994, for a detailed description of this process). In fact, content analysis can also be subject to subgroup analysis—for example, an analysis of the findings by participant gender, organizational level, or age. With or without these subgroup analyses, the final result of content analysis is a mixture of qualitative and quantitative data. This type of information can be very rich and provide the OD practitioner with many insights and valuable opportunities for discussions with the client. However, one caution should be noted: the ability to

Exhibit 5.3. Sample Content Analysis of Organizational Culture Descriptions.

The following statements represent current aspects of the PetroCorp culture that people would like to see changed.

Management Committee Responses (12 responses)
- Risk aversion due to job security fears (4 responses)
- Blindly following the leader; we bring in people who support our views and systems (3 responses)
- Lack of integration of ideas; strong silos; "not invented here" syndrome (3 responses)
- Our arrogance, bureaucracy, and narrow focus (2 responses)

Leadership Council Responses (26 responses)
- Conservative, formal, technocratic, and risk-averse culture (6 responses)
- Orientation to points of authority; strong chain of command (5 responses)
- When you are trying to reach a decision, anyone can say no and no one can say yes (5 responses)
- We are heavily burdened by protocol and too bureaucratic to survive (4 responses)
- "Emotional moonlighting"; people are disengaged from PetroCorp on and off the job because of layoffs and an excessive workload (2 responses)
- The parent-child mentality (senior management is parent and employees are children); this has fostered an atmosphere of limited ownership (2 responses)
- Arrogance—we like to think we are better than average and unique, but we are not (2 responses)

---

generalize the findings from this type of analysis to other settings can be somewhat limited because sample sizes are often small and questions asked during the interview process are often specific to the problems or issues present in the organization with which the OD practitioner is working.

Step 4: Presenting the Interview Results and Facilitating Action

In the OD context, interview results are typically reported in both written and verbal form. The basic elements of a written interview report are the same as any other data-based report: a cover page, table of contents, listing of participant demographics, executive summary, statement of the problem, results, conclusions and recommendations, and appendixes (for more detailed descriptions, see Church & Waclawski, 1998, 2001; Krueger, 1994; Kvale, 1996; Rea & Parker, 1997).

In almost all cases, however, the written report is designed for communication in support of the verbal presentation made by the OD practitioner and to provide additional input for group discussion and action planning purposes (Kvale, 1996). For the OD practitioner, the oral report or presentation and ensuing facilitated group discussion is the primary medium for communicating results. This format presents many more opportunities for group interaction and brainstorming, and the process facilitates the ultimate goals of the OD practitioner: the transfer of ownership of the data and group action planning. Therefore, in keeping with the OD assumption that increased involvement leads to increased commitment, the group presentation is the method of choice.

Moreover, with respect to action planning, because the OD practitioner is not generally a content expert, his or her role is to help the client come to conclusions regarding what the data mean and how to act on them. This means that the primary role of the OD practitioner is as a facilitator. This approach is different from that of the traditional management consulting and I/O method of delivering findings, in which the researcher or consultant is often a content expert. In OD, the practitioner is merely the instrument of change. The client owns and must act on the data. The practitioner's expertise lies not in prescribing actions based on the data but in aiding the client in arriving at conclusions about what the data mean and what needs to be done as a result. For all of these reasons, the verbal presentation of the interview findings to the large group is most appropriate for OD work.

Interviews for Diagnosis: A Case Example

Several years ago, the first author was consulting to a global oil company headquartered in the United States. The purpose of this consulting work was to help the client change its culture through a series of activities that included the development of a new company business model, an action research–based change program, and a series of diagnostic interviews. These were conducted with the top team (twelve members of the organization management committee) and members of the organization's leadership council (a consortium of twenty-six high-potential employees and a diverse cross section of leaders from the organization). It was through this series of activities, all of which converged on new ways of running and leading the business, that an effective change in the organization's culture would be determined.

The specific role of the interviews in this context was to enable the culture change by identifying and highlighting the similarities and differences between the top teams' perception of the organization and its culture and those of other leaders and key employees in the company. Specifically, the goal was to compare the response themes of the management committee members with those of the leadership council members to pinpoint areas of similarity and difference with respect to these groups' perception of the current organizational culture and the desired future culture. Through this comparison process and the presentation of the interview results, joint strategies and action planning activities could be undertaken to move the organization forward. Two additional factors were also assessed during these interviews: the teamwork (or lack thereof) exhibited by the management committee members and perceptions of the effectiveness of the new chief executive officer (CEO). These factors were deemed critical elements to assess during the interview process because they would clearly have a significant impact on the organization's ability to achieve the desired culture change. (Exhibit 5.1 contains the list of actual interview questions used.)

In terms of the interview process, the first author conducted all interviews (one-on-one) over a month. Each interview lasted approximately one hour and was conducted at the client organization's headquarters. Among other things, the results of the interviews yielded some interesting perceptions about the organization's culture (see Exhibit 5.3). These findings, in addition to those that resulted from the other interview questions, were used for action planning at an off-site meeting for the senior team in which the CEO and management committee were active participants. The results from these interviews were used to help top management understand and ultimately bridge the gap between its current culture and its ideal culture. Moreover, the results were very useful in helping the senior team better understand how it was functioning—or at least how others in the organization perceived them to be functioning, which led to additional team-building work for this group.

Using Focus Groups in OD

Interviews are an effective means for diagnostic and exploratory OD work; however, they are not without limitations. Perhaps the biggest problem is the amount of staffing required, which is why focus groups represent a good alternative.

Sometimes referred to as a focus group interview (Morgan, 1997), a focus group is "a carefully planned discussion designed to obtain perceptions on a defined area of interest in a permissive nonthreatening environment" (Krueger, 1994, p. 6). Focus groups have a long history as a primary method of inquiry in market research as a means for investigating customer preferences and potential buying patterns (Krueger, 1994); their use in the fields of I/O psychology and OD has been relatively minor until recently years (Morgan, 1997).

Uses of Focus Groups

Unlike interviews, focus groups are not generally used as a tool for diagnosing teams because of the sensitive nature of the information that is often revealed in an effective team diagnosis. In other words, much of the information that can be openly shared in a candid and confidential one-on-one interview cannot and should not be shared in a group discussion where other team members are present.

However, much like interviews, focus groups are often used in OD for exploratory purposes. For example, one of the most common uses is in the context of an organization or culture survey. The use of focus groups can be invaluable at the beginning of an organizational culture survey effort by providing information that is essential to the development of survey items. Moreover, focus groups can be of benefit at the conclusion of the same survey effort as a means for investigating its success or failure (Church & Waclawski, 1998, 2001).

In general, the uses of focus groups for OD practitioners are many and almost endless. For example, focus groups are a powerful tool for collecting employees' thoughts, opinions, attitudes, and feelings on a host of organizational issues ranging from current salary levels and compensation, to perceptions of senior leadership, to intentions to leave the organization, to opinions about the company's annual appraisal process, to perceptions of other teams and work units. No matter what the purpose of the focus group, the process itself is seen as an invaluable one to many OD practitioners because it allows for a maximum of group interaction, discussion, debate, and sharing with a minimum demand for time (especially in comparison to one-on-one interviews). In addition, good facilitation skills (an area of expertise for many OD practitioners) are an important part of the focus group experience, thus making this technique one that OD practitioners find highly enjoyable as well as useful. For these reasons, focus groups are a commonly used technique in the OD practitioner's tool kit.

Four Steps to Using Focus Groups in OD

The four steps to conducting an effective focus group in OD work are much the same as those described with respect to interviews: (1) preparing for and staging the focus group, (2) conducting the focus group, (3) analyzing the focus group results, and (4) presenting the focus group results and taking action. However, because the nature of a focus group is substantially different from that of the OD interview (especially with respect to how it is conducted), we will spend the majority of the remainder of this chapter discussing the two steps in this process that are most dissimilar to those already discussed: the staging and conduct of the focus group session.

Step 1: Preparing for and Staging the Focus Group

In order to prepare for the focus group, the practitioner first needs to determine its purpose. For example, is the practitioner interested in obtaining detailed information on a topic to be used for building an organizational assessment survey instrument, collecting employees' opinions about the effectiveness of a current organizational change initiative, or asking a group of employees about the most recent organizational survey that was just completed to find out how the survey can be improved before the next administration? Determining the purpose is essential; it will drive the nature of the focus group questions, group composition, and ultimately the success or failure of the session and outcomes.

In addition to the purpose, it is important to determine who will have access to the information or data collected during the focus group and how this material can and will ultimately be used. For example, if the nature of the focus group information collected is somewhat confidential (say, perceptions of the new CEO's policy on work-life balance), then access to the data collected will need to be more restricted than if the focus group were conducted for a less sensitive purpose (such as employee benefits).

Once these factors have been decided, it is time to determine the appropriate sample of employees and the general scheme for group composition. This is a natural next step, as the nature of the questions being asked should always play a part in determining to whom these questions are directed. Although there are many considerations to address in selecting a focus group sample (see Krueger, 1994, and Morgan, 1997, for more on focus group sampling), some important factors to consider are geographic location, age, gender, income, organizational level, and organization tenure.

One issue that has received a good deal of debate over the years among practitioners and researchers alike is the age-old question as to whether it is better to use homogeneous (similar) or heterogeneous (mixed) groups when conducting focus groups. Although there are conflicting opinions on this subject—some OD practitioners like to use mixed groups in which participants vary considerably on key demographic variables in order to get a diversity of opinions—the general consensus is that homogeneous groups, in which members are selected based on their similarity on a key demographic variable such as organizational level, are preferable to heterogeneous groups. The general thinking in support of this argument is that generalizability is better sought by using a series of homogeneous groups that, when combined, comprise a heterogeneous mixture of people. For example, if a practitioner is conducting fifteen focus groups to determine the impact of the most recent organizational survey on employees' perceptions of top management, he or she will not want to conduct fifteen groups in which management levels are mixed. A better design would be to conduct five focus groups composed of top management, five with middle management, and five with nonmanagerial employees. In this way, a diverse and representative sample of employees can still be obtained without jeopardizing the confidentiality and openness of responses between management levels.

Next, the size and scope of the OD initiative must be determined. This means discussing with the client the budget or resources for the project; determining a mutually acceptable time frame for organizing, conducting, and completing the focus group process; and coming to agreement on the deliverables of the focus group process—that is, what tangible outputs the client will receive at the conclusion of the initiative. A discussion of all of these elements is essential to the OD practitioner and client alike because focus groups can take a considerable amount of time to conduct, analyze, and feed back and be costly as well (Morgan, 1997).

The final step in the preparation phase is the development of the focus group script and accompanying questions (also known as the facilitator's guide). With respect to item preparation, there are several important factors to consider when developing a focus group protocol. They include the purpose of the focus group, time considerations (that is, the amount of time spent with each group), and issue coverage (whether to focus on a broad spectrum of topics or an in depth approach to a limited number). In the end, it is better to err on the side of specificity when designing focus group questions. In our experience, no matter how detailed the questions seem to be, invariably someone else will find them too vague.

Step 2: Conducting the Focus Group

When conducting a focus group for OD, the facilitator (that is, the person leading the session) needs to be aware and on top of two very important considerations: the physical layout of the session and the step-by-step process of leading a focus group.

With respect to the basics of the physical layout, in general, most focus groups range in size from ten to twelve people, with an ideal size of between six and nine for complex topics (Krueger, 1994). Generally, focus groups conducted for OD purposes last anywhere from one to two hours. They are typically conducted in an off-site location or in a closed-door on-site location. Either way, it is essential for the facilitator to create an environment in which employees feel they can share their thoughts, opinions, and feelings openly. This is no simple task. Therefore, it is important that the facilitator take every measure possible to ensure the confidentiality of the process. This means having only participants present in the focus group. In addition, members of the same work group should not participate in the same focus group if confidentiality is an issue. On a related matter, participants should be informed as early on in the focus group as is possible that their individual remarks are completely confidential. Often this means that the facilitator will need to provide participants with an explanation of the content coding or force-field analysis process (depending on which will be used to analyze results) to reassure them.

Finally, in the OD context, focus groups are usually conducted in a circular or semicircular formation (see Figure 5.1), with the facilitator and scribe (the person taking session notes, often on a flip chart) at the front of the room. This type of physical arrangement allows for maximum eye contact, interaction, and sharing among participants, which is essential to the focus group and the quality of the information collected from it. Without significant group interaction, discussion, and even debate, the focus group does not offer more than the one-on-one interview, and in fact it can even yield less!

Figure 5.1. Focus Group Session Setup.

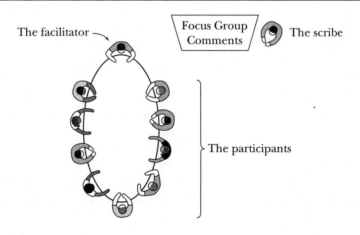

The focus group session can be as structured or unstructured as the facilitator chooses (Krueger, 1994). This means that the facilitator need not follow a verbatim protocol in terms of process and questioning. Although many OD practitioners prefer this approach, we do not recommend it. In our experience, a more structured approach is preferable because it creates a consistent experience for focus group participants and generally yields more reliable results. Therefore, we advise the use of a facilitator's guide—a detailed script for the facilitator to follow when conducting a series of similar focus groups. This guide typically has a consistent format for leading each focus group from beginning to end (see Exhibit 5.4).

However, given the informal nature of much OD work, it is uncommon for a facilitator to create an actual script like the one in Exhibit 5.4. Instead, it is more likely that he or she will develop (through years of experience) a personal style for leading focus groups and focus on the development of specific questions to ask during the sessions. Nevertheless, this informal approach will often include many of the elements detailed in the exhibit.

Focus groups usually begin with an introduction to the session, which often opens with the introduction of the facilitator and scribe and their respective roles. Typically, the facilitator's role is to ask questions and moderate the discussion, with the scribe recording verbatim comments from group members on a flip chart. In our experience, the use of a flip chart, a popular OD tool, is essential because it offers participants the opportunity to see exactly how their responses are being recorded and allows them the opportunity to correct the scribe if necessary. This also serves an equally important function of allowing participants to see what comments have already been made (if they forget them) and add to them if desired.

Once the facilitator and scribe have introduced themselves and the objectives of the session, it is customary to provide a detailed explanation of the data analysis and reporting process—that is, how the comments will be concatenated and how they will be presented to the organization. It is usually during this discussion that the subject of confidentiality is explained in detail. A discussion of ground rules for the session should also occur at this juncture.

Exhibit 5.4. Sample Focus Group Facilitator Guide.

Good afternoon. My name is Jane Doe, and I will be your focus group facilitator for this meeting, which will last approximately ninety minutes. My associate John Doe will be the scribe, which means he will be taking notes and recording your responses so that we can use the results of this focus group to improve the quality of your organization's annual survey.

Before we begin, please be advised that all of your individual comments will be completely confidential and will not be released to others within your organization. So please be as candid and honest as possible in your responses, since this will be essential to us in creating your survey.

My associate is now distributing three important items: (1) our business cards with our contact information in case you have any questions or concerns about this focus group after we conclude today, (2) a series of questions we would like you to answer individually at your seats, and (3) an attendance sheet on which you should record your name and function. Please take the next fifteen minutes to write down your answers to these questions individually. Then we will go around the room, and I will ask each of you to share your answers, and we will have a group discussion about each. Any questions?

Questionnaire

1. Describe the qualities of a survey at its best.
2. Describe your survey nightmares (perhaps a bad past experience with the annual survey).
3. What will make your company's annual survey more meaningful?
4. What are the critical issues facing your company that need to be incorporated into the annual survey?
5. What were the results in terms of actions taken of last year's survey?
6. Were you satisfied with the actions taken from last year's survey?
7. Did these actions make a difference? How do you know when you are making a difference?
8. If you had one wish for the annual survey, what would it be?

Closing Remarks

Thank you for your participation in this focus group. We will provide each of you with a summary report via e-mail of our findings and our recommendations for the improvement of your annual survey by the end of the month.

The last item that should be covered before launching into the actual focus group questions should be participant introductions. Typically, the facilitator asks all participants to introduce themselves briefly. In so doing, they will each get a better sense of the nature of the group composition and begin the process of group participation.

The actual questioning can range from very informal (the facilitator has only a few prepared questions that he or she asks in no particular order) to more formal (the facilitator has a longer list of structured questions to ask in a particular sequence). In fact, short quantitative surveys can even be administered as part of the focus group session, thus adding more formality to the meeting and hard data to the results. We recommend a more structured approach. In either case, however, the moderating style of the facilitator is of paramount importance to the success of the focus group. Among other things, this means having a nonjudgmental approach to participants and their viewpoints, keeping the group on task, soliciting input from less vocal members, monitoring time and objectives closely, watching nonverbal behaviors, monitoring the flow of the session, and focusing on facilitating the session, not leading it or the results obtained.

Challenges that facilitators often face include dealing with overly dominant participants, encouraging the participation of introverted or shy participants, keeping the group conversation focused on the topic at hand, making sure that all of the focus group questions receive coverage, and, the most difficult task of all, overcoming participant resistance to the focus group session itself. Whatever the roadblocks may be in a particular session (and there are always some of these), the ability of the facilitator to manage the group and the dynamics associated with it is the most important factor in determining the ultimate success of the focus group and the utility of the resulting data. One commonly used approach that is helpful when working with reticent participants is to start with more general questions first and funnel down into specifics as the session progresses. This approach can be particularly useful if participants are wary of the process and need to be eased into sharing their thoughts and opinions in a group setting.

Steps 3 and 4: Analyzing the Results and Delivering the Findings

These two steps are similar to those described in the discussion of interviewing. The principal difference is that in analyzing focus group results, the facilitator and scribe work together to debrief their impressions and review the group transcripts as soon as possible after each session. For this reason, it is imperative that the facilitator and scribe determine how participants' comments and responses will be coded prior to the conduct of the focus group session. This increases the accuracy and ease of coding of the results obtained. It should be noted, however, that both interviews and focus groups have advantages and disadvantages to their use and application. Table 5.1 presents a brief summary of some of the issues in using these methodologies.

Conclusion

Interviews and focus groups are essential tools for OD practitioners. The quality and quantity of data provided by these techniques can be used to drive many OD interventions as varied as team building, organizational assessment, and the assessment of the impact of OD work itself. Although the data are qualitative in nature, they can be highly descriptive and detailed and, through the use of force-field and content analysis, quantitative or hard as well.

Practice Tips

1. Explain in detail the purpose and ultimate use of the interview or focus group to those who are participating.
2. Set ground rules for participation, and gain agreement on these rules at the outset of the interview or focus group.
3. Let the participants see the notes you are recording, and make changes to them if the participants are uncomfortable.
4. Follow a structured series of questions to ensure comparability of experiences for the interviewee or focus group participant and results.

Table 5.1. Advantages and Disadvantages of Interviews and Focus Groups in OD practice.

Methodology	Advantages	Disadvantages
Interviews	Effective for team diagnosis	Useful only for smaller rather than larger groups
	Effective way to explore concepts and issues in detail	Interviewers may bias responses
	More adaptive and participative than surveys	Coding and interpreting them can be more costly, time-consuming, and biased than surveys
	Used in diagnosis to get at root causes and symptoms	
	Provide remarks in context by using actual quotes for feedback	
	Facilitate empathy and openness with the interviewee to get richer data and to cement the consulting relationship	
Focus groups	More adaptive than surveys (the facilitator can make on-the-spot adjustments to questions and probes)	Can be fraught with self-report bias
	Can be more time efficient and less expensive than interviews	Typically more expensive and time-consuming than surveys
	Can stimulate more creative thinking among participants than surveys or interviews	Groupthink can be a problem
		Can inhibit the participation of less vocal people
		Must be led by a skilled facilitator

Practice Tips, cont'd.

5. Give interviewees or focus group members the opportunity to ask questions—for example, regarding what will be done with data, when they will receive data, and what form the data will take.
6. Thank people for their participation and candor (perhaps sending each of them a thank-you note), and communicate the next steps.
7. Make sure that the interview or focus group questions are designed to address the problem you are looking to solve with the OD effort.
8. Do not allow interviews to get off track or allow a single individual to monopolize group time during focus group sessions
9. Do not breach participants' confidentiality by identifying their comments in the final report.
10. Guard against letting the focus group discussion turn into an argument or a griping session by forgetting to focus on actionable ideas.
11. Provide detailed contact information to interviewees or focus group participants in case they have question or concerns.

References

Babbie, E. R. (1973). *Survey research methods.* Belmont, CA: Wadsworth.

Burke, W. W. (1982). *Organization development: Principles and practices.* Glenview, IL: Scott, Foresman.

Church, A. H., & Waclawski, J. (1998). *Designing and using organizational surveys.* Aldershot, England: Gower.

Church, A. H., & Waclawski, J. (2001). *Designing and using organizational surveys: A seven-step process.* San Francisco: Jossey-Bass.

Cummings, T., & Worley, C. (1997). *Organization development and change* (6th ed.). St. Paul, MN: West.

Fordyce, J. K., and Weil, R. (2000). In W. L. French, C. H. Bell, Jr., and R. A. Zawacki, *Organization development and transformation: Managing effective change* (5th ed., pp. 161–170). Boston: Irwin/McGraw-Hill.

French, W. L., & Bell, C. H., Jr. (1990). *Organization development: Behavioral science interventions for organization improvement* (4th ed.). Upper Saddle River, NJ: Prentice Hall.

Hyman, H. (1955). *Survey design and analysis.* New York: Free Press.

Krueger R. A. (1988). *Focus groups: A practical guide for applied research.* Thousand Oaks, CA: Sage.

Krueger R. A. (1994). *Focus groups: A practical guide for applied research* (2nd ed.). Thousand Oaks, CA: Sage.

Krueger R. A. (1998). *Moderating focus groups.* Thousand Oaks, CA: Sage.

Kvale, S. (1996). *InterViews: An introduction to qualitative research interviewing.* Thousand Oaks, CA: Sage.

Lewin, K. (1951). *Field theory in social science.* New York: HarperCollins.

Miles M. B., & Huberman, A. M. (1994). *Qualitative data analysis: An expanded sourcebook.* Thousand Oaks, CA: Sage.

Morgan, D. L. (1997). *Focus groups as qualitative research.* Thousand Oaks, CA: Sage.

Morris, R. (1994). Computerized content analysis in management research: A demonstration of advantages and limitations. *Journal of Management, 20,* 903–931.

Rea, L. M., & Parker, R. A. (1997). *Designing and conducting survey research: A comprehensive guide* (2nd ed.). San Francisco: Jossey-Bass.

Schuman, H., & Kalton, G. (1985). Survey methods. In G. Lindzey & E. Aronson (Eds.), *The handbook of social psychology* (3rd ed., Vol. 1, pp. 635–697). New York: Random House.

Seidman, I. E. (1991). *Interviewing as qualitative research.* New York: Teachers College Press.

Van Maanen, J. (1988). *Tales of the field.* Chicago: University of Chicago Press.

CHAPTER 6

Organization Development and the Bottom Line
Linking Soft Measures and Hard Measures

Steven H. Cady
Mark J. Lewis

Beckhard (1997) defined organization development (OD) as a planned systemwide change program that uses behavioral science knowledge to move the organization to a new state. Interestingly, he found that this definition did not sit too well with some OD practitioners. He noted that most of the practitioners at the time of his writing focused on increasing skills and not on the client system or incorporating the bottom line.

Beckhard's assertion is valid and supported by the unrelenting and unnerving challenge to practitioners who work in OD and related fields. Although values debates regarding the primary focus of OD interventions have long plagued the field (Church, Burke, & Van Eynde, 1994; Greiner, 1980; Margulies & Raia, 1990), the notion of demonstrating the impact of OD efforts regardless of their focus has arisen only in the past decade, largely as a result of the changing nature of business.

Managers working in today's organizations with flatter, less hierarchical structures are often faced with multiple projects and competing demands, and they are under pressure to take action, often any action. Time is their most prized resource. Managers, under constant pressure, often look to their cross-functional peer as the cause of their problems without first looking in the mirror. The proverbial "they" and "we" are used to explain a multitude of performance-related outcomes. Furthermore, these two culprits, "they and we," are often the sole justification for initiating various interventions intended to improve performance. When working with a manager faced with competing priorities, the OD practitioner needs to be able to provide value to the manager by helping to identify meaningful actions that will strengthen the organization. If the manager or organization is not able to recognize the value provided, the OD practitioner will lose credibility.

Although many leaders within organizations are challenging the value of OD and its interventions, there is a renewed interest in empirically driven change (Cady, 1998). Rather than being a threat, this challenge presents a tremendous opportunity. Relating soft measures to hard measures or bottom-line results provides tangible evidence of the OD practitioner's value to the organization. Empirically driven change speaks in a language that managers understand, providing a vehicle to drive behavioral change systematically that leads to improved individual and organizational performance (see also Chapter Two). This chapter examines linking soft measures to the bottom line using an innovative whole system performance management (WSPM) approach.

A Case Study: All Industries Performance Improvement Process

All Industries was a manufacturing organization that had grown from a single facility to a midsized organization with thirty-seven sites and seven thousand employees located throughout North America. Rapid growth through acquisition during the past twelve years had created a diverse culture with a wide range of behavioral and performance-related norms and expectations. Growth brought with it the need to move from an entrepreneurial environment to a more professional, consistent, and systematic management style. As part of this evolution, the management team at the founding site developed a set of behavioral expectations that would apply to managers at all levels of the organization. The Performance Improvement Framework was developed to lay the foundation of a strong culture that would value continuous improvement and superior customer service.

The Performance Improvement Framework explicitly defined openness, respect, accountability, adult behavior, and participation as behavioral expectations that were intended to guide managers in achieving business objectives. An important feature of the model was clearly defining each of the behaviors identified on the framework. For example, *openness* was defined as follows

> Openness means communicating with each other directly, honestly, and completely. Trust between people is developed and supported by explaining the facts and issues around a decision, speaking plainly in a way that is easy to understand, telling a person what he or she needs to know when he or she needs to know it, and by being truthful and honest with people when discussing all types of issues. Communicating plainly and providing the required details of a situation in a timely manner allow others to take appropriate action, minimizing the possibility of surprises.

Each manager was expected to model this behavior. The organization believed that superior results would be achieved if all managers were capable of treating each other with respect, openly tabling and discussing issues in an adult manner, involving the workforce in decision making, and then holding one another accountable for doing what was agreed on.

Although the logic of the model was intuitively appealing, like most other leadership theories and practical treatments of the subject, the framework focused on "the what" of leadership but did not provide a systematic approach to "the how" of leadership development. The model had not been tested to determine the strength of the relationship between the behavioral expectations and actual bottom-line results. There was no mechanism in place to provide managers with a baseline of their current performance, and there was no consistent understanding of the performance expectation. There was no method in place to provide regular feedback to managers, feedback that would allow them to assess their effectiveness in modeling the expected behavior. Managers acted with the best of intentions, doing what they thought was right and in the best interests of the organization. Finally, there was no method to implement the framework systematically in multiple, geographically dispersed sites. Managers were expected to read the behavioral definitions, recognize the inherent value of the statements, and consistently apply and model the behavior in their managerial practices.

There was a need for a tool that would increase managerial performance by supporting them in dealing more effectively with situations at work. Dealing more effectively with work-related situations would increase the effectiveness of the workforce, resulting in a measurable improvement in business results. WSPM provided the solution. This model, drawn from previous work conducted by Cady (1998), has subsequently been further developed and refined to provide managers with a predictive tool that develops a complete understanding of performance and performance-related issues and identifies appropriate actions that will lead to sustainable performance improvement.

An Integrated Whole System Performance Management System

Figure 6.1 presents the whole system performance management model. This model is designed to relate behavior to bottom-line performance and is particularly useful in organization development and change settings.

WSPM captures six key components that are predictors of performance: performance, morale, emotion, critical customer service behaviors, organizational climate, and personal characteristics. Each of these components falls into one of two categories of measurement: soft or hard. Soft measures are perceptual in nature. That is, the scoring of soft measures is based on an individual's judgment or opinion. For example, an employee is asked to respond in a survey (see Chapter Four for more on this method) to the statement, "I am satisfied with my job." The employee chooses a number on a 7-point Likert scale ranging from Strongly Disagree with the statement (equal to 1) to Strongly Agree with the statement (equal to 7) (Church & Waclawski, 2001; Rea & Parker, 1997). Hard measures are observable and can be objectively counted, often based on behavior or units of some kind; they are not based on opinion. Of the measures in the WSPM model presented in Figure 6.1, most of the performance and some of the

Figure 6.1. Whole System Performance Management Model.

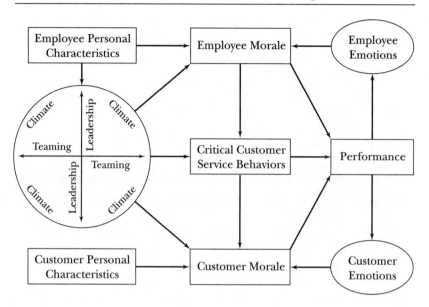

personal characteristics (for example, biographical characteristics) are typically measured as hard measures.

An example of a hard measure is the number of products sold to a customer by an employee, department, or store. Each of the six components can be assessed using either hard or soft variables, which represent critical measures of the component's performance. The variable number of products sold to customers is a hard measure of external performance related to productivity.

WSPM is designed to develop a manager's or organization's understanding of how managerial actions and behavior (soft measures) influence important bottom-line outcomes (hard measures). This model can be used to provide meaningful, ongoing feedback to managers at all levels, diagnose departmental or organization-wide performance issues, and identify appropriate interventions that will positively impact performance. In short, it helps bring all of the various data sources together into one model that can be used for diagnosis and change in an OD context (for more examples, see Chapter Two; Waclawski, 1996; and Wiley, 1996).

Component 1: Performance and the Bottom Line

Profitability immediately comes to mind in any discussion of the bottom line. In this chapter, profitability is part of a broader definition of performance that is based on a balanced approach to assessing the bottom line.

There are three performance measures, and the first is profitability. Profit is one measure of performance that has dominated throughout the history of economic ventures, and it remains a central focus. However, there is growing recognition that profit is not the only indicator of the real bottom line (Kaplan & Norton, 1996; Collins & Porras, 1995). There are other measures that provide a more balanced approach to assessing the bottom line. That is why, in the proposed WSPM, we use the word *performance* in place of *bottom line*. In addition to profit, there are internal and external performance measures. Some of these might include turnover, market share, net sales, product shrinkage, and even equipment damages, as in Church's study of airline service performance (1995). In general, profitability is influenced by internal and external performance measures, each of which can be assessed using the measures listed in Table 6.1.

Component 2: Morale

These measures are soft by nature. That is, each measure is assessed by asking the employees or customers their opinions regarding a variety of issues. Measures of morale address attitudes

Table 6.1. Selected Performance Measures.

External Performance Measures	Internal Performance Measures
Customer retention	Quality (time, defects, customer expectations)
Number of new customers	
Productivity (units and dollars)	Employee retention
Innovation (new products and services)	Organizational learning (knowledge and skills, process improvement, change initiatives)

and intentions from both the employee and customer perspective. Attitudes focus on such matters as job satisfaction or reward and recognition for employees, and product and service speed and satisfaction for customers. Intentions focus on such factors as intention to leave a job or intention to return to buy a product or service again. These measures tend to focus on a degree of agreement or disagreement using a survey or feedback based measure of some sort (see Chapter Four for more examples of these measures).

Component 3: Emotion

Emotions are similar to yet distinct from morale. These basic emotions tend to be related to discrete events and are reactionary in nature. The reason that they are considered similar to morale is that they are known to affect morale. For example, a failed performance by an employee (for example, a lost sale) can lead to anger and guilt. These emotions can subsequently lead to an exaggerated low level of job satisfaction and a heightened level of intention to leave the position. Over time, these levels of satisfaction and intention to leave can return to the original levels prior to the failed performance. That is, emotions can have a temporary influence on morale yet generally not a permanent influence. Measures of emotion include happiness, sadness, anger, guilt, and fear.

Component 4: Critical Customer Service Behaviors

Customers have certain expectations when receiving products and services. There are all sorts of support required and questions to be asked. In the process, the customer can define a set of employees behaviors that add value to the product or service. These behaviors are applicable across industries, yet must be customized to fit a particular industry (service or product). Based on our research, we have identified five critical behaviors that will lead to higher levels of customer satisfaction and retention: response time, personalized attention, professionalism, expertise, and comforting.

Component 5: Organizational Climate

A considerable amount of research and survey measures are directed toward a better understanding of the factors that directly influence task performance. These task-dependent measures fall into three variables: job climate factors, teaming behaviors, and leadership behaviors.

- Job climate factors—those things that directly relate to the work being done, such as environmental support, personal capabilities, and reward systems.
- Teaming behaviors—the critical behaviors that team members should exhibit that lead to a high-performing team (see also Chapter Eight). Teaming behavior measures include anticipating and fulfilling team needs, managing one's own personal contribution, displaying a positive attitude, and effectively communicating.
- Leadership behaviors—critical behaviors that leaders should exhibit to create a high-performing team (see also Chapter Two). They include supporting, informing, monitoring, recognizing and rewarding, empowering, and clarifying.

Component 6: Personal Characteristics

There are two types of personal characteristics, each of which contains different measurable variables. First are biographical characteristics, which are considered hard measures and are usually found in most personnel files. Biographical characteristics include age, race, sex, tenure, and function. The second type of personal characteristic is personality, which refers to the more stable behavioral traits that people exhibit. For example, there are a variety of personality models such as the Myers-Briggs Type Indicator (MBTI), the big five (extroversion, emotional stability, agreeableness, conscientiousness, and openness to experience), along with other nondimensional measures such as locus of control and pessimism (see Chapter Three for more on the use of personality measures).

Integrating the Six Components

Each of the major components in the model is statistically interrelated. Through applied analysis and making data linkages, a piece to the puzzle is put in place. In the end, the puzzle is the whole system predictive model. Putting all of the pieces together paints a descriptive (and predictive) picture of the organization. It provides diagnostic feedback at each of the individual, department, site, and organizational levels. Each relationship can be valuable for the organization, particularly where the organization integrates these relationships in order to unearth more compelling findings. Moreover, the nature of these relationships provides an important set of levers for change for the OD practitioner in working with the client.

Moving from Model to Action: The WSPM Process

The WSPM process comprises five basic steps. As you look at the five steps, you should be reminded of theoretical development concepts and the field of research methodology. These are important components to creating a whole system predictive model for an organization. WSPM extends these approaches by focusing on creating a systemic model comprising multiple change initiatives and measures. While action research focuses diagnose and intervene to solve a problem in the organization (see Chapter One), WSPM focuses on diagramming the entire system. The steps are summarized in Table 6.2.

Step 1: Evaluate Existing Model and Measures

The goal in this step is to map the explicit and implicit relationships. Mapping the perceived relationships is important to future steps. Most people have an innate need to express and hypothesize their own working beliefs about relationships between variables. For example, someone may believe that as the organization's employee job satisfaction increases, the turnover rate will decrease. This is a hypothesis, because it is proposing a relationship between two variables. Clarifying existing hypotheses gets people involved in exploring additional relationships and other performance-related questions (for more information, see Hedrick, Bickman, & Rog, 1993; Keppel, 1982; Mendenhall, Reinmuth, & Beaver, 1993). In general, there are five key questions that OD practitioners should ask when assessing these beliefs:

**Table 6.2. Whole System
Performance Management Steps**

Step	Objective	Benefits
1. Evaluate existing model and measures.	Understand implicit and explicit relationships; get perceptions on the table.	Generate interest and understanding Foster learning
2. Enhance existing model and measures.	Clarify understanding of whole system performance for sound thinking	Increase confidence in WSPM process and develop appreciation
3. Install and initiate data collection process.	Gather reliable, relevant, efficient, and accurate data	Centralization of data Benchmarking of current performance
4. Diagram the predictive model.	Validate model, and identify significant relationships	Understand actions that affect results Build organizational learning
5. Take action.	Facilitate healthy and constructive discussion leading to actions	Sustainable improvement in bottom-line results

- What types of data are being collected?
- What are the location, retrieval mechanisms, and quantity of stored data?
- How are the data being collected?
- Why are the data being collected?
- What are the expected relationships among the variables?

Forcing people to verbalize their internal existing frameworks and beliefs always stirs up cognitive dissonance and resistance with other key stakeholders. A rigorous examination and use of information can be intimidating to organizational members, including leaders (Harrison, 1994).

Sometimes this step indicates the pace and method for proceeding. And in some cases, it might be advisable for the OD practitioner not to proceed with the linkage work. In the end, the leaders of the organization or units using this process must embrace the reality that there will be positive and negative findings.

A data-driven OD process such as this is based on the value of truth and objectivity. While the truth can set you free, developing and maintaining effective performance management systems requires more effort and discipline than many managers and executives believe. Moreover, going by intuition may be quicker, but it is not easily verified and lends itself to political maneuvering. That is, a disjointed performance management system with unreliable measures empowers leaders to make quick decisions and move their agendas forward without much justification. The decisions can be supported by anecdotal evidence that may or may not be reliable. This is where the proverbial "we and they" surface.

Step 2: Enhance Existing Model and Measures

Based on the analyses conducted in Step 1, a new set of questions should surface, and a better idea of the whole performance system should begin to emerge.

In general, the three prongs of sound thinking are instrumental in developing a more thoughtful and testable model and can be easily framed as questions.

Prong 1: What do you currently know about X? Most people go on a hunch by using easily accessible information. It may be effective, but it will not be helpful in more complex decisions and modeling like the approach being proposed here.

Prong 2: What do the experts, research findings, and theories say about X? Some people will review expert research findings. This will get at important research and relevant theoretical issues, but it lacks the necessary practical implications associated with benchmarking.

Prong 3: What are best and worst in class doing with regard to X? Benchmarking is a valuable tool, but it must be assessed with the unique knowledge that exists in the organization (prong 1) and expertise outside the organization (prong 2).

The three prongs of sound thinking should be conducted completely and in the order described. The questions can be posed in a variety of forms and are presented as examples. The results for people using an exercise like this are confidence in the decisions made, better decisions, and an appreciation for sound thinking.

Step 3: Install and Initiate Data Collection Process

The process by which data are gathered and stored can be overwhelming. This focus of this step is on getting the most reliable, relevant, efficient, and accurate data. It is important to consider where to house the organization's data. Many organizations keep their information decentralized. In some cases, information is kept from other parts of the organization (and OD consultants attempting to make these linkages), which can raise political concerns and turf wars, which the practitioner will need to resolve (Church & Waclawski, 2001).

Fundamentally, however, creating a whole system model requires that all information be centralized. There are exceptions to this prescription, but it should be explicitly addressed and agreed on. Even when data warehousing is centralized, the collection process can be decentralized. Because there are various ways to measure something, the previous steps should be used to choose the best measurement protocol. As for timing of data collection, decisions need to be made about frequency, date, and time.

Step 4: Diagram the Predictive Model

Diagramming the predictive model requires conducting statistical analyses and visually mapping the significant and meaningful relationships. Examining relationships in the whole system model requires that at least two questions be answered.

First, what relationships are significant? As relationships are shown to be significant or not significant, the model's validity becomes apparent, and the opportunity for refinement becomes clearer. For relationships that are not significant, the variables in question may need to be revised or removed.

Second, how important and meaningful is the significant relationship? This is determined by statistical tools that provide information as to the amount of variance explained by the predictors in the performance variables of interest. Meaningfulness also refers to the degree of impact a predictor variable has. That is, as the predictor variable moves, what degree of change does it create in the outcome variables?

For example, a 3 percent increase in an employee's perceptions of environmental support may lead to a 2 percent increase in critical customer service behaviors, thus leading to a 3 percent increase in customer intention to return. This 3 percent increase in customer intention to return may then lead to a 4 percent increase in actual customer retention and a 2 percent increase in sales. A relatively small change in a predictor variable can translate into a large leap in performance.

Step 5: Take Action

Feeding back the results from performance modeling can be both productive and challenging. The objective is to facilitate a healthy and constructive discussion that leads to significant action (see Chapters One Through Four). Figure 6.2 presents a simple model that can be used to facilitate the discussion. It is based on clearly separating the facts of the situation from judgments and emotions.

Figure 6.2. Components for Facilitating Healthy Feedback.

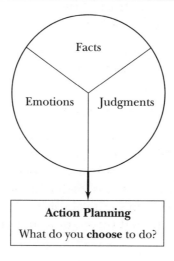

To begin, identify the relevant facts. Facts are objective, measurable, and observable information. Second, draw judgments (also called conclusions) from agreed-on facts. Judgments are value-laden opinions related to the relative importance of the information. The modeling process provides facts related to causal relationships among the soft and hard measures.

These facts can be helpful in evaluating long-standing judgments that have existed in the organization. Judgments based on empirically based facts are more objective, and the emotional ramifications can help to build consensus. Therefore, it is important to connect facts to judgments clearly.

Next, it is important to share the emotions—happiness, sadness, fear, and guilt, for example—that are surfacing as the facts are shared and judgments are formed. Using the performance model to facilitate the sharing of emotions can be helpful in eliminating the static that often interferes with interpersonal communication.

Finally, after coming to consensus on judgments regarding the facts, ask the following question: "What do you choose to do?" This is the step that promotes action and accountability. We recommend that the model in Figure 6.2 be presented at the beginning of the feedback session as part of the ground rules. Use the model explicitly as a tool for keeping discussion focused and constructive. (For more on using an OD model to drive these types of analyses, see Chapter Four.)

Key Principles to Support the Implementation of WSPM

There are six practice principles to consider when implementing WSPM's bottom-line approach in OD.

Principle 1: Diagram the System

WSPM requires diagramming the entire system. It is based on the research questions, "What is high performance, how is it measured, and then how can we predict it?" It identifies valued outcomes and meaningful predictors. It helps leadership to define success and focus on the organization's critical success factors. Both soft and hard measures are aligned throughout the organization. Those who describe OD in terms of applied experimentation and more contemporary interpretations support this notion (see Chapters One and Ten). Experimentation lends itself to objective systems thinking, proactive planning, and organizational learning, leading to an organization's honest self-assessment (Ulrich, 1998).

Principle 2: Understand Relationships

This approach requires practitioners and leaders alike to have a predictive understanding of the complex relationships among the organization's systems and design, employees who maintain those systems, customers' perceptions and actions, shareholders' confidence, and revenue growth. Numerous consulting firms and internal OD practitioners move future organizational leaders toward improved understanding of the important content and appreciation for the need to design effective processes. But after advising and coaching leaders to plan, analyze, evaluate, and decide, they leave the leaders alone. Just how are leaders supposed to select intelligently from among so many attractive and information-rich options?

Here is where a bottom-line approach can make a difference. WSPM integrates high-performance theories, theoretical development processes, research methods, statistical modeling, and management theories. Theoretical development processes build hypothetical models that are scientifically studied and validated. Research methodologies are used to ensure the rigor necessary for reliable and valid information. Statistical modeling approaches are used to understand and predict complex relationships based on the gathered data. Management theory is used to develop the hypothesized model and understand the results of data analysis.

Principle 3: Integrate Stakeholder Knowledge

Building a whole system's performance model requires integrating the collective knowledge of key stakeholders for the organization: employees, customers, stockholders, and other relevant groups. Such engagement encourages the organization's members to bridge functional silos and focus on the relevant performance drivers. As a result, the stakeholders become more accountable to each other and the organization as a whole. Furthermore, WSPM advocates centralizing the data storage, while the data collection and dissemination is decentralized. This allows the modeling process to work efficiently. It provides leadership with the necessary information to make quick decisions by having accessible information. In addition, it creates better data collection coordination, therefore removing redundant and cumbersome data collection activities, such as multiple surveys administered by a variety of uncoordinated groups.

Principle 4: Master Statistical Techniques

Develop the knowledge and skill set necessary to use statistical techniques (for example, general linear modeling, causal modeling, factor analysis, and regression) in order to analyze, validate, and determine how best to use the whole system model. This allows for various ways to examine the quality of the data so that they can be reduced and improved. It also provides the necessary information to quantify the organization's performance model.

Based on our experience working with hundreds of executives who have pursued their master's degrees in OD, we have come to the conclusion that OD practitioners and leaders of organizations lack the basic skills necessary to tie soft measures to the bottom line. Rather than face this skill set limitation, they devalue or undermine empirically based methods. Others believe the OD should not be concerned with organizational goals or that there is not enough time to assess the impact of OD initiatives on the organization (for more on evaluation issues, see Chapter Fourteen).

The reality, however, is that change is inevitable, turbulent, and fast. It cannot be realistically or practically evaluated. We must have faith in its efficacy. These views can be seen in comments like, "That can't be realistically measured" or "What will that tell us anyway? It doesn't work." We believe that underneath these criticisms of empirically based approaches is a desire not to face one's own limitations in the area.

Statistical modeling and rigorous analysis within the field of OD are here to stay. Software and hardware are advancing at a pace that makes it hard to ignore the cutting-edge statistical approaches. Those who do so are running the risk of being left behind.

Some OD practitioners are getting on board. Sears, Roebuck and Co., for example, uses its own WSPM process called Total Performance Indicators. The model shows that employees' perceptions and behaviors lead to customers' perceptions and actions, which in turn lead to revenue growth (Rucci, Kirn, & Quinn, 1998).

Principle 5: Start Low and Work Up

Start with the lowest level of analysis and work up. Measures can be taken at the individual or the group level. Soft measures like job satisfaction are normally measured at the individual level. That is, each employee fills out a survey that leads to computing his or her own job satisfaction score. Because soft measures start at the individual level, we recommend building the WSPM from the individual level and then moving up to the group and organizational levels.

Performance, however, is not always as easy to measure at the individual level (for example, as units sold, produced, or packaged). Rather, the output can be measured only at the group level. Measures that can be obtained only at that level are those where the team is highly interdependent in producing the output, such as producing a car. In these situations, aggregate the soft measures up to the group level and conduct the analysis there (see also Chapter Two). When it is possible to build a performance model at the individual level, do not stop there. Aggregate up to the group level so that examination and comparisons can be made across various groups (teams and departments) and locations (plants, factories, and other outlets). Although this can be difficult at times due to data management or political reasons, linked results will yield important relationships and provide the OD practitioner with a competitive advantage.

Principle 6: Adopt a Bottom-Line Approach

A bottom-line approach is a necessary but not sufficient condition for creating an effective organization. Without rigorous organizational improvement initiatives, OD will become obsolete. However, there are many other important factors that affect the success of

OD initiatives, such as leadership support, communication, and a sense of urgency. These too are necessary and should be validated through scientific approaches. It is only through this rigor that we will be able to build an enduring case for the importance of OD.

Case Study: A Practical Application of the Model and Learning Points

In the end, All Industries successfully implemented the WSPM. The modeling process identified the strengths and weaknesses of its data collection and measurement systems. Completion of the WSPM cycle identified a general weakness within managerial cross-functional working relationships and provided the focus and support for an intervention designed to strengthen these relationships. Individual multisource feedback to managers allowed them to see their strengths and weaknesses through the eyes of others (see Chapter Two for more on this method). The implementation of the WSPM cycle was challenging and provided some key learning.

Conclusion

This chapter advances a view that is emerging as a new mandate for OD: for OD practitioners to move beyond the *or* of the soft versus hard sides of OD (Collins & Porras, 1995). We see two types of perspectives on this issue.

On one hand, there are nonvisionary practitioners, who like to pit the soft and hard components against each other. They believe that OD cannot be studied empirically and should not be concerned with organizational goals and the bottom line. In their view, time is critical since change is inevitable, turbulent, and swift, thus making assessment of OD interventions unrealistic. We must have faith in its efficacy.

Visionary practitioners, on the other hand, embody the principle of improving the individual and the organization using the most advanced means available. Properly implemented, OD can ensure that change is a results-oriented experience. Getting leaders to embrace this concept, however, can be a challenge. Therefore, our aim should be to demonstrate how OD, a fundamental component in an organization's change initiatives, can result in a measurable long-term competitive advantage through the use of applied modeling and linkage analyses.

Practice Tips

1. There is a trade-off between maintaining individual and department confidentiality of multisource feedback results and holding managers accountable for taking the necessary follow-up actions.
2. Because linking behavior to results can create apprehension, introduce the concepts and steps at a pace that matches the organization's willingness to discuss and accept the need for change.
3. Working through the WSPM cycle provides a tremendous opportunity to foster organizational learning about the application of data, the value of a rigorous approach, and the impact that behavior has on operating results. The opportunity to provide this learning can be lost if the learning points and methods are not planned during the cycle.
4. The WSPM cycle must not be considered finished after the results are presented. There needs to be a mechanism to drive actions based on the results.
5. Clearly explain results to all participants. Communicating the results and benefits provides the logic for changes and allows others to learn from the process.

References

Beckhard, R. (1997). *Agent of change: My life, my practice.* San Francisco: Jossey-Bass.

Cady, S. H. (1998). Whole System Predictive Modeling: An integrated approach to designing an effective high-performance organization. *Organizational Development Journal, 16,* 43–56.

Church, A. H. (1995). Linking leadership behaviors to service performance: Do managers make a difference? *Managing Service Quality, 5,* 26–31.

Church, A. H., Burke, W. W., & Van Eynde, D. F. (1994). Values, motives, and interventions of organization development practitioners. *Group and Organization Management, 19,* 5–50.

Church, A. H., & Waclawski, J. (2001). *Designing and using organizational surveys: A seven-step process.* San Francisco: Jossey-Bass.

Collins, J. C., & Porras, J. I. (1995). *Built to last.* New York: HarperBusiness.

Greiner, L. (1980). OD values and the "bottom line." In W. W. Burke & L. D. Goodstein (Eds.), *Trends and issues in organization development* (pp. 319–332) San Diego, CA: University Associates.

Harrison, M. I. (1994). *Diagnosing organizations: Methods, models, and processes.* Thousand Oaks, CA: Sage.

Hedrick, T. E., Bickman, L., & Rog, D. J. (1993). *Applied research design: A practical guide.* Thousand Oaks, CA: Sage.

Kaplan, R. S., & Norton, D. P. (1996). *The balanced scorecard.* Boston: Harvard Business School Press.

Keppel, G. (1982). *Design and analysis: A researcher's handbook* (2nd ed.). Upper Saddle River, NJ: Prentice Hall.

Margulies, N., & Raia, A. (1990). The significance of core values on the theory and practice of organization development. In F. Massarik (Ed.), *Advances in organization development* (Vol. 1, pp. 27–41). Norwood, NJ: Ablex.

Mendenhall, W., Reinmuth, J. E., & Beaver, R. J. (1993). *Statistics for management and economics* (7th ed.). Belmont, CA: Duxbury Press.

Rea, L. M., & Parker, R. A. (1997). *Designing and conducting survey research: A comprehensive guide* (2nd ed.). San Francisco: Jossey-Bass.

Rucci, A. J., Kirn, S., & Quinn, R. T. (1998). The employee-customer-profit chain at Sears. *Harvard Business Review, 76,* 82–97.

Ulrich, D. (1998, Jan.). A new mandate for human resources. *Harvard Business Review,* pp. 125–135.

Waclawski, J. (1996). Using organizational survey results to improve organizational performance. *Managing Service Quality, 6,* 53–56.

Wiley, J. W. (1996). Linking survey results to customer satisfaction and business performance. In A. I. Kraut (Ed.), *Organizational surveys: Tools for assessment and change* (pp. 330–359). San Francisco: Jossey-Bass.

PART 2

Process-Based Approaches to Organization Development

CHAPTER 7

Process Consultation
A Cornerstone of Organization Development Practice
William M. Kahnweiler

Organization development (OD) practitioners have widely varying opinions about the field's definition, purpose, goals, and theoretical underpinnings, among other dimensions (see Chapter One, and French & Bell, 1995). Furthermore, there has been considerable debate as to whether this vast diversity in perspectives strengthens the field, weakens its foundations, or has no effect at all (Bazigos & Burke, 1997; Goodstein, 1999). However, there is general consensus among OD practitioners and scholars that working with the human processes in organizations—how people relate to, communicate with, and affect each other—is a mainstay of OD practice. Uncovering, observing, analyzing, and improving these human processes is the essence of process consultation (PC). It can thus be assumed with some degree of assurance that most, if not all, OD practitioners use PC to one degree or another in their work with clients. PC is thus a cornerstone of the field.

Schein, considered by many to be the Father of PC, defined it as "a set of activities on the part of the consultant that help the client to perceive, understand, and act upon the process events that occur in the client's environment" (1987, p. 34). PC focuses on the "how" (that is, processes) rather than the "what" (that is, content) within the client system. It occurs solely through face-to-face interactions between the consultant and the client, who can be an individual or a group of people but not an entire organization (since one cannot have face-to-face interactions with a non-human entity such as an organization).

Typically, though not exclusively, PC is directed toward human rather than task-oriented processes in organizations. For example, it often targets how people, individually and collectively, approach, identify, and solve problems and make decisions and how they communicate with each other, as opposed to how the organization develops products or services, analyzes potential acquisitions, hires people, or allocates resources. Suppose a team has interpersonal conflicts among its members, and these conflicts lead to team meetings that deteriorate to finger-pointing sessions. PC may be employed to assist team members in discussing and ultimately resolving these conflicts, thereby enabling the team to focus on achieving its goals (see also Chapter Eight). PC may be used as a stand-alone intervention or in conjunction with other OD strategies. Although it is often viewed as soft, the data it elicits comprise observable client behaviors and are typically qualitative in nature. This data are collected and analyzed throughout a PC intervention (Schein, 1995).

Goals of PC

The cornerstone of PC is being as helpful as possible to clients. Although it is likely that every OD intervention has being helpful to clients as the primary, overarching goal, the process consultant continually asks himself or herself and the client, "Am I being helpful, and if so, how?" Such an evaluation, though often informal, occurs throughout a PC intervention and is not limited to an evaluation phase toward the end of a project (Coghlan, 1988; Schein, 1999).

Furthermore, being helpful in PC is often at odds with what is seen as being helpful in other forms of OD and organizational consultation. While the latter often employ specialized tools and procedures that imply a high degree of expertise, PC considers being helpful as helping clients to help themselves. As such, the process consultant avoids giving advice, using overly complex and esoteric methods, and creating a client's dependency on the consultant for assistance in fostering individual and group change (Huffington,

Cole, & Brunning, 1997). Whether deliberate or not, many forms of organizational consultation seem to create the situation where the client is dependent on the consultant for particular areas of expertise—for example, skills in particular methodologies such as multisource feedback, culture surveys, or large system change (see Chapters Two, Four, and Eleven). PC views such dependency as both unhealthy and unnecessary. In fact, a key indicator of the "Am I being helpful?" issue is how quickly the process consultant can finish a client engagement. This is akin to the adage about fishing for a person to achieve a short-term objective (relieving immediate hunger) or teaching a person how to fish (to relieve hunger for the rest of his or her life). At its core, PC teaches clients how to solve their human process problems on their own. This goal is similar to that of the humanistic psychology movement in general and client-centered therapy (Rogers, 1951) in particular. Furthermore, the distinction between PC and client-centered therapy can become even more blurred in that both frequently seek to help clients be aware of and understand their behavior and how it affects others. Since PC focuses on interpersonal dynamics, such as the unintended negative results of an executive's management style with subordinates, a staff group's evasiveness in response to probing questions from the consultant, or a work group's dysfunctional communication patterns, it can resemble psychotherapy closely. Indeed, the very roots of PC are embedded in the early works of Rogers that are now a half-century old.

Enablers and Obstacles

The efficacy of PC is maximized when the following conditions exist in the client organization:

- The client owns the problem (Dougherty, 1990; Schein, 1987, 1999).
- The client and consultant share equally in diagnosing the presenting problem further (Schein, 1987, 1995).
- The client agrees that the diagnosis and the intervention cannot and should not be separated (because such a distinction is artificial) (Altier, 1987).

These three conditions may seem to be rather easy to satisfy. Let us take a look at them more closely by first examining some situations that do not satisfy these conditions but are nonetheless commonplace in OD consulting.

Many, if not most, OD consulting interventions begin by having a prospective client make some statements to the consultant that portray the presenting problem. The consultant may be an insider, that is, an employee of the organization, or external to the organization. Here are some examples of typical initial statements:

"The finance operation has some real morale problems."

"Division G's attitude survey results show they need to improve downward and lateral communications."

"I can't get my staff to buy into my vision."

"Our call center desperately needs some leading-edge customer service training."

All of these statements either imply or explicitly state that the client has performed a diagnosis, believes the diagnosis is accurate and thorough, and through a modest conceptual leap, the solution to the problem uncovered in the diagnosis is clear. Thus, the client wants assistance in the form of a pair of hands (Block, 2000)—that is, someone who can come in and boost morale, improve communications, motivate people to support a vision, or deliver training. This model is also referred to as the *purchase of expertise* (Schein, 1987; Sidley, 1997).

Alternatively, and also common, are situations where the client either does not know precisely what the problem is or is not interested in participating in a process to uncover it. In these situations, the client typically has more pressing things on the agenda or for whatever reason simply does not want to devote time and energy to deal with the problem that needs to be solved. Thus, the client purchases in the OD consultant both diagnostic expertise to identify the problem and solution expertise to eradicate it. This model has been referred to as "doctor-patient" (Schein, 1987), and one can readily see why. Suppose you have a recurring headache. Despite your attempts to obtain relief, such as altering your diet or employing stress-reduction techniques, the headaches continue to bother you, so you decide to seek the counsel of a physician. More than likely, the doctor will ask you some questions about the frequency and duration of these headaches, their intensity, your activities when the headaches occur, and so forth. Then he or she will likely perform a series of tests to uncover the cause of your headaches, which are treated as symptoms of some underlying medical condition. Assuming that the tests uncover a root cause, the treatment will become clear by default and then administered by the physician (or another specialist if deemed appropriate). As the patient, you have handed over to someone else the power to both diagnose what the problem is and then solve it. Organizational clients who have "a headache" (for example, poor morale, dysfunctional communications, lack of teamwork) do the same thing when engaging an OD or other consultant as their "doctor."

A variation of this occurs when the client has only a vague sense of what the symptoms are but nonetheless wants a solution while being uninvolved in identifying the solution as well as executing it. I call this the *car mechanic model.* I am grateful for the many conveniences cars offer and am equally uninterested in how they work. Let us say my car starts making some strange noises one day. Because I need reliable transportation, I do not hesitate to take my car into the mechanic as soon as possible. When I pull into the shop, I inform my mechanic of the noises, tell her to find out what is wrong, and then call me. More often than not, I have no idea if the diagnosis is accurate, so I usually say to go ahead and fix the problem and then call me when my car is ready to be picked up.

Organizational clients often act in this way as well. They do not want to be involved in disentangling symptoms from causes or implementing solutions that attack the causes. They delegate those tasks to the OD consultant, to whom they attribute particular expertise in the realm of human issues. A statement such as, "Communication [or training, morale issues, and a host of others] is your area of expertise, so go find the exact problem and then fix it," illustrates this delegation. In other words, the OD consultant is told to see what is causing the noises in the organization and then get rid of them.

Although these situations are common, they do not represent ideal conditions for PC to be efficacious. The first reason is that either the diagnosis of the problem has already been made by the client or the client is unwilling to partner with the consultant to identify the real problem. Second, there is a clear distinction made between the diagnosis and the intervention or treatment phases. Third, in some situations, the problem is seen as someone else's issue (that is, the finance department's or the call center's).

As a stand-alone intervention or combined with others, PC relies heavily on a joint venture between the client and the OD consultant. Thus, the minimum antecedents necessary for PC to be optimally effective involve the client's willingness to admit there is some sort of problem, admit that he or she is not sure what exactly the problem is, work in partnership with the consultant to diagnose the real problem, be open to alternative explanations of the problem throughout the diagnosis, own the problem and ultimately decide which solutions to employ in solving it, and learn the skills that will be useful in diagnosing and solving similar problems in the future. Alternatively, when the client's diagnosis is accurate, the client cannot or will not participate in diagnostic data collection and analysis, and the problem's solution is very straightforward, PC is likely to be inappropriate. In these instances, a doctor-patient or expert consulting approach is warranted.

Fundamental Techniques

Although PC in its pure form eschews techniques (the process that occurs between the consultant and client *is* the product), there are a number of procedures that the process consultant typically employs. Readers who have some graduate education in counseling, clinical psychology, or a related field will probably find these techniques quite familiar. In one way or another, all these techniques are applied to help clients express themselves directly, clearly, and honestly; to uncover hidden agendas and underlying meanings; to help clients become more aware of what the real problem is (and ultimately what the right solution is); and to support clients in choosing possible solutions (Donovan & Letize, 1993; Margerison, 1992; Schein, 1995).

Facilitating—"I wonder what you mean by 'morale problems?'"

Eliciting—"Tell me more about what those morale problems look like. What would I see if I encountered one of them?"

Probing—"You seem bothered and upset about the customer service reps' performance. What exactly bothers you? Why?"

Self-disclosing—"I've worked with several clients who resisted the idea of process consulting, so you are by no means the first one. I understand there are real risks in your taking this approach with me. In fact, I'm somewhat scared too, for I really have no idea what will come out of our sessions. I can't guarantee what I'm offering you will work."

Observing—"For the past fifteen minutes, I've watched how the group doesn't allow the person who's talking to finish what he or she is saying."

Confronting—"This group conveys a lot of energy, and it seems that much of it is directed toward attempts to look good to each other rather than to say what's really on our minds. I wonder if some of us feel it's unsafe in here to be real? What do you think?"

Obviously, the examples are somewhat trite and for illustrative purposes only. In practice, these techniques are often combined with one another, as well as with other OD interventions, such as survey feedback or team building. The key point to remember is that any technique that the process consultant uses has a single goal: to be as helpful as possible to the client at all times. Being helpful, from a PC perspective, is not about giving advice or providing solutions but helping clients to help themselves.

Despite this admittedly cursory overview of some key techniques, it can be seen that the process consultant is "the instrument" in PC's most uncontaminated form. That is, attitude surveys, questionnaires, and other commonly used data collection instruments are really superfluous in a pure process consulting endeavor. It is the consultant who manages the data—that is, observes, stores, synthesizes, retrieves, and reports client behaviors. These data are collected in an ongoing way (as opposed to a discrete phase of a project), and it is the consultant who is the data collection instrument through these techniques.

Key Skills in Process Consultation

Because a helping relationship is the foundation of any PC intervention, the skills necessary to perform PC effectively mirror those
embraced by other helping professions, such as counseling, clinical psychology, and social work. Most assuredly, self-awareness ranks
at or near the top of the list in importance. Process consultants
must not only know themselves in a general sense; they must be
cognizant of what they are thinking and feeling virtually all the
time. This is because they are the instrument in PC. As such, they
must separate their own emotional baggage from the data that
emerge from the client. Similarly, because the major goal of PC is
to help clients help themselves, the process consultant must be
constantly vigilant in ensuring that his or her own needs, opinions,
biases, and feelings do not contaminate the helping process. Only
through keen and constant self-awareness is this possible.

Behavioral observation skills are also necessary. Because PC
relies on data emerging from the client, the consultant needs to
be able to note what people are doing throughout an intervention,
as this is important information. The ability to give and receive
feedback in helpful ways is another major skill in PC. This takes
considerable practice and experience, especially since minimal resistance to problem ownership is paramount.

Implied in this skill package is the ability to listen, including
active listening (that is, hearing verbally unexpressed yet real messages) and empathy (the ability to get in another's shoes). These
skills are needed to demonstrate the PC consultant's genuine interest in the client and the client's issues, as well as his or her desire to be helpful at all times. Along with these, the sense of
knowing when to be more directive (for example, using confrontation) and when to be nondirective (for example, simply listening and allowing the client to talk) is needed. Often, this artful
skill comes only with considerable experience. There are no
recipes or guidelines that an aspiring process consultant can rely
on in choosing how directive to be at a particular time.

Although some PC skills parallel those used by a competent
consultant grounded in fields such as industrial/organizational
psychology or human resource development, the truly high-caliber
process consultant is by and large an OD professional who has

amassed years of experience performing PC. Most, if not all, high-caliber process consultants have received formal training in PC skills at one time or another. Such training is usually intensive and extensive. Groups such as the National Training Laboratories and the Tavistock Institute have been in the business of training and educating current and aspiring process consultants for years and have earned solid reputations. Because PC requires such finely tuned, seasoned, and varied skills (including, but not limited to, self-awareness and interpersonal savvy), a case can be made that an aspiring process consultant needs to undergo individual psychotherapy, group psychotherapy, both, or some form of intense interpersonal experience supervised by a competent veteran consultant. What is necessary and sufficient preparation and training of process consultants is a highly debatable issue. What is not debatable is the need for process consultants to be constantly learning from their experiences. It is generally agreed within various strands of OD that no one can legitimately claim he or she has learned everything about PC or has reached his or her full potential as a process consultant. Being teachable is a lifelong process for a process consultant.

Certain traits or attitudes are key elements that assist a process consultant to be optimally helpful to clients. First, PC requires the consultant to want to be helpful to clients. While this may seem a moot point, it is difficult, if not impossible, for a process consultant (and perhaps other types as well) to feign wanting to be helpful. Most clients are intelligent and perceptive. Eventually, they will know whether the consultant truly wants to help or has more self-serving interests. Related to this is a form of humility on the part of the consultant. Specifically, he or she needs to be able and willing to avoid the seduction of being seen as an expert. This seduction is often difficult to resist, especially when clients seek expertise. It should also be clear by now that PC is usually an ambiguous, unpredictable journey. Even the data that emerge are informally obtained and qualitative in form. Thus, having high tolerance for ambiguity, a trait that is likely useful in any OD consulting venture, is certainly imperative when conducting PC. Having low control needs is also helpful, since the client drives the process while the consultant takes a less directive stance. Patience on the part of the consultant, particularly one who believes he or she knows "the answer" to the client's problem, is needed so that the client ultimately defines and solves the problem rather than being dependent on the consultant to do so.

Helpful Antecedents in the Client System

The key enablers of PC are that the client owns the problem, is willing to participate in the diagnosis, and realizes that diagnosis is continuing and cannot be separated (except artificially) from the intervention and solution. In addition, other conditions in the client system facilitate PC's efficacy. Conversely, the absence of these conditions will result in PCs' being less effective and appropriate. These conditions can be boiled down to four:

- *The client should have sufficient trust in the consultant.* Of course, trust is earned over time and not bestowed immediately. Suffice it to say that if the client fails to have adequate trust in the consultant as a person (along with their skills), PC will have minimal positive impact.
- *The client should have minimal dependencies on the consultant.* There is a fine line between dependency and willingness to be helped. *Dependency* in the context of PC means looking to the consultant for expertise, the answer, direction, and advice without significant involvement in diagnosis and treatment of the problem.
- *The client should be willing and able to admit defenses and explore them* (Schein, 1999). This condition parallels that posited for many forms of psychotherapy. Often, PC will unravel data that suggest it is the client who is the problem, or at least a factor that contributes to the problem. Through the use of the skills described previously, the process consultant can assist clients in facing their own behaviors that are exacerbating or even causing the problem.
- *The client and client system should not be in a crisis mode.* PC places considerable demands on the client, not the least of which is emotional investment. Thus, if an individual client or the organization is in the midst of considerable turmoil, relentless crises, or constant churning, PC will have minimal chances of succeeding. Time, reflection, investment in establishing and maintaining trustful relationships, and other elements of PC make it difficult

to coexist when people and their organizations are in a continual firefighting posture.

Some readers may be wondering how long a successful PC intervention takes. The definitive answer is, "It depends." Factors that affect PC's duration include those of the consultant (for example, degree of skills, attitudes, and traits), the client (for example, level of commitment, effort, and teachability), and the organization (for example, the number of helpful antecedents and obstacles that exist). Taking into account that these and other factors will vary widely among consultants, clients, and organizations, effective PC can often be accomplished in three to ten sessions, each session (with an individual or a group as the client) lasting one to three hours. Thus, it is probably safe to assume that in most situations, PC does not take as long as deep, highly introspective, nonbehavioral approaches to psychotherapy. It is also reasonable to expect that PC will require more time than a two-hour orientation session for newly hired employees or a one-day workshop on using a spreadsheet program.

Limitations and Pitfalls of PC

Like any other intervention, PC is not a panacea even under ideal conditions. In addition to the absence of helpful antecedents, there are three major limitations to PC even when these antecedents are present.

Client Resentment and Resistance

Although resentment and resistance can occur with any form of consultation, PC is particularly susceptible to them because it is relatively nondirective and requires a high level of client involvement (Akkermans, 1995). When clients get stuck, the diagnosis becomes murkier, or the solution becomes more elusive, clients can become frustrated. They can then easily switch into the mode of wanting expert advice from the consultant. The PC consultant will be aware of this and resist the temptation to extricate the client from the frustration. This can create even more frustration for the client and ultimately lead to blaming the consultant. From the client's point of view, it is easier in many ways to buy the consultant's expertise. Recall the car mechanic model.

Client Perceptions of Consultant Inefficiency and Apathy

These attributions can occur because PC is relatively nondirective and the consultant is often throwing back data to the client to process. This is not unlike a Rogerian therapist's saying, "Hmmm. So you are saying you think the problem is _____." Sooner or later the client can easily begin to suspect the consultant does not know anything worthwhile, is incompetent, or is merely dancing by refusing to offer suggestions, advice, or guidance.

A Dearth of Research on Effectiveness

Empirical research on the effectiveness of PC is sorely lacking (Dougherty, 1990; Kaplan, 1979). One acute challenge in this regard is creating well-designed studies. Furthermore, because PC is such a relationship-intensive endeavor and the data it elicits are usually very soft (that is, qualitative), conducting studies that are sufficiently rigorous in the traditional sense is extremely difficult, and maybe impossible (Bowers, 1973). Nonetheless, the OD profession needs to come up with some creative research designs that can evaluate PC accurately without being overly intrusive to clients. Certainly, more case study research is needed to provide empirical evidence of PC's claims. And although most field research prevents true experimental designs to be employed, consideration needs to be given to longitudinal studies, such as time-series designs. Such research can enhance the credibility of PC within the OD profession, as well as with prospective clients, while providing some broad guidelines to assist practitioners in assessing what elements of PC work with which clients at which time with what problems.

Practice Tips

1. Provide specifics, not generalities, when giving feedback.
1. Try to be helpful at all times.
2. Do not allow your ego or need to be seen as an expert to get in the way, and never overstate your expertise.
3. Be authentic; don't falsely represent yourself.
4. Respect the client, and show that respect.
5. Do not foster or create client dependency, and never give the client answers. When in doubt, ask questions instead.
6. Make it simple for the client to participate in the diagnosis.
7. Never assume that the client knows what the real problem is.
8. Manage the client's expectations. Never expect the results to be immediate and easily measurable.
9. Keep an open mind. Be sure not to allow your own and your client's biases to influence you.

Conclusion

The core of OD in general and PC in particular is helping clients achieve success. The bottom-line question for the process consultant is, "Has my helping been helpful?" Collaborative goal setting with the client at the beginning of a PC project (or another OD effort that uses PC as an adjunct) can help address this important question. Innovative research designs can be employed as well. However, because PC is such a client-driven endeavor, ultimately the answer to this question will have to come from clients themselves. After all, it is their organization, their problems, and their willingness to partner with the process consultant to discover what the real problems are and then do something constructive about them. Thus, often it is simply a matter of asking the client on a regular basis, and not just near the end of the engagement, "Have I been helpful?" and then using other techniques (for example, probing) to uncover to what degree PC has been helpful, how it has been helpful, and why.

For centuries, the helping professions have sought answers to the issue of what works with which clients. This chapter has presented some parameters that may assist readers in determining when PC is and is not a viable tool in the OD professional's arsenal. And while the debate rages about OD's rightful place in organizational life, its effectiveness, and even its definition, one aspect of OD on which most experts agree is that OD is a process-oriented craft conducted in largely content-oriented, results-driven workplaces. Perhaps this explains some of OD's struggles to be credible and valued and why OD professionals sometimes feel like they are all alone despite having people around them all the time. We are square pegs trying to assist clients who are round holes. And some of those clients question why square pegs even exists, while others do not even want to find our what square pegs might offer.

Nevertheless, because OD is a process-oriented craft, PC is a major cornerstone. Indeed, without PC, it is difficult to conceptualize, much less, practice OD.

References

Akkermans, H. (1995). Developing a logistics strategy through participative business modeling. *Journal of Operations and Production Management, 15,* 100–112.

Altier, W. J. (1987). We're glad we don't know your business. *Journal of Management Consulting, 3,* 28–32.

Bazigos, M. N., & Burke, W. W. (1997). Theory orientations of OD practitioners. *Group and Organization Management, 22,* 384–408.

Block, P. (2000). *Flawless consulting.* San Francisco: Jossey-Bass.

Bowers, D. G. (1973). OD techniques and their results in 23 organizations. *Journal of Applied Behavioral Science, 9,* 21–43.

Coghlan, D. (1988). In defense of process consultation. *Leadership and Organization Development Journal, 9,* 27–31.

Donovan, M., & Letize, L. (1993). Lessons from the wizard. *Journal for Quality and Participation, 16,* 4–17.

Dougherty, A. M. (1990). *Consultation: Practice and perspectives.* Pacific Grove, CA: Brooks/Cole.

French, W. L., & Bell, C. H., Jr. (1995). *Organization development: Behavioral science interventions for organizational improvement* (5th ed.). Upper Saddle River, NJ: Prentice Hall.

Goodstein, L. D. (1999). Customer value: The linchpin of organizational change. *Organizational Dynamics, 27,* 21–36.

Huffington, C., Cole, C. F., & Brunning, H. (1997). *A manual of organizational development: The psychology of change.* Madison, CT: Psychosocial Press.

Kaplan, R. E. (1979). The conspicuous absence of evidence that process consultation enhances task performance. *Journal of Applied Behavioral Science, 15,* 346–360.

Margerison, C. (1992). Counseling and advice in management development. *Management Development Review, 5,* 22–26.

Rogers, C. R. (1951). *On becoming a person.* Boston: Houghton Mifflin.

Schein, E. H. (1987). *Process consultation* (Vol. 2). Reading, MA: Addison-Wesley.

Schein, E. H. (1990). A general philosophy of helping: Process consultation. *Sloan Management Review, 31,* 57–64.

Schein, E. H. (1995). Process consultation, action research, and clinical inquiry: Are they the same? *Journal of Managerial Psychology, 10,* 14–19.

Schein, E. H. (1999). *Process consultation revisited: Building the helping relationship.* Reading, MA: Addison-Wesley.

Sidley, N. A. (1997). Some things I've learned about changing behavior in a Fortune 100 company. *Journal of Organizational Behavior Management, 17,* 99–108.

CHAPTER 8

The Heart of It All

Group- and Team-Based Interventions in Organization Development

Richard W. Woodman
William A. Pasmore

The effective functioning of groups and teams is central to the effective functioning of organizations. That simple observation lies at the heart of organization development (OD) practice, a good percentage of which is team related in two respects: many interventions are designed to create more effective teams or groups, and interventions often rely on using teams to facilitate various transitions or transformations to a higher state of effectiveness. We will deal with team-based interventions in both respects in this chapter. Although it is increasingly common to distinguish between the terms *groups* and *teams* in the management literature, we draw no such distinction for this chapter and use the terms interchangeably.[1]

From its inception, the practice of OD has had a strong focus on groups and teams as both the focus of change and as vehicles for changing the organization (Cummings & Worley, 2001). A recent survey of internal OD practitioners in the Fortune 500 industrials found that human processual change interventions, such as team building and process consulting, occupied over one-third of the OD professional's time in these firms (McMahan & Woodman, 1992). An unpublished survey of the Fortune 500 service firms yielded similar findings with regard to the continued emphasis on groups and teams. Given the centrality of team-based interventions to OD and effective change management, it is crucial for practitioners to have a strong grounding in the family of interventions with this focus. In addition, it is important for practitioners to have insight into the dynamics of groups and teams, including how to harness the strong potential influences of groups on individual behavior in complex social settings.

A Primer on Group Dynamics

From a systems perspective, all organizational groups or teams exist within an environment or context. The context of any organizational group provides both the resources the group needs to accomplish its work and ultimately judges the success of the group's effort. Five elements of group work are crucial if a group is to succeed (see Table 8.1):

- *Directioning*—understanding what it is expected to accomplish
- *Organizing*—agreeing on an approach to using the group's resources to complete the task
- *Exploring*—exploring options and alternatives to perform the work
- *Converging*—deciding on the best approach or solution
- *Executing*—satisfactorily completing the work or implementing the solution

Much of what we do in OD to build more effective teams or to use teams to intervene in organizational issues addresses one or more of these five elements of group work. Goal-setting interventions, for example, help teams clarify what is expected of them (directioning); role clarification interventions help team members understand how the team is organized to perform its work (organizing); brainstorming methods help groups explore alternatives (exploring); decision-making techniques assist teams in reaching higher-quality decisions (converging); and action planning interventions help teams to plan the execution of their solutions (executing).

Conditions remaining equal, it would seem logical that teams facing the same challenges, with comparable membership and

Table 8.1. Task-Related and Group Dynamics Issues for Teams.

Issue	Examples
Task-Related Issues	
Directioning	Framing, goal setting, visioning, setting measures of success
Organizing	Planning, staffing, choosing methods to accomplish task
Exploring	Learning, thinking, brainstorming, creating, generating alternatives, scenario planning
Converging	Problem solving, deciding among alternatives
Executing	Communicating, action planning, engaging others, monitoring outcomes, revising solutions, implementing
Group Dynamics Issues	
Fit	Membership, capabilities, representation, connections
Power	Leadership, authority, influence, control
Affect	Emotions, commitment, conflict, motivations

using similar methods, should achieve similar outcomes. Yet we know this not to be the case. Different teams composed of similar members vary greatly in their level of performance. Even the same teams that are performing roughly the same work produce different outcomes at different times. What accounts for these phenomena? We know that emotional affect plays a large role in group performance. Teams that are fired up, highly cohesive, and make full use of the resources at their disposal usually outperform teams that are unmotivated, contentious, and lacking synergy. Thus, we have also created interventions that are intended to address the emotional reality of groups. T-groups, for example, are intended to help group members explore interpersonal relationships; ice-breakers help new groups get to know each other so that they can better understand how to apply their resources to the task at hand; conflict resolution techniques help groups overcome divisiveness; and visioning exercises can help enhance motivation.

Emotional issues in groups come in three basic forms:

- *Fit*—issues that refer to membership and belonging
- *Power*—issues of influence and control
- *Affect*—issues of group members' sentiments toward one another

Our model is similar to Schutz's framework (1958) for inter-personal relationships in groups. As in Schutz's formulation of group development theory, we believe that most groups develop over time by working through cycles of these emotional issues, beginning with who is qualified to be in the group to work on the task, who controls the applications of resources and decisions, and how members feel about each other and their experience of working together. Highly developed groups, in our view, are those that are aware of these emotional issues and are able to address them effectively as they skillfully reorganize themselves to deal with each unique task they perform.

Because each group faces a unique challenge in its specific context and is composed of different members, no single inter-vention or set of OD interventions can guarantee success. Instead, diagnosis is required to understand the situation the group is facing and to tailor the appropriate set of interventions to the needs of the group and setting. Thus, although all groups face similar task–related challenges and must overcome a predictable set of emotional hurdles, interventions cannot be undertaken in a me-chanical fashion. Nor do we believe that interventions can succeed that are addressed narrowly to the team's work or emotional ex-perience or even more narrowly to a single aspect of either. The most effective interventions are those that deal with the group in a holistic manner, with multiple methods to help the group ap-proach its full range of task and emotional issues.

The Focus of Group- and Team-Based Interventions

Interventions in groups to improve their effectiveness or with groups to change organizations must begin somewhere. With that in mind, we propose a framework that targets promising places for interventions to begin, depending on the type of group and situation provided by the intervention opportunity.

Table 8.2 lists nine important varieties of groups and teams that exist in organizations. These teams are grouped into two major categories: permanent and temporary. The list is not intended to capture every type of team that could exist; however, these nine represent a significant portion of the groups and teams that organizations use. For each type of team, we identify promising intervention targets in terms of task-related issues and group dynamics issues. These are intended to be illustrative only. Although we think the areas shown are likely to be high-payoff targets for interventions, only a valid diagnosis can identify the most crucial change levers in each particular organizational instance. The primary theme here is one of context. To design an effective group- and team-based intervention, it is essential to appreciate differences among types of groups and teams, differences in terms of team tasks, and differences in terms of group dynamics.

Two examples of our thinking with regard to the entries in Table 8.2 are illustrative. Cross-functional teams can be described as composed of members from different functions, departments, and areas of expertise (Lam, Bischoff, Higgins, & Persing, 1999). Although these teams may be temporary, organizations increasingly are creating cross-functional teams that become a permanent part of the organizing structure. The teams are created when organizational boundaries interfere with communication and coordination among organizational members regarding shared responsibilities. Because cross-functional teams are intended to identify common issues, explore different ways of dealing with them, and recommend solutions to the problems and opportunities they uncover, we would consider issues of exploring to be central to the effective functioning (and indeed the reason for existence) of cross-functional teams; thus, we identify this area as potentially a high-payoff intervention focus. If the team is not

**Table 8.2. High-Payoff Focus of
Group- and Team-Based Intervention.**

Type of Team	Primary Focus of Task-Related Issues	Primary Focus of Group Dynamics Issues
Permanent Work Teams		
Cross-functional	Exploring	Fit
Departmental, functional	Executing	Power
Knowledge	Exploring	Power
Leadership	Directioning	Power
Self-managing	Organizing	Affect
Virtual	Converging	Fit
Temporary Teams		
Change management	Executing	Affect
Design, parallel	Organizing	Power
Task forces	Exploring	Fit

effective in its exploration activities, much of the rationale for its existence disappears. Furthermore, we would expect emotional issues of fit to be crucial in cross-functional teams. These teams must establish the legitimacy of members' claims to influence over the issues they address. Because cross-functional teams are not controlled by a single leader or chain of command, the identity and competence of their members must be established. Connections to salient parts of the organization and its environment will be paramount. Thus, interventions may often be focused on issues of fit to create an effective working team.

Change management teams are typically charged with the responsibility of directing some significant change effort through to completion. As such, issues of executing may provide a high-payoff focus for intervention. The success of the change management team will ultimately be determined by how well they implement the changes desired. Significant organizational changes are complex, challenging, and problematic. Thus, we might expect group dynamics issues under the category of affect to be particularly important for the effective functioning of the team. Individuals must rely on their teammates to maintain strong levels of motivation and commitment during the long, difficult change process.

All types of teams engage in all five of the task-related activities at one point or another in their work. Similarly, all group dynamics issues are salient for every team. However, we believe that a useful starting point for diagnosis is to understand the type of team, the key task-related challenge for the team, and the most crucial emotional issues facing the team at the current phase of its development. Understanding these elements is key in planning successful group- and team-based interventions.

Interventions with Teams and Groups

Effective organizational change begins with valid diagnosis. Certainly that is a truism that exists in almost every published model of an OD change process. However, recognizing the importance of diagnosis does not mean that it is always done well or is well integrated with other intervention activities. Valid organizational diagnosis is a tricky business, with many pitfalls that can derail a change effort. While any information is almost certainly better than none, simply gathering data about organizational problems does not yield a valid diagnosis. With group- and team-based interventions, the change agent needs a valid framework or perspective to understand the role and effective functioning of teams within the context of the organization's strategy and goals (Woodman, 1990). We would argue that the framework presented in Tables 8.1 and 8.2 provides such a useful diagnostic tool.

From this context-based perspective, we suggest that every intervention with groups or teams should address both task and emotional issues. As a corollary, it should be obvious that the performance of any group depends on the ability of its members to perform the five task-related skills and help manage the impact of emotional dynamics on teamwork. Thus, an additional set of interventions that are commonly applied to improve team performance is related to training members in these skills and competencies.

Training, we believe, is most effective when performed in conjunction with actual work on tasks with intact groups that experience emotional dynamics on a firsthand basis. Generic training that is delivered in a piecemeal, disassociated manner generally has less impact and sustainable benefit in our observation. Thus, we believe that in general, team interventions should be tailored to the specific group and situation, comprehensive in addressing both task and emotional issues, and combined with targeted, real-time training as required.

Practice Tips

1. Provide specifics, not generalities, when giving feedback.
1. Group- and team-based interventions are the means, not the end result, whereby organizations become more effective.
2. Do not engage in team-building training for the sake of training.
3. Be a BIG OD person. Create the capacity in the organization to reinvent and transform itself as needed to remain effective.
4. Group and team interventions that are designed to create more effective work teams should not be used when the individuals involved have little or no actual need to work interdependently.
5. Effective interventions always begin with valid organizational diagnosis.

A Guide to Interventions

In our own practice, we often yearn for the same magic bullet types of solutions. But there are no magic bullets outside the pages of superhero comic books. Effective change management is a tricky, and sometimes quite messy, business. Following are some philosophical observations that might serve as a useful guide to the effective practice of group- and team-based interventions. An example highlights why we think each is important.

• Group- and team-based interventions are the means, not the end result, whereby organizations become more effective.

An older, conservative senior team was faced with a dramatic change in its competitive environment. Solutions that worked before were no longer working; the organization was in trouble. The consultant, sensing that the senior team needed to become looser and more creative, intervened with a number of activities intended to change the dynamics of the group, including using music to help the members of the group explore physical movement as a spur to creative thinking. The consultant was fired. The senior group wanted help with its business issues, not its own dynamics. The consultant's diagnosis was correct: the group did need to think outside the box. The problem was that the consultant chose an intervention that was not sensitive to the group's composition and perspective. He would have been more successful if he had started from a discussion of desired business outcomes and engaged the group in determining the best ways to stretch the limits of its thinking.

Clearly, process skills are one of the major areas of expertise that the OD change agent brings to the table (see Chapter Seven). In a very real sense, these process skills provide much of the OD consultant's competitive advantage. This could result in a troubling goal displacement phenomenon with regard to creating effective groups and teams in an organization. Let us explain as follows: A quarterback might occasionally attempt to force a pass when a receiver is not open, change the coach's play at the line of scrimmage (audible), call a pass when another option makes more sense, and so on. In the world of professional football, a critical commentator might describe such a situation as one where the quarterback "falls in love with his arm." An individual or change team engaged in group or team interventions could easily be guilty of a similar goal displacement. Any process-based intervention should always be used in the service of systemwide change—that is, to advance toward the goals and vision the organization is pursuing. The goal of the organization is not to have effective teams; rather, effective teams are needed in order for the organization to attain its goals (Woodman, 1993). This distinction is subtle, but crucial, for effective change agentry.

• Do not engage in team-building training for the sake of training.

A full year after a major corporation had spent a fortune on classes for every employee to attend a diversity management program, employees reported that little had changed. The glass ceiling was still in place, and there were few visible signs that senior leaders of the organization really cared about the circumstances that women and minorities encountered in the company. People on teams reported that decisions continued to be made by the same people as before. Minority turnover actually increased after the program.

We would argue that every team- and group-based intervention should have a training component. However, this should never be the only component of the intervention. The kiss of death in human resource training programs comes when these efforts are conducted in isolation from the strategy and goals of the firm. This represents a serious form of goal displacement.

• Be a BIG OD person. Create the capacity in the organization to reinvent and transform itself as needed to remain effective.

At the height of the quality improvement movement, almost every major corporation kept track of its progress in improving quality by counting the number of quality circles that it had formed. Today, few quality circles still exist. Most found that they could change small things to affect quality locally, but were unable to address larger issues that cut across departmental lines. A few organizations, like GE and Allied Signal, took quality to another level with their Six Sigma programs, which trained and empowered people to go after big issues that really mattered. In those companies, quality has become a way of life, not a program that came and went.

BIG OD is what the founders of the field thought they were doing. *BIG OD* means creating the capacity in the organization to reinvent and transform itself as needed to remain effective. BIG OD is sustainable, systemwide change (see Chapter One). It has no beginning and no end; it is a way of managing complex organizations so that they are able to survive in a world of constant change. *Small od* is a variety of techniques and interventions, often done in isolation, having no congruent linkage with the strategy and goals of the firm. Small od is counting how many workshops were held last year. Small od also is what the detractors of the field think OD is (Woodman, 1993). Unfortunately, the arena of action occupied by group- and team-based interventions may lend itself to lots of small od thinking. It is easy to get caught up in the minutiae of conducting team-building workshops and interventions with small groups of individuals and lose sight of the critical linkage between these activities and the overall effectiveness of the system. Do not let that happen.

• Group and team interventions that are designed to create more effective work teams should not be used when the individuals involved have little or no actual need to work interdependently.

A newspaper company formed a group composed of people from each of the major departments in the company to look at ways to improve company performance. Members of the group suggested ideas, but they tended to fall within the responsibilities of managers of different departments. These ideas were handed off to the departments for consideration, and the group went on looking for other ideas to improve the organization. After some time, the group was floundering, and a consultant was brought in to help the group improve its motivation and effectiveness. The consultant provided the group with methods for brainstorming and problem solving that improved its efficiency, but the work still failed to generate much excitement among its members or in the larger organization. It was not until the group was asked to refocus its attention on creating a series of future scenarios for the paper that its members became excited. For the first time, they were working on ideas that would require each of their departments to contribute to new ways of doing things, all at the same time. The group took on a life of its own.

Many of the activities normally associated with team building are appealing and perhaps even fun to use. They also have the advantage of being task focused, relatively low in cost, and nonthreatening (usually) for participants. As such, group- and team-building activities may be used, at the margin, when other interventions would be more useful. We have occasionally experienced situations when team-based interventions were being used because that was what people knew how to do, team interventions were being used because action needed to be taken and these approaches seemed active, or team-based interventions were being used because collections of people were involved, although these folks were not really a group or team in any meaningful sense of these terms. If the only time the employees have to coordinate their work is during team-building training, for example, this should be a clue that something is wrong with the choice of intervention.

- Effective interventions always begin with valid organizational diagnosis.

> An external consultant using a standardized methodology she had been taught started to create a series of teams to engage in the change management work that would be required to implement a new enterprise resource management system. The establishment of these teams was met with resistance by the vice president of organizational effectiveness, who had previously established a network of teams to work on a variety of other change initiatives. He wondered why the existing teams could not be used to carry out the change management work for the new system. The external consultant insisted that the membership of the existing teams was not what was called for by the current intervention. The vice president of information technology, who sponsored the project, met with the vice president of organizational effectiveness to discuss the issue. The external consultant was informed that she would need to work with the existing change management teams and that the work on the new system would have to be made seamless with work on other organizational initiatives that were already under way.

With team- and group-based interventions, context is the key. It is not possible to intervene effectively in the system without a careful diagnosis that results in a deep understanding of the types of teams needed in the system, the issues that these teams will be addressing, where in the team process the greatest value can be created by improvement efforts, and so on. The high-payoff intervention strategy stems from valid diagnosis of context.

Conclusion

Teams are at the heart of many OD interventions, whether the goal is to improve team performance or to use teams to improve organizational performance. We have proposed a framework that consultants can use to optimize the starting point for their interventions and shared some tips based on our experience that we hope will help new practitioners avoid common mistakes. Our most important advice is to ensure that a valid diagnosis is conducted before team-based interventions are initiated and that all team-based interventions address the task, emotional, and educational needs of the groups involved.

Note

1.   The most meaningful difference between the two constructs seems
to be with regard to the closeness of working relationships, with
groups denoting collections of employees that are related in a somewhat looser fashion than teams. Teams, on the other hand, are typically thought to be collections of individuals whose working
relationships require close coordination, higher levels of cooperation, greater cohesiveness, and the like. Nevertheless, we see little
practical significance in the distinctions being drawn with regard to
the issues addressed in this chapter and thus choose to use the
terms as synonyms.

References

Cummings, T. G., & Worley, C. G. (2001). *Organization development and change* (7th ed.). Cincinnati, OH: South-Western.

Lam, L. L., Bischoff, S. J., Higgins, L. H., & Persing, D. L. (1999). Implementing effective cross-functional teams: A multilevel framework
for analysis. In W. A. Pasmore & R. W. Woodman (Eds.), *Research in
Organizational Change and Development* (Vol. 12, pp. 171–203). Greenwich, CT: JAI Press.

McMahan, G. C., & Woodman, R. W. (1992). The current practice of organization development within the firm: A survey of large industrial
corporations. *Group and Organization Management, 17,* 117–134.

Schutz, W. (1958). *FIRO: A three dimensional theory of interpersonal behavior.*
Austin, TX: Holt, Rinehart & Winston.

Woodman, R. W. (1990). Issues and concerns in organizational diagnosis. In C. N. Jackson & M. R. Manning (Eds.), *Organization Development Annual: Vol. 3. Diagnosing client organizations* (pp. 5–10).
Alexandria, VA: American Society for Training and Development.

Woodman, R. W. (1993). Observations on the field of organizational
change and development from the lunatic fringe. *Organization Development Journal, 11,* 71–74.

CHAPTER 9

Action Learning

Victoria J. Marsick
Judy O'Neil
Karen E. Watkins

Action learning (AL) is an approach to working with people to develop, and sometimes change and transform, them and their organization. This development takes place as individuals work in small groups on an actual project or problem as the way to learn. AL builds a laboratory for learning around real-life issues that are complex and messy. These issues can take the form of an individual project or problem for each participant or one project or problem for the group. In its ideal form, AL is peer learning that the learners themselves manage. Learning coaches work with AL groups in many programs and can be drawn on as resources.

Table 9.1 shows one of many possible AL program designs. This design was used to develop some 260 managers and line staff by Public Service Electric and Gas Company between 1996 and 1999. In each program cycle, four small teams of seven to ten people worked on one project or problem per team. The teams met with a learning coach during the program session days and on their own during the interim days. The program took place over a six-week time frame (Marsick & Watkins, 1999). This program, and some of its elements, are discussed later in the chapter.

In the Public Service Electric and Gas program, as in many other AL programs, the primary role of the learning coach was to create situations in which group members could take control of their learning (O'Neil, 1999). Table 9.2 identifies situations in which

177

**Table 9.1. Program Design for
Public Service Electric and Gas.**

Program/Back on Job Days	Content and Process
Half-day orientation	Presentation of the business case supporting the program
	What is action learning?
	Project presentation
	Action learning team meeting
	Participants establish personal learning goals
One-week interim period	
Two-day jump start	Action learning team meetings
	Programmed learning focusing on such areas as learning styles and communication
Two-week interim period	Work on action learning project and personal learning goals
Two-day interim session	Action learning team meetings
	Programmed learning focusing on such areas as conflict and uncovering personal assumptions
Two-week interim period	Work on action learning project and personal learning goals
Two-day final session	Action learning team meetings
	Programmed learning focusing on such areas as barriers and enablers to project recommendations
	Presentation of project recommendations to sponsors

Table 9.2. Learning Coach Interventions.

Intervention Need	Learning Coach Intervention
Creating an environment for learning	Emphasis on confidentiality Work with an individual, but only within the group setting Create a supportive environment
Specific interventions for learning	Questioning Reflection Critical reflection Programmed knowledge and just-in-time learning Make work visible Create ways to help think differently Challenge the group
Transfer skills needed for learning	Share role of expert with group members Help participants to give and receive help and feedback to each other Transfer of learning Help rather than teach Say nothing and be invisible Transfer of learning adviser skills

Source: O'Neil, 1999, p. 181.

AL learning coaches might intervene and the likely focus of their interventions. Other examples of AL programs can be found in Boshyk (2000), McGill and Beaty (1995), Mumford (1996), Pedler (1997), and Yorks, O'Neil, and Marsick (1999).

Action Learning and Other OD Interventions

AL shares some features with other kinds of OD interventions, for example, other task-oriented strategies, other development initiatives, and on-the-job learning that is not part of a development program. By differentiating these somewhat similar interventions and an AL intervention, OD practitioners can help organizations make better decisions about when to use AL or one of these other strategies.

Task-Oriented Strategies

Some task-oriented strategies also help people learn from work, but that is not their main focus. They exist primarily to get a job done. Examples include work groups that use a process consultation facilitator, cross-functional task forces, and quality circles (see Chapters Seven and Eight). Learning and data collection often take place through work in these groups, but little direct attention is specifically given to learning as the main focus of the work or to enhancing the learning that occurs.

When facilitators are invited to help the group with their work, they bring expertise to improve process and productivity. They are less concerned with developing learning capability in people or the organization. Learning coaches can sometimes take a role similar to that of a process consultant in that they use interventions to help the group with their process, particularly early in the program, (O'Neil, 1997). They do not, however, take an active role in the process; they are primarily focused on the learning of the individual and the group.

Development Initiatives

Some development interventions incorporate work, but unlike AL, real work is not the primary vehicle for learning. In these interventions, work or tasks may be in the form of simulations; tasks may be like the real job but are not actually real, or tasks may be real but included primarily to practice new knowledge and skills.

In addition, people often use the term *action learning* to describe any intervention that involves both action and learning. This might include physical activities undertaken outdoors to challenge people's limitations and fears (for example, an Outward Bound experience, whitewater rafting, or scaling mountains); experiential learning during which a team might engage in an exercise and learn from its debriefing; or the simple inclusion of an actual life case study in which learners apply concepts. AL is not a simulation; it is the real work of the individual or organization, and although an AL program may provide a chance to practice new skills in a safe setting, it is more than a practice opportunity.

Learning from Work

Finally, AL shares features with learning that is more fully integrated with work. For example, coaching might be provided to bring a team member up to speed on some aspect of a new engagement as the work progresses. Or learning reviews might be held to debrief important or unusual events and extract lessons learned. The After-Action Review (Sullivan & Harper, 1996), which was created by the U.S. Army, is now used in many corporations for this purpose. During After-Action Reviews, key stakeholders answer four questions: (1) What did we intend to happen? (2) What happened? (3) Why did it happen that way? (4) How can we improve what happened?

When learning takes place on the job rather than in an AL program, the intervention is typically focused on meeting specific needs. The organization often provides the impetus and structure for on-the-job learning. By contrast, an AL program takes place over time, and the program puts learners more directly in charge of recognizing their own learning needs and finding ways to meet them. The difference is similar to distinctions often made between training, which is short term and specific, and education, which is broader and more developmental in nature.

When to Choose AL

AL should not be used when it is better to get expert advice, save time, resolve an immediate crisis, meet a clearly identified specific need, or import a once-in-a-lifetime solution. AL is not effective for simple skill development, although it may well be used when people need to develop the capacity to adapt simple skills to complex, messy realities of daily work life. AL is always a good choice when a major reason for the intervention is to develop the capacity of people, work groups, and the organization to understand and manage their own learning and work better. Even when an organization decides that AL is an appropriate intervention, however, OD practitioners need to make choices about the nature of the AL program design.

Choosing Among Different Action Learning Program Types

Even when practitioners can differentiate between AL and other kinds of interventions, they can still be confused because of the different ways AL is practiced. O'Neil (1999) identified four schools of AL based on differences in the learning philosophy of those who practice it: the tacit school, the scientific school, the experiential school, and the critical reflection school. Each school builds on some of the practices advocated by the prior school and adds a unique dimension (Yorks et al., 1999). These philosophies lead people to value and use data differently.

Tacit AL School

In the tacit AL school, people assume "that significant learning will take place so long as carefully chosen participants are put together, some team building is done, and information is provided by experts" (Yorks et al., 1999, p. 12). Little is done intentionally to structure opportunities for learning outside of what would result incidentally from work on the project (O'Neil, 1999). Boshyk (2000), who has organized a network of companies that use this model, calls it *business-driven action learning*.

Tacit programs primarily focus on OD and as a result are designed with group projects. Two of the three objectives in the tacit program at Johnson & Johnson, for example, deal with generating business ideas and applying them to the organizational issues (Bossert, 2000). The third objective, "to assist participants develop the leadership and team skills necessary to work across organizational boundaries" (p. 95), deals with individual development to achieve company goals.

Most of these programs are run in a condensed time frame—Johnson & Johnson's is over a three-week period—and the typical program might begin with instruction from experts on topics that support the objectives of the initiative, along with activities to build the team's ability to work together. Teams then work on their project. They collect data and often interview stakeholders about the project, perhaps traveling to sites to observe interaction among staff or with customers. They then present their recommendations to one or more senior executives who probe the report and their thinking, as would be the case in the normal course of business.

The tacit school does not have a process for explicitly helping individuals to focus on their learning. In the other schools, the learning coach takes this role, at least at the start of programs, and helps individuals learn how to learn from their action through reflection.

Scientific AL School

The scientific AL school is based in the work of Reg Revans (1970), who is often called the Father of AL. Revans was a physicist, and his training shows in this model, which centers on the interplay of three interactive systems that Revans called Alpha, Beta, and Gamma. System Alpha involves the interplay of a manager's values with the external and internal organizational environment in decision making. System Beta is a five-step action research and learning process for reaching decisions: a survey stage, hypothesis or trial decision stage, experiment or action stage, audit stage, and review stage leading to action. System Gamma focuses on personal development and change. Practitioners who follow Revans's approach use a question-based learning design. Revans felt that too many educators emphasize programmed wisdom from the past, which he referred to as *P learning*, rather than insight that comes from asking fresh questions, which he called *Q insight.*

Programs following the scientific school often take place over an extended period of time because they involve diagnosing and acting on a complex actual problem that probably cannot be solved quickly. Teams meet periodically as they address the issue, sometimes with a learning coach and often on their own. Peers work together to diagnose the problem, collect and interpret data, and test out proposed solutions.

The scientific school builds an overlayer of explicit research and learning on top of the tacit school's model. The tacit school leans toward task accomplishment, whereas the scientific school adds more emphasis on the way in which a person's self-understanding influences task accomplishment.

An example of a scientific program was the General Electric Company (GEC) program that took place in England in the early

1970s (Casey & Pearce, 1977). The program extended over eight months, during which participants devoted themselves full time to their individual problems. The first three months of the program were given to the diagnosis of the business problem and an equal amount of time to implementation of the solution. During both phases of the program work, specific problem solving and experimentation processes were used often.

One day a week, individuals met in a group, or *set* as it was called, with four or five other participants to share with and help one another. Two project advisers, or learning coaches, one of them an internal person, also met with the group. There were two residential courses, one at the start of the program and one at midpoint, and several two-day workshops at participant instigation. An external college faculty provided these courses.

Experiential AL School

Practitioners of the experiential AL school believe in an explicit process for learning from experience that can be traced to Kolb (1984), who built on the work of Dewey (1938), Piaget (1971), and Lewin (1951). Kolb hypothesized that learning begins with an experience that people then reflect on, conceptualize, and act on through experimentation and practice with feedback.

These practitioners believe that learners co-construct their own reality. The key to change is helping people recognize that they draw conclusions based on the data of their daily lives all the time, and often do so unconsciously. Learning coaches help people become more effective at improving the way they inductively reason about these personal data. Learning coaches are aware that the here and now can be used to understand much more about oneself and the culture of organizational systems. The design therefore emphasizes personal understanding. Personal learning goals can become the vehicle for understanding a larger change agenda and are often central to these programs.

In the experiential design, groups of peers meet periodically over a specified time frame that is adequate for addressing the challenges being faced. With individual problems, participants discuss their problems and receive help and support, as in the scientific school. With group or team projects, the participants as a group address a problem, usually sponsored by a high-level executive. They investigate the problem, decide on action, take the action, and then reflect on that action to learn and make decisions about next steps. Reflection and just-in-time learning are facilitated by the learning coach, who also looks to create other situations in which participants can learn.

Critical Reflection AL School

Advocates of the critical reflection AL school agree that people need to learn from experience, but they suggest that reflection be taken to a deeper level than the experiential school. They seek to make taken-for-granted opinions explicit so that these views can be analyzed and challenged. Yorks et al. (1999) write that Mezirow (1991) "calls this process critical reflection, through which people recognize that their perceptions are filtered through uncritically accepted views, beliefs, attitudes and feelings inherited from their own family, school, and society" (p. 10). This school emphasizes both personal and organizational transformation in order to nurture breakthrough thinking and innovation in the midst of discontinuous change.

A variant called action reflection learning is typical of this school of thought. Learners usually work on group projects, and as they do so, learning coaches actively seek to help them question their viewpoints and probe the culture of the organization. As is the case in the experiential school, these programs often combine work on projects with work on personal learning goals. The program provides disorienting dilemmas in many ways in order to encourage people to get outside their frames of reference. For example, participants may explore a question about leadership by engaging in a mini-anthropological field visit to a different culture (either in a different country or through exploring the arts or a very different kind of social setting). Participants are encouraged to use the arts to get in touch with and express their thoughts, for example, by painting or doing skits.

An example of a program that falls in both the experiential and critical reflection school was with Public Service Electric and Gas (PSE&G). (The program design is shown in Table 9.1.) PSE&G used a company-developed problem-solving process that was adapted by the learning coaches to have additional emphasis on learning as a part of the process. There were a number of just-in-time learning elements that the learning coaches used, and reflection times were integrated into the work processes. There was an emphasis on surfacing, examining, and challenging both project and personal assumptions. Participants also had individual learning goals on which they worked during the course of the program (Marsick & Watkins, 1999).

Choosing Among the AL Schools

Practitioners should choose a school for their AL program based on the kind of learning they would like to have take place in the program and the outcomes that are desired. Yorks et al. (1999) provide an action learning pyramid (see Figure 9.1) to help practitioners make decisions about the design of their AL program.

Beginning at the bottom, if the practitioner wants to focus on improved problem solving and improved solutions to important strategic issues but without any explicit or implicit examination of the existing culture, then the tacit school is the best design. The scientific school fits best when the practitioner would like to focus on examining problems differently through problem framing and problem posing in addition to problem solving. The third level, the experiential school, adds the element of personal development, so it could be chosen if the practitioner wants that as an outcome. The critical reflection school encompasses the rest of the pyramid and adds to it the possibility of personal and organizational transformation. Practitioners need to ensure that the organization is prepared to deal with the ramifications, or noise, of participants' questioning and challenging organizational norms if they decide to implement a program in this school (Yorks et al., 1999).

Data Use in Action Learning Programs

AL programs help people and organizations develop their learning capacity by engaging team members in an inquiry into a problem or challenge for which there is no known solution or about which reasonable people might disagree. Inquiry necessarily requires the collection, analysis, interpretation, and discussion of

Figure 9.1. Action Learning Pyramid.

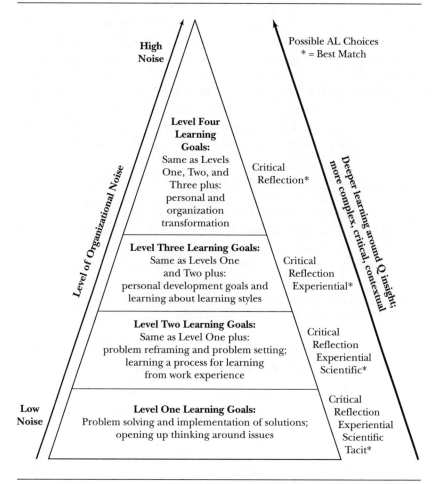

Source: Adapted from Yorks, O'Neil, & Marsick (1999, p. 14). Used with permission.

data so that groups can better understand their problem or challenge and agree on the steps they need to take to address it. However, the word *data* has many meanings, and in AL programs, groups collect both hard data about the tasks they undertake and soft data about their own interaction within the group.

AL team members in a financial services company, for example, consciously set out to collect and analyze data that were directly related to their project focus: identifying alternative investment strategies during an economic downturn. The team collected information on economic trends and examined the financials associated with many alternative investments. They scoured the writing of financial analysts and consulted experts within their company and at universities about the economics of downturns. The team was also engaged in data collection of another kind when members confronted one another over power, work preferences, leadership, and group dynamics. Both kinds of data collection and analysis were essential to their ability to meet the project goals successfully.

Data Forms

Data can take many forms. Table 9.3 sets out two distinctions that are helpful in understanding data use in AL programs: whether data are quantitative or qualitative and whether data come from and can be used to address the life experiences of an individual or the group (often called experiential data) versus whether data are used to address the AL problems taken on by the group.

Table 9.3. Types of Data Used in Action Learning Initiatives.

	Data Needed to Address AL Problems of Group	Experiential Data from Life Experiences within AL Group
Qualitative Data	Perceptions reported or observed by others outside of oneself	Perceptions that come from direct interaction with others
Quantitative Data	Directly observable data that are numerical and not personal; may or may not be subjected to rigorous quantitative data analyses using statistical methods	Directly observable data that can be quantified but are also personal and not subjected to rigorous quantitative data analyses using statistical methods

People collect and make use of both quantitative and qualitative data as they work on and learn from their projects or problems. Because AL participants are usually not experts on their problem, these data are usually collected from sources external to the project group. Participants may collect data to address problems in programs in an unsystematic fashion, or they may use a more rigorous, statistically oriented research design for their applied research.

In addition, people use their subjective perceptions of experiences in the group to learn. Most of the time, such data are qualitative in nature and have to do with feelings, intuition, and hunches that are not based on systematically collected data. However, sometimes these experiential data can be quantified, as is done, for example, if a record is generated to track certain viewpoints or opinions or the number of interactions among people in the group.

Data in AL programs can also be viewed as implicit and tacit or as explicit. According to Polanyi (1967), tacit knowledge is ill defined and not explicitly codified. Because it often resides in one's taken-for-granted reality, it may not be readily accessible to the individual, and it may include unexamined beliefs, values, and assumptions. By contrast, when data are explicit, they are usually codified, objectively verifiable, and more easily quantifiable.

Selecting the Data to Use in an AL Program

Several factors stand out when thinking about how data get selected and used in an AL program: (1) whether the focus is on individual development or organizational change, (2) the length of the program, and (3) the learning philosophy of people who staff programs.

Although all AL initiatives help individuals grow and develop, some programs also use the program as an organizational change initiative. When the focus is primarily on individual development, learning coaches may make suggestions about data type, but they are more likely to leave the ultimate choices to the individual about which data are collected, when, and how. Coaches then help people inquire into the soundness of these choices by helping them to see how results were affected by the quality of these choices.

If the initiative is also being used for organization development or change, however, the learning coach may push the group harder about data choices because the consequences could have broader systemic ramifications. The organization might also ask that certain tools be used to guide data collection that they want to have adopted throughout the organization. GE, for example, has developed recommended guidelines for identifying problems and working through projects that are used throughout the world. These formats influence choices about data collection focuses and methods.

Another key factor is the length of the program and whether it is designed to take place in one consecutive block or sandwiched in between regular work responsibilities over a period of several months. AL programs are often longer than structured training because they are built around real challenges, most of which unfold over time. Opportunities are scheduled as people tackle the problem to gather data and learn in consultation with one another. However, initiatives may be condensed because of time or resource constraints. In short programs, participants learn through framing the problem and creating a set of recommendations, but they cannot learn by carrying the project through to its conclusion. Data choices are influenced by these time considerations.

Finally, the learning philosophy of the staff of an AL program plays a part in influencing the choice and use of data. In some AL schools, learning coaches deliberately hold back their expertise so they do not "steal the learning"; in other schools, learning coaches may take a more directive role based on program objectives.

Examples of Data Use in AL Programs

In general, each of the practices in the four schools creates different opportunities for learning and needs for data that run the gamut of all the kinds of data we have described.

Tacit School

Returning to the Johnson & Johnson program design, we can examine the types of data that the project groups would have collected and used in the course of the program. Because the projects are organizationally based, there are a lot of quantitative data that exist and need to be collected and examined. One project discussed dealt with accelerating market development and growth. The program design called for two days of business environment analysis to gather and analyze the existing quantitative data. The design also called for five days of interviews to collect qualitative and quantitative data in a variety of countries. Both sets of data were then analyzed over two days in order to develop the recommendations.

Team development is facilitated through the collection and use of explicit experiential data. However, in the tacit school, there is often no plan, or intention in the design, to help implicit data get surfaced. To develop their leadership and team skills, members of groups thus use data that are obvious through observation and feedback. It is expected that the urgent nature of the problem and its solution will help members become aware of things that otherwise might remain hidden. One participant stated, "Hopefully the outcome of the information is applicable to your learning going back to where you came from, but also the leave-behind document and presentation and plan that you leave for the operating business and company" (Bossert, 2000, p. 100).

Scientific School

Practitioners in this school believe that learning takes place when the project is explored with a systematic, methodical process, along with the supportive help of peers in the set (Casey, 1977). This philosophy translates into participants' collecting explicit quantitative and qualitative data for use in the problem-solving process. Through this process, they come to understand both the business and the problem better.

One of the managers in the program at GEC worked on a problem in a part of GEC with which he was not familiar. He laid out a plan to help deal with this unknown entity. He was able to have such a comprehensive data collection plan because of the length of the program (Scott, 1977, pp. 63–64):

What is the business?   2 weeks
How is it performing?   4 weeks

How could its performance be improved?	4 weeks
What are the objectives?	2 weeks
What should be done to achieve this improvement?	2 weeks
Implementation of recommendation.	12 weeks

This school also advocates personal development through interaction with peers in the set. It is similar in this to the experiential school of personal development, so participants uncover and make use of both explicit and tacit experiential data through reflection on the interaction among themselves and with others in the organization as they address the project. This school usually does not delve more deeply into assumptions and beliefs—personal and organizational—as does the critical reflection school. One participant at GEC discussed how "the project turned out to be a very effective means of getting to know about myself," but "I do not believe this type of programme produces a 'before' and 'after' man" (Prince, 1977, p. 31).

Experiential and Critical Reflection Schools

The PSE&G program, which addressed team projects connected to the organization's business plan, was significantly shorter than that in the scientific school, so although participants did collect explicit quantitative and qualitative data to address the project, they were not able to collect as many data or carry out the implementation of their recommendations during the time frame of the program. Many teams did implement their recommendation after the program ended.

Qualitative, experiential data for the project were also collected through a process in which the assumptions of the team were surfaced and examined. One team charged with lowering the cost of running overhead wire felt that they knew the solution already and that the company simply was not implementing it. Through the process of surfacing and examining the assumptions they held about the problem and gathering the data necessary to check those assumptions, they found that their answer had already been done and that they needed to investigate other options.

Learning coaches used reflection during the work the team did together. This experiential process helped collect explicit and tacit experiential data for use by the team. "We are not a lot of hotheads anymore. We are using more reflection to understand the situations. It is more of an 'us' concept." Experiential data of this type included observations of team members and learning coaches about personal behaviors and attitudes, leadership, and group dynamics. Group members sometimes reported views they would otherwise suppress because they created trust-filled relationships in the AL group.

The program also focused on personal development through personal learning goals. With the use of a questioning process that at times led to critical reflection, participants were able to uncover tacit data about themselves and their work that led to personal change and transformation. One participant noted, "The people who knew me were surprised with the way I acted. It was not, 'Let's get it done.' It was, 'Let's get it done and learn from this experience.'"

Data-Driven Tools

The quantitative and qualitative data that are usually needed to address the AL problem are collected using surveys, interviews, document reviews, and so on. These tools are discussed elsewhere in this book (see Chapters Two through Five) and in many other sources.

Here we concentrate on tools that we have used in AL groups to collect experiential data from the life experiences of the group, for use in understanding both the project or problem, as well as the dynamics of the group, with particular emphasis on tacit data:

- Group reflection
- Raising, examining, and challenging assumptions
- Questioning process for exploring individual problems or personal learning goals
- Reframing the problem
- The TALK model for improving people's ability to elicit and use data in work conversations

Guidelines for Group Reflection
Reflection is central to AL programs, but people in organizations often feel more comfortable taking action than taking the time to

stop and think. Organizational cultures often do not reward reflection. We regularly ask AL groups to take time to reflect on their perceptions of work they do together and then to share these perceptions publicly and set joint goals for improving their work together. Group members are often surprised to learn how differently others think. Sometimes a single powerful idea—new data—that would otherwise remain hidden takes the group in utterly new directions and helps them either to prevent mistakes or improve outcomes significantly.

The learning coach creates space for reflection. She typically poses one or two questions to the group to help focus their thinking. These questions might probe new ways of thinking about the problem in the light of data being examined, or questions may focus on eliciting feedback about the way the group is working together or individuals are interacting with one another. The learning coach:

- Provides time to stop and reflect.
- Asks probing, reflective questions.
- Asks group members to record thoughts and feelings before speaking.
- Asks all group members to share their reflections.
- Guides the group in thinking about the implications of these reflections on action and on the group process.

Among the questions that the learning coach might ask are the following:

- What worked, and why?
- What did not work, and why?
- What are some alternative strategies?
- How will you use these new insights on the job?

Raising, Examining, and Challenging Assumptions
This process begins by educating the AL participants about the concept of assumptions: "An assumption is any belief, idea, hunch, or thought you have about a subject. We use our assumptions to guide our behavior. We get into trouble when we start believing that our assumptions and inferences are fact" (Partners for the

Learning Organization, 2000, p. 12). When a group is dealing with individual problems, the process continues as follows:

1. Have the group listen to the problem holder discuss his/her problem and respond to group questions.
2. Have the group members reflect and write down the assumptions they have about the problem that they think may be different than those of the problem holder.
   "I assume that . . ." "I think I am right when I say . . ."
3. Tell the problem holder each group member's assumptions. Allow the problem holder to question, react or just listen so he/she can use the assumptions to help him/her think differently about the problem.
4. An alternative approach is to have the group reflect and write down those assumptions that they think the problem holder may have that he/she does not recognize he/she has [Partners for the Learning Organization, 2000, p. 12].

When the group or team is dealing with a team project, the assumptions they focus on have to do with that one project. The process is slightly different (Partners for the Learning Organization, 1998, p. 5):

1. Have the team agree on a statement of the project as they now understand it.
2. Have the team members reflect and write down the assumptions they now hold.
   "I assume that . . ."
   "I think I am right when I say . . ."
3. Analyze assumptions
   As a group, record on easel sheets your assumptions until all assumptions have been listed.
   How can you check out each of these assumptions? What difference would it make if your assumptions are incorrect? Not shared by others?
   To what extent do you think that each of these assumptions is challengeable?
   After your discussion, how might you change these assumptions?
4. Refer back to the "Problem as the Sponsor Defines It" worksheet to determine if the definition of the project/problem has changed or been further clarified.

This tool, or process, enables tacit data to be made explicit. The AL participants can then use the data to understand and investigate their problem better. Without these data, the wrong problem may be pursued or the group may find working together more difficult.

Questioning Process

This tool, or process, is used to help participants examine and re-examine some of the tacit data that they hold about their problem or themselves and better recognize how it may be affecting their ability to solve their problem or change themselves. Whether it is used with the individual problem model of AL or in addressing personal learning goals, the process is basically the same. Table 9.4 shows the two sides of the process.

Each person takes a turn having the floor. The objective of the process is not to give advice but to use questions to help the participant critically reflect on the tacit data about the problem. We advocate using the following kinds of questions (Partners for the Learning Organization, 2000):

Table 9.4. The Questioning Process.

When You Have the Floor	When Someone Else Has the Floor
Describe your problem and why it is important to you.	First, ask objective, reflective, and interpretative questions.
Discuss the result or outcome you are hoping for.	Avoid giving advice.
	Do not interrupt.
Describe what success would look like.	Avoid taking over the floor.
Focus the group on what help you would like from them.	Do not bombard the presenter with too many questions.
	Provide your assumptions.
Listen closely to the group's questions.	Help reframe the problem.
	Ask decisional questions last.
Reflect and answer, or reflect and consider later.	
Describe what action you plan to take.	

- Objective—for example, "You said, 'Everyone always does X.' Do you mean 'everyone' and do they 'always'?"
- Reflective—for example, "What do you think would happen if you did X?"
- Interpretive—for example, "What do you think is really going on?"
- Decisional—for example, "What's stopping you from doing X?"

Once the participant begins to uncover tacit data, he or she can begin to unpack the problem. This may result in a reframing of the problem into a new or different problem. If the participant is working on a personal learning goal, it may result in new insights into his or her behavior and the decision to try new or different actions to test the outcome. This action may result in new explicit, experiential data that participants can then use to continue their investigation into their problem or behavior.

Reframing the Problem

As groups probe deeply into the root underlying dynamics of a problem, they begin to see that their original frame on the problem was inadequate, incomplete, or otherwise incorrect. As a result, one of the most important steps in critical reflection is that of reframing the problem. This step is also one that may be iterative, with several possible takes on the problem offered and explored before all agree that they have fully redefined the problem.

The learning coach helps the group to take the time to test alternative explanations of the problem by taking them through the following steps:

1. Ask the group to identify additional information or data that they need in order to define the problem better.
2. When they think they have enough information, they should each redefine the problem as they now see it. Each group member should offer a theory of what he or she believes is the real problem in the case and explain why he or she thinks that this is the underlying problem or issue.
3. The group examines these different versions of the problem and comes to consensus about what they now believe is the best formulation of the problem at hand.

4. The group suggests at least three different approaches they might take to address the problem. They should argue for each approach, clarifying how each best responds to the dimensions of the problem.
5. The group weighs the advantages and disadvantages of each approach. They help to identify criteria for making a judgment about the best alternative. It sometimes helps to weigh some criteria as more important than others in coming to a decision.
6. The group selects one approach. They can do this by assigning each person a small number of votes that can be assigned to one of the alternatives or divided among several alternatives.
7. The group identifies steps they need to take action on to try out this approach. They also identify data they will need to collect to assess the adequacy of this approach at their next meeting.

TALK Model

We often use a simple variation of a learning strategy created by Argyris and Schön (1978): combining advocacy with inquiry in order to improve outcomes. *Advocacy* refers to the way in which people influence one another by arguing for a solution or set of actions. *Inquiry* refers to the need to ask others about their view of the solution being advocated so that all information is put on the table to craft the best solution. Argyris and Schön (1978) have found that people unconsciously construct their conversations in ways that make it difficult to get all data and reasoning out into the open so that the best decisions can be made.

We use a data-based model called TALK (tell, ask, listen, keep open):

Tell the person what you are thinking from the start Illustrate what you are thinking with examples of what you have directly heard or observed that led you to your conclusions.

Ask whether he or she has the same interpretation of the situation. If not, ask about alternative views.

Listen to his or her response. Listening also involves stating what was understood, checking to see if this is what was meant, exploring differences, and working to reach joint agreement of what was meant.

Keep open to others' views. Recognize that each person's view
is but one possible interpretation of a situation. Shared meaning can come only from accepting and surfacing multiple
understandings.

TALK is designed to help people become more aware of their
thinking and reasoning, make their thinking and reasoning more
visible to others, and ask about others' thinking and reasoning.
The model helps people construct clear conversations that are
aimed at inquiry. Using TALK, we help people to analyze problematic conversations, design new ones, and practice in this new
way through role play.

Conclusion

AL programs are hard to evaluate for all of the reasons that make
evaluation of any learning initiative in organizations difficult. It is
possible to measure changes in specific desired behaviors, often
through behavioral measures of practice before and after an intervention, but it is much more difficult to determine whether the
change is long-lasting and far-reaching. In AL programs aimed at
organizational change, an added challenge is measuring this organizational impact.

A review of some of the qualitative studies of AL programs suggests that these initiatives affect at least three areas: project results;
a cluster of interrelated leadership, group dynamics, and interpersonal skills; and the ability to engage in reflective learning practices at work. The first area is one that easily speaks to most
organizations; that is, the money saved by employees acting as internal consultants to the organization is often equal to or greater
than that reaped by engaging external consultants. AL projects
generate both good ideas and the goodwill of key stakeholders who
have to implement these ideas. Buy-in from internal consulting is
often greater, and the capacity for implementation is affected by
early engagement in generating the project solutions.

Second, no matter what the topics are that are addressed by the
program, AL initiatives always improve a basic cluster of interrelated
leadership, group dynamics, and interpersonal skills. Many of the
qualitative data collected around personal and group interaction

provide participants with feedback they seldom get and a relatively safe environment in which to interpret these data and try out new behaviors.

Third, AL tools and strategies incorporate many of the reflective learning practices that need to be transferred to the workplace in order to increase the general learning capacity of the organization. The program provides many opportunities to practice these skills. Participants often speak of ways in which they begin to use these skills with their own staffs. Learning practices are quickly multiplied, and the climate in which people work is opened up to healthy learning skills.

As an OD intervention, action learning has continued to grow in use and popularity. It is now seen as one of the more significant ways to develop leadership capabilities (Conger & Benjamin, 1999; Giber, Carter, & Goldsmith, 2000), as well as change and transform organizations (Marquardt, 1999; Marsick & Watkins, 1999; Watkins & Marsick, 1993). The types of data and the tools used in collecting those data have played an important role in establishing that prominence. By enabling leaders and organizations to surface previously unused tacit data and by using those tacit and explicit experiential data to examine organizational issues, action learning creates the unique ability within participants to see themselves and their organization anew and opens previously unseen opportunities for change and transformation.

Practice Tips

1. Gather the data to determine if there is a need for AL and if so, what school would best address the need. Do not use AL if it is not the appropriate intervention.
2. Design an AL program that will enable participants to gather the type of data appropriate for their and the organization's needs—for example:
   Tacit school—provide participants with the opportunity to interact with executives in the company so the executives can help participants better understand the culture they need to support.
   Scientific school—allow enough time for the process of problem framing and problem posing to happen.

Practice Tips, cont'd.

Experiential school—have participants establish personal learning goals through which the group and learning coach can help them to develop.

Critical reflection school—include exercises that enable the learning coach to help participants learn how to surface, examine, and challenge their own and the organization's assumptions and norms.

3. Ensure organizational support for the program by engaging top leadership as participants and project sponsors; communicating with the entire organization regarding the purpose, objectives, and potential outcomes of the program; and putting processes in place that will help with the transfer of learning and solution implementation.

4. Do not have an AL program as a stand-alone intervention; there needs to be a strategic linkage.

5. Implement the program only if there are support for and understanding of the outcomes in the organization as a whole.

References

Argyris, C., & Schön, D. (1978). *Organizational learning: A theory of action perspective.* San Francisco: Jossey-Bass.

Boshyk, Y. (Ed.). (2000). *Business-driven action learning.* Old Tappan, NJ: Macmillan.

Bossert, R. (2000). Johnson & Johnson: Executive development and strategic business solutions through action learning. In Y. Boshyk (Ed.), *Business-driven action learning* (pp. 91–103). Old Tappan, NJ: Macmillan.

Casey, D. (1977). Programme outline. In D. Casey & D. Pearce (Eds.), *More than management development: Action learning at GEC* (pp. 7–14). Aldershot, England: Gower Press.

Casey, D., & Pearce, D. (Eds.).(1977). *More than management development: Action learning at GEC.* Aldershot, England: Gower Press.

Conger, J. A., & Benjamin, B. (1999). *Building leaders.* San Francisco: Jossey-Bass.

Dewey, J. (1938). *Experience and education.* New York: Collier.

Giber, D., Carter, L., & Goldsmith, M. (Eds.). (2000). *Best practices in leadership development handbook.* San Francisco: Jossey-Bass.

Kolb, D. A. (1984). *Experiential learning.* Upper Saddle River, NJ: Prentice Hall.

Lewin, K. (1951). *Field theory in social sciences.* New York: HarperCollins.

Marquardt, M. (1999). *Action learning in action.* Palo Alto, CA: Davies-Black.

Marsick, V. J., & Watkins, K. W. (1999). *Facilitating learning organizations: Making learning count.* Aldershot, England: Gower Press.

McGill, I., & Beaty, L. (1995). *Action learning: A practitioner's guide* (2nd ed.). London: Kogan Page.

Mezirow, J. (1991). *Transformative dimensions of adult learning.* San Francisco: Jossey-Bass.

Mumford, A. (1996). Effective learners in action learning sets. *Employee Counselling Today, 8,* 5–12.

O'Neil, J. (1997). Set advising: More than just process consultancy? In M. Pedler (Ed.), *Action learning in practice* (3rd ed., pp. 243–256). Brookfield, VT: Gower Press.

O'Neil, J. (1999). *The role of learning coaches in action learning.* Unpublished doctoral dissertation, Columbia University, New York.

Partners for the Learning Organization. (1998). *Action learning toolkit.* Warwick, RI: Author.

Partners for the Learning Organization. (2000). *An introduction to action learning.* Warwick, RI: Author.

Pedler, M. (Ed.). (1997). *Action learning in practice* (3rd ed.). Aldershot, England: Gower Press.

Piaget, J. (1971). *Psychology and epistemology.* New York: Penguin Books.

Polanyi, M. (1967). *The tacit dimension.* New York: Doubleday.

Prince, B. (1977). The project is everything. In D. Casey & D. Pearce (Eds.), *More than management development: Action learning at GEC* (pp. 31–39). Aldershot, England: Gower Press.

Revans, R. (1970). The managerial alphabet. In G. Heald (Ed.), *Approaches to the study of organizational behavior* (pp. 141–161). New York: Tavistock.

Scott, B. (1977). Communication is the key to getting commitment. In D. Casey & D. Pearce (Eds.), *More than management development: Action learning at GEC* (pp. 62–70). Aldershot, England: Gower Press.

Sullivan, G. R., & Harper, M. V. (1996). *Hope is not a method: What business leaders can learn from America's army.* New York: Broadway Books.

Watkins, K. E., & Marsick, V. J. (1993). *Sculpting the learning organization: Lessons in the art and science of systematic change.* San Francisco: Jossey-Bass.

Yorks, L., O'Neil, J., & Marsick, V. J. (Eds.). (1999). *Action learning: Successful strategies for individual, team, and organizational development.* San Francisco: Berrett-Koehler.

Appreciative Inquiry
The New Frontier
Stephen P. Fitzgerald
Kenneth L. Murrell
H. Lynn Newman

Appreciative inquiry (Ai) is the new frontier! What a provocative and bold assertion. So what is this appreciative approach, and what's new about it? Is it a current fad or truly something new in organization development? Many people have called Ai "groundbreaking." Certainly, as conceived of and described in some of the foundational work of David Cooperrider and colleagues at Case Western Reserve University, in the doctoral program in organizational behavior created in 1960 by Herb Shephard, and at the Taos Institute, Ai reflects the core values of organization development (OD) practice and theory developed over the past half-century. At a minimum, it encourages us to rethink and enlarge how OD professionals approach this work, possibly leading to a reinventing of OD itself.

Cooperrider and Whitney (1999) offer the following practice-oriented definition of Ai:

> Appreciative Inquiry is the cooperative search for the best in people, their organizations, and the world around them. It involves systematic discovery of what gives a system "life" when it is most

Note: We thank David Cooperrider for his feedback on this chapter and helpful additions to it.

effective and capable in economic, ecological, and human terms. Ai involves the art and practice of asking questions that strengthen a system's capacity to heighten positive potential. It mobilizes inquiry through crafting an "unconditional positive question" often involving hundreds or sometimes thousands of people [p. 10].

Ai is not a technique or method, although there is a basic Ai approach that has been articulated in the literature and practiced in various settings. Most important, Ai is an affirmative worldview that shapes what we look for in organizational inquiry. It involves a conscious value choice to seek the most affirmative, valuing, and generative information available. The intention is to discover and build on the strength and vitality of human systems as experienced and reported by their members.

Ai is a novel approach to organizational change work. The affirmative value choice is what distinguishes it from other forms of OD. It influences every aspect of Ai, from the design of topics and questions to explore, to data analyses and feedback. As a strategy of change, Ai inspires collaborative action that engages and serves the whole system.

Ai's Historical Roots and Basic Principles

Ai is relationally linked to contemporary forms of action research. It is rooted in radical social constructionism, appreciation, and the generative power of positive imagery. These historical roots are the bases of Ai's five basic principles (constructionist, simultaneity, poetic, anticipatory, and positive). In addition, there are complementary innovations in other fields that are co-constructing a similarly affirmative worldview (for example, solution-focused therapy in counseling psychology; De Shazer et al., 1986).

Action Research

Action research underlies most current OD approaches for studying and simultaneously changing social systems (see also Chapter One). Lewin (1946) introduced this scientific process as a way of generating knowledge about a social system while simultaneously attempting to change it. He initially described action research as a "spiral of steps, each of which is composed of a circle of planning, action, and fact-finding about the result of the action" (pp. 34–35).

Cooperrider and Srivastva (1987) first articulated the idea and coined the term *appreciative inquiry* as they reenvisioned the possibility of action research. They noted that action research had not "achieved its potential for advancing social knowledge of consequence and [had] not, therefore, achieved its potential as a vehicle for human development and social-organizational transformation" (p. 130). They claimed that this was due to the problem-oriented view of organizing that pervaded the approaches to action research that were current when they wrote. Their argument was essentially that action research had become too focused on the client and the solving of the client's problem, to the exclusion of the theory-generating aspects so critical to the definition of action research that Lewin had outlined. It remains true to this day that practitioners too often focus exclusively on linear problem solving of immediate organizational issues, which is what clients most readily understand and expect.

Other contemporary forms of action research have also emerged, among them participatory action research, action science, and action learning. All of the contemporary approaches, including Ai, emphasize full client-consultant partnership, collaborative learning throughout the action research process, the importance of local tacit knowledge, a willingness to examine assumptions in the system, and organizational transformation. These newer approaches might be viewed as extending an action research continuum that ranges from more traditional, consultant-directed, linear applications toward increasingly collaborative, systemic, transformational change processes (Newman & Fitzgerald, 2000).

Appreciation

Beyond sharing these characteristics of contemporary action research, Ai selectively values appreciation. The work of Sir Geoffrey Vickers, published in the late 1950s and early 1960s in the United Kingdom and United States, offered what was for many a completely new understanding of the concept of appreciation. For Vickers, appreciation is a process of developing a full and penetrating understanding of a particular world, as well as a focus on what one wants to make of it. His concept of appreciated worlds provided the impetus to go deeply into the meaning of the ideas or events one is trying to assist in changing. He encouraged us to focus on what is right and not just what is lacking. Today the Ai practice of creating dialogue helps to bring out what a fuller and deeper appreciation means.

Social Constructionism

Social constructionism is a fundamental underpinning of Ai. This philosophy of science (Berger & Luckmann, 1966) suggests that we have considerable influence over the nature of the realities that we perceive and experience, and to a great extent we actually create our realities through collective symbolic and mental processes.

Cooperrider's initial inspiration for Ai rose from the more radical forms of social constructionism (Gergen, 1982), out of which Ai emerged as a theory-building process. The notion of generative theory is central to this in that it "has the capacity to challenge the guiding assumptions of the culture, to raise fundamental questions regarding contemporary life, to foster reconsideration of that which is taken for granted, and thereby furnish new alternatives for social action" (Cooperrider, 1999, p. 1, citing Gergen, 1982).

Reflecting on Ai's early history, Cooperrider (1999) wrote, "It was later, partly because of social constructionism's relational view of knowledge that [we] began doing 'theory building' with organizations . . . literally creating the theory and propositions with the organizations we were working with . . . making the theory-building totally collaborative. We invited people to challenge the status quo, to stretch, to provoke new ways of thinking and talking about the future" (p. 1).

Five basic principles have been described as central to Ai's theory base of change (Cooperrider, Barrett, & Srivastva, 1995; Cooperrider & Srivastva, 1987; Cooperrider & Whitney, 1999). Social constructionism serves as the primary theoretical foundation for at least three of those five principles: the constructionist principle, the principle of simultaneity, and the poetic principle. The constructionist principle holds that human knowledge and organizational destiny are intricately interwoven. To be effective as executives, leaders, and change agents, we must be adept in the art of understanding, reading, and analyzing organizations as living, human constructions. Knowing (organizations) stands at the center of any and virtually every attempt at change. Thus, the way we know is fateful.

Because organizations are living human constructions, inquiry and change cannot be separated; they occur simultaneously. This is the principle of simultaneity. The seeds of change—the things that we think and talk about, discover and learn together, and that inform our dialogue and inspire our images of the future—are implicit in the very first questions we ask. Those questions set the stage for what we find, and what we discover (the data) becomes the linguistic material, the stories out of which the future is conceived, conversed about, and constructed.

Thus, human organizations are a lot more like an open book than, say, a machine. An organization's story is constantly being coauthored. Moreover, pasts, presents, and futures are endless sources of learning, inspiration, and interpretation—much like the endless interpretive possibilities in a good piece of poetry or literature. This is the essence of Ai's poetic principle. The important implication is that we can study virtually any topic related to human experience in any human system or organization. We can inquire into the nature of alienation or joy, enthusiasm or low morale, efficiency or excess. There is not a single topic related to organization life that we could not study.

The Power and Role of Image

The Ai approach is based on the formidable power of cognitive image to create action. Consider two different settings: anticipating what we expect may be a conflictual meeting with a friend versus anticipating sharing a favorite activity with a friend. Each of these images creates different expectations and feelings in us that are likely to result in different behaviors. Anticipation is a potent, generative force. It is the basis for Ai's fourth principle.

One of the basic theorems of this anticipatory principle is that the image of the future guides what might be called the current behavior of any organism or organization. Much like a movie projector on a screen, human systems are forever projecting ahead of themselves a horizon of expectation (in their talk in the hallways, in the metaphors and language they use) that brings the future powerfully into the present as a mobilizing agent. To inquire in ways that refashion anticipatory reality, especially through the artful creation of positive imagery on a collective basis, may be the most productive thing any inquiry can do.

Furthermore, research from diverse fields substantiates the power of positive imagery to generate positive action (see Cooperrider, 1990, for a thorough treatment of these concepts). For example, in medicine, the well-documented placebo effect results from people's positive expectancy about the healing potential of medication that they are given, even when, without their knowledge, it contains only sugar.

Classic research in the field of education found that a so-called Pygmalion effect occurred when teachers were told that some of their students had high potential when in fact they were no different from other students. In study after study, the supposedly high-potential students significantly outperformed their classmates. This positive expectancy effect has been demonstrated in the workplace as well as in the world of sports. It is the basis for Ai's fifth principle.

This positive principle grows out of years of experience with Ai. Building and sustaining momentum for change requires large amounts of positive affect and social bonding—things like hope, excitement, inspiration, caring, camaraderie, sense of urgent purpose, and sheer joy in creating something meaningful together. We have found that it does not help to begin inquiries from the standpoint of the world as a problem to be solved. Instead, we have seen that the more positive the questions are that we ask in our work and the longer we can retain the spirit of inquiry of the everlasting beginner, the more long-lasting and successful are our change efforts. The thing that makes the most difference is to craft and seed, in better and more catalytic ways, the unconditional positive question. Changes never thought possible are suddenly and democratically mobilized.

In sum, Ai is relationally linked to contemporary forms of action research. It is rooted in radical social constructionism, appreciation, and the generative power of positive imagery. These historical roots are the bases of Ai's five basic principles. In addition, there are complementary innovations in other fields that are coconstructing a similarly affirmative worldview (for example, solution-focused therapy in counseling psychology; see De Shazer et al., 1986).

The Essential AI Process

Ai's five underlying principles (constructionist, simultaneity, poetic, anticipatory, and positive) come to life through the design of the basic Ai process, which is typically presented as a cycle of four phases known the *4-D cycle* (Cooperrider, 1996):

Phase 1: Discovery of people's experiences of their group, organization, or community at its most vital and alive and what made those experiences possible

Phase 2: Dreaming together to envision a future in which those exceptional experiences form the bases for organizing

Phase 3: Designing appreciative systems and structures to support the manifestation of the co-created dreams

Phase 4: Destiny or delivery, which involves implementation of those systems and structures in an ever-expanding positive-feedback loop of appreciative learning

Ai practitioners have developed several variations on the 4-D cycle involving additional phases for use in a variety of settings. One addition that had always been considered the cycle's precursor is an initial defining phase in which three to five topics are collaboratively selected to focus the inquiry. Key practitioner guidelines on each of these five phases are described below.

Phase 1: Define

Based on Ai's underlying principles, the most powerful tools at our disposal are our capacity to inquire together and focus the nature of the inquiry. Hammond (1996) notes that "what we focus on becomes our reality" (p. 20). Therefore, defining the topics for an appreciative inquiry is perhaps the most critical phase of the process.

To ensure broad-based support and whole system impact, include representatives of all stakeholder groups in defining the topics for the inquiry. For large applications, topic definition may require a preliminary two-day Ai retreat or systemwide Ai interviews. During this process, value-rich, locally meaningful topics are collaboratively developed—for example, "transform leadership development into open, just, and inclusive leadership" (Newman & Fitzgerald, 2000, p. 7). As a general rule of thumb, three to five broad topics are the maximum for an Ai process. Ai interview questions are then developed out of the chosen topics.

Phase 2: Discover

The discovery phase typically begins with paired appreciative interviews exploring participants' peak experiences of each topic and what made those experiences possible. The interview questions and process are designed to elicit and revitalize the positive affect associated with participants' stories, which nurtures intrinsic motivation.

The highlights and most "quotable quotes" from participants' stories are then shared in small and large groups. This essentially builds a live, collective database of organizational excellence that includes metaphor, imagery, and affect, in addition to concrete examples. Capturing these elements graphically on large surfaces in addition to or instead of expressing them in verbal and written words greatly amplifies their impact throughout the process.

Phase 3: Dream

During the dream phase, the best of the past is amplified into collectively envisioned and desired futures. Working together in groups, participants review the images, metaphors, hopes, and dreams that were generated in the discovery phase. (Paired appreciative interviews typically conclude with questions that elicit individuals' hopes and dreams regarding the Ai topics.) Participants are then encouraged to expand, stretch, and elaborate their collective dreams and to embody them creatively through skits, art, songs, and other forms, which are then shared with the entire group.

Phase 4: Design

During the design phase, participants identify key facets of organizational systems and structures that will be needed to support the realization of their collectively generated dreams. The facilitator may introduce a model of organizational structure for participants to work with or may support participants in generating their own models.

Working again in groups, participants craft bold, affirmative possibility statements, also known as *provocative propositions* (PPs), that express their expansive dreams as already realized in the present tense. Language, imagery, and examples from the discovery and dream phases are incorporated into these design statements, each crafted around a facet of the organizational structure. The finished PPs are then visually displayed and shared with the entire group. Together, the PPs form the basis for developing vision-guided action plans.

Phase 5: Deliver

This fifth phase may begin prior to the conclusion of an Ai summit (see Chapter Eleven), but it extends into the ongoing life of the group, organization, and community. Participants self-select into task groups according to the design statements that they feel most strongly drawn to. They then work together to ground those design statements in action steps. Action plans may be shared with the entire group. Participants then self-select projects or tasks that they would like to work on or otherwise support. Actions are implemented over time in an iterative, appreciative learning journey.

Organizational Applications

Ai processes have been successfully implemented in a wide variety of organizational settings in the business, government, and nonprofit sectors. Ai applications have ranged from appreciative human resource practices, team development, diversity initiatives, and strategic planning, to the transformation of global corporate cultures and social change organizations (Hammond & Royal,

1998; Head, 2000; Mohr, Smith, & Watkins, 2000; Newman & Fitzgerald, 2000; Whitney & Cooperrider, 1998; Williams, 1996). The diversity of these applications continues to increase as practitioners explore Ai approaches in a wide variety of organizational settings.

Given the breadth and diversity of Ai applications, some may protest that Ai is being hailed as a magic bullet that works in all situations. Yet to make this same claim for the highly accepted problem-solving orientation is not that unusual. The problem-identification-analysis-solution approach is so firmly grounded in our culture of critique that it is seldom questioned as to the overall effect it has on the way we characterize the world as a problem to be solved.

There are at least four reasons for choosing Ai for large-scale applications: (1) high levels of participation and cooperation are required, (2) the change process needs to be accelerated, (3) the work requires innovation among diverse groups in a high-stakes environment, or (4) multiple change initiatives need to be synthesized (Whitney & Cooperrider, 1998). Even when these conditions are met, however, Ai may not be appropriate if sufficient resources are unavailable for adequate implementation or leadership does not support affirmative approaches or full system participation. Some successful organizational applications are briefly described.

Large-Scale System Change

In its fullest expression, Ai is an approach to large-scale system change. Whole system Ai transformation is the ideal because it affects the mind-set and culture of the entire enterprise, influencing every facet of organizational life. Thus, Ai is approached not as an intervention or event but as a continual, systemic, self-reinforcing learning journey.

A cornerstone of large-scale Ai system change is the Appreciative Inquiry Summit, which integrates the best of current large group change processes (see Chapter Eleven) into an appreciative framework. (Whitney & Cooperrider, 1998) It is typically a four-day event that includes the entire organization and its customers, suppliers, and other community stakeholders. An Ai Summit incorporates the full 4-D cycle. It also provides unstructured time for informal relationship building, which is crucial to the effectiveness of any significant change initiative.

Ai Summits have proven to be effective in a wide variety of organizational settings—for example, "launching a union-management partnership throughout GTE; strategic planning for the entire company, Nutramental; for culture change in numerous organizations in health care, government, and consulting services; for economic development in a region of the country; for citywide community development and for drafting a charter for a newly emerging global organization" (Whitney & Cooperrider, 1998, p. 21).

Team-Based Applications

Whole system, large-scale Ai implementation may be ideal, but applications with teams can also be successful. Furthermore, Ai success with one or more teams can lead to wider organizational implementation.

That is exactly what happened in the case of an Ai strategic planning session with the executive team of a 120-person nonprofit health care facility (Newman & Fitzgerald, 2000). A large-scale organizational change effort had been in process at the clinic since 1996. Traditional action research approaches (for example, customized survey to identify organizational issues, and executive coaching) were used in the first years. A trusting relationship between the executive director and lead consultant developed over time, allowing for the implementation of increasingly collaborative action research processes.

By the third year, the executive team wanted to increase creativity in its problem solving and strategic planning. An Ai design was incorporated into the executive retreat. The interview questions focused on the topic of "open, just, and inclusive leadership" so as to address issues that had been identified in that year's employee survey.

Results far exceeded expectations. Team members generated a powerful vision of inclusive leadership. They created fundamental structural changes that addressed key organizational issues from a place of vision expressed through their PPs.

Ai has also been used effectively with teams experiencing significant conflict. In one case, an engineering design team was six weeks behind schedule at the eleventh month of a strategically critical twenty-month project. At that point, Ai was employed in a team retreat. As a result, the team finished a month ahead of schedule and "delivered a product that performed significantly above specifications for less than the expected cost" (Brittain, 1998, p. 228). As a result of the team's success, Ai was implemented for all product design teams throughout the organization.

A recent empirical study (Head, 2000) substantiates the efficacy of Ai in fostering the development of heterogonous teams. Three interventions—Ai, team building, and a control group—were divided among eighteen new management teams in the U.S. Postal Service. The Ai teams exhibited the largest decline in self-directed behaviors and greatest increase in team-related behaviors on the Group Style Instrument, the best results (although not statistically significant) on external measures of team performance, and significantly more positive imagery regarding their future interactions and performance. Furthermore, a statistically significant, strongly positive correlation ($r(34) = .74$, $p < .001$) was observed between group image and performance, indicating that the more positive a team's image of itself, the better is its performance. "The results lend support to the theory that Ai aids in assisting groups to improve their image of the future and that allows groups to more quickly develop and perform" (Head, 2000, p. 66).

Program Evaluation

Program evaluation has traditionally been approached as a past-focused critique. However, Mohr et al. (2000) collaborated to develop a vital, appreciative program valuation for the R&D division of SmithKline Beecham. Over a six-week period, they conducted 109 appreciative interviews with research scientists in two countries who had participated in an innovative simulation-based training program. To their surprise, they found that the scientists were very receptive to the appreciative approach, the process "increasingly became a forward-focused intervention in its own right, rather than the backward look of a typical evaluation study" (p. 39), and "not only were these traditional evaluation questions effectively met with this approach, but the corporation benefited from both the learning reinforcement that occurred and the richness of data which would not have been captured in a normal evaluation process" (p. 49).

In another example, an appreciative approach was used in a follow-up evaluation for the Academy of Management's Theme-Summit, from the design of the survey instrument to the analysis, display, and discussion of the data (Fitzgerald, 1999).

Human Resource Practices

Many traditional human resource practices have been redesigned from an appreciative framework. For example, Bosch (1998) describes her experiments in approaching exit interviews with "an appreciative eye." Based on learning derived from her experience, she provides detailed ideas for improving Ai-based exit interviews.

In addition, many innovative Ai applications such as using multi-source feedback processes (see Chapter Two) have not yet found their way into books or journals. The Ai listserv and newsletter are prime sources for current information on the development of Ai theory and applications around the world.

Deliverables

Traditionally, OD consultants contract with their clients to produce specific tangible products, known as *deliverables*. Examples are customized surveys and data analysis reports. Consistent with the positivist worldview, these deliverables are generally prepared independently by the consultant serving as a neutral observer of the client system. As in any other OD consultation, clarifying Ai deliverables is a vital, integral part of the contracting process.

Ai deliverables are dependent on the nature of the particular consultation. Consistent with more participatory forms of action research, the consultant may support the client in producing deliverables in order to promote ownership and organizational learning or may co-create them in full partnership with the client (Mohr et al., 2000). In either case, the Ai practitioner serves as a participant with client co-participants rather than as a neutral observer.

Ai deliverables may be tangible or intangible. Potential tangibles include a compendium of best practices and stories, visual displays, customized appreciative interview protocols or surveys, organizational design and action plan statements, train-the-trainer plans and meetings, skill-building activities for client personnel, customized Ai workshop curricula, meeting designs, and special events such as a whole system meeting.

Intangible deliverables may range from process consultation (see Chapter Seven) and appreciative data analysis approaches to culture change and organizational transformation. In his detailed rendering of an Ai proposal for large-scale organizational change, Cooperrider (1996b) provides vivid, real-life examples of intangible deliverables (which he calls *objectives*)—for example, "to build an affirmative atmosphere of hope and confidence necessary to sustain, over the next several years, the largest whole-system transformation in the company's history" (p. 25).

Slaying Ai's Mythical Dragons

As the affirmative "knight in shining armor" of OD, Ai has surfaced its share of mythical dragons that appear as fearsome threats to its validity and applicability.

Warm-Fuzzy Dragon

This most formidable dragon labors under the unfortunate misconception that while Ai excels at facilitating warm and fuzzy "group hugs," it has no basis in or use for hard data. In fact, Ai is as data driven as any other OD application. However, the nature of the data, and how they are collected and analyzed, is different.

Ai thrives on rich, qualitative data, but quantitative data are often incorporated as well. As in traditional OD applications, qualitative data from interviews and focus groups may be used to support the development of a quantitative survey instrument for wider organizational implementation (see Chapters Four and Five). Williams (1996) illustrates the efficacy of such an approach using an Ai framework in transforming a serious crisis situation (significant loan losses leading to a 10 percent downsizing, hostile takeover attempt) in an $11 billion regional commercial banking institution with eight thousand personnel.

Scaredy-Cat Dragon

This dragon's fire is fueled by the illusion that Ai cowers behind a security blanket of positive thinking and therefore cannot, and should not, be used to address difficult organizational challenges. That dragon evaporates in the light of the banking institution (Williams, 1996) and product design team (Brittain, 1998) cases already described and others. Furthermore, Ai differs from positive thinking in that meaning is collectively and continually co-created, whereas positive thinking is an individual practice that strives to maintain affirmative thought patterns and hold fast to particular affirmative images.

Wildly Imbalanced Dragon

This dragon thunders that Ai is dangerously lopsided in its unwavering devotion to the affirmative and that so-called problem-solving OD approaches have always balanced a search for problems with a search for strengths (Golembiewski, 2000). Three points may help to tame this dragon.

First, although many traditional OD applications include a search for strengths, scant attention is given to discovering the factors that make the strengths possible and how they might be profitably amplified. Furthermore, as a by-product of the pervasiveness of our deficit-elimination continuous improvement culture, negative data automatically and unconsciously steal focus, no matter how positive the overall results may be.

Second, the rationale for a balanced design may be predicated on the underlying assumption of a normal bell curve. That assumption may fuel the unconscious co-construction of a purposefully normative organizational reality that strives to reduce or eliminate behavioral variations to the mean. Such a homogenization process substantially subdues the human spirit so vital to effective organizations.

Third, Ai is grounded in at least three legitimate forms of qualitative sampling: a search for the extreme or exceptional, in which learning derives from "highly unusual manifestations of the phenomenon of interest" (Miles & Huberman, 1994, p. 28); a dedication to maximizing the diversity of the positive exceptions discovered in the inquiry, a form of "maximum variation sampling" (p. 28);

and (3) a delight in "taking advantage of the unexpected," that is, "opportunistic" sampling (p. 28).

Conclusion

Clearly, Ai is a powerful new OD approach. Yet it is not a disembodied miracle worker. As with all other OD work, results are dependent on the practitioner's experience with the approach, attunement with self and others, and his or her overall physical, spiritual, mental, and emotional well-being. Furthermore, effective Ai practice is built on living a solid foundation of traditional OD values like inclusiveness, integrity, developing trusting relationships, challenging the status quo, collaboration, and contracting effectively (see also Chapters One and Fourteen).

True to its philosophy, Ai is in a constant state of experimentation, learning, and self-reflective appreciation for innovation. Creating and exploring this new frontier can be an exciting and challenging evolution for OD practitioners. It requires continual change, development, and renewal within both ourselves and our field.

Practice Tips

1. Begin with yourself. Practice being appreciative of yourself and others. Catch people doing something right, and acknowledge them for it.
2. Experience Ai, and get more Ai training. Take an Ai workshop. Partner with a seasoned Ai practitioner.
3. Read everything you can about Ai and its foundations and applications.
4. Practice crafting appreciative questions.
5. Try some Ai interviews with your coworkers and family.
6. Begin meetings with appreciative questions like, "Describe something that you did really well this week, something that made you excited and proud of your work. What made that possible? What can we learn from this?"
7. If you do not have access to the top of the organization, start where you are; it may lead to the top.

Practice Tips, cont'd.

8. Always educate clients on Ai's basic assumptions and research foundations. Make sure you include enough time in your contract and design for this.

9. Make sure your clients are on board philosophically and that they are fully committed to including the voices of all stakeholders.

10. Encourage your clients' (and your own) sense of adventure and innovation. Make sure they understand that no one really knows precisely where this (or any other real change process) will lead.

11. Let your light shine, and share your enthusiasm. Participate fully. Act consistently with Ai principles.

12. Codesign an iterative, ongoing Ai learning journey rather than a one-time event.

13. Establish a mutual learning partnership with your clients rather than contracting to serve as an Ai expert or vendor.

14. Pay careful attention to facilitation of the design phase, which is a challenging exercise in social construction. Allow ample time for this when designing an Ai process.

15. Avoid the following: mixing Ai with problem-solving approaches, pressing forward in an inhospitable environment (for example, with autocratic leadership, lack of support for inclusion of all stakeholders, or inadequate resources), and analyzing Ai data or finalizing the provocative propositions on behalf of the client without their direct participation and ownership.

References

Berger, P., & Luckmann, T. (1966). *The social construction of reality.* New York: Doubleday.

Bosch, L. (1998). Exit interviews with an "appreciative eye." In S. A. Hammond & C. Royal (Eds.), *Lessons from the field: Applying appreciative inquiry* (pp. 230–244). Plano, TX: Practical Press.

Brittain, J. (1998). Do we really mean it? In S. A. Hammond & C. Royal (Eds.), *Lessons from the field: Applying appreciative inquiry* (pp. 216–229). Plano, TX: Practical Press.

Cooperrider, D. L. (1990). Positive image, positive action: The affirmative basis of organizing. In S. Srivasta & D. L. Cooperrider (Eds.), *Appreciative management and leadership: The power of positive thought and action in organizations* (pp. 91–125). San Francisco: Jossey-Bass.

Cooperrider, D. L. (1996a). The "child" as agent of inquiry. *OD Practitioner, 28,* 5–11.

Cooperrider, D. L. (1996b). Resources for getting appreciative inquiry started: An example OD proposal. *OD Practitioner, 28,* 23–33.

Cooperrider, D. L. (1999, Mar. 31). "Re: Provocative Propositions." In Appreciative Inquiry listserv. Available at: appreciative-inqry @utdallas.edu.

Cooperrider, D. L., Barrett, F., & Srivastva, S. (1995). Social construction and appreciative inquiry: A journey in organizational theory. In D. Hosking, P. Dachler, & K. J. Gergen (Eds.), *Management and organization: Relational alternatives to individualism* (pp. 157–200). Aldershot, England: Avebury Press.

Cooperrider, D. L., & Srivastva, S. (1987). Appreciative inquiry in organizational life. In R. W. Woodman & W. A. Pasmore (Eds.), *Research in organizational change and development* (Vol. 1, pp. 129–169). Greenwich, CT: JAI Press Inc.

Cooperrider, D. L., & Whitney, D. (1999). Appreciative inquiry: A positive revolution in change. In P. Holman & T. Devane (Eds.), *The change handbook* (pp. 245–263). San Francisco: Berrett-Koehler.

Cooperrider, D. L., & Whitney, D. (2000). A positive revolution in change: Appreciative inquiry. In D. L. Cooperrider, P. F. Sorensen Jr., D. Whitney, & T. F. Yaeger (Eds.), *Appreciative inquiry: Rethinking human organization toward a positive theory of change* (pp. 3–27). Champaign, IL: Stipes.

De Shazer, S., Berg, I. K., Lipchik, E., Nunnally, E., Molnar, A., Gingerich, W., & Weiner-Davis, M. (1986). Brief therapy: Focused solution development. *Family Process, 25,* 207–222.

Fitzgerald, S. P. (1999, Aug.). *Academy of Management ThemeSummit '99: A pluralistic program evaluation.* Paper presented at the annual meeting of the Academy of Management, Chicago.

Gergen, K. J. (1982). *Toward transformation in social knowledge.* New York: Springer.

Golembiewski, R. T. (2000). Three perspectives on appreciative inquiry. *OD Practitioner, 32,* 53–58.

Hammond, S. A. (1996). *The thin book of appreciative inquiry.* Plano, TX: Practical Press.

Hammond, S. A., & Royal, C. (Eds.). (1998). *Lessons from the field: Applying appreciative inquiry.* Plano, TX: Practical Press.

Head, R. L. (2000). Appreciative inquiry as a team-development intervention for newly formed heterogeneous groups. *OD Practitioner, 32,* 59–66.

Lewin, K. (1946). Action research and minority problems. *Journal of Social Issues, 2,* 34–46.

Miles, M. B., & Huberman, A. M. (1994). *Qualitative data analysis* (2nd ed.). Thousand Oaks, CA: Sage.

Mohr, B. J., Smith, E., & Watkins, J. M. (2000). Appreciative inquiry and learning assessment: An embedded evaluation process in a transnational pharmaceutical company. *OD Practitioner, 32,* 36–52.

Newman, H. L., & Fitzgerald, S. P. (2000, July). *Appreciative inquiry with an executive team: Moving along the action research continuum.* Paper presented at the Seventh International Conference on Advances in Management, Colorado Springs, CO.

Whitney, D., & Cooperrider, D. L. (1998, Summer). The appreciative inquiry summit: Overview and applications. *Employment Relations Today, 25,* 17–28.

Williams, R. F. (1996). Survey guided appreciative inquiry: A case study. *OD Practitioner, 28,* 43–51.

CHAPTER 11

Understanding and Using Large System Interventions

Barbara Benedict Bunker
Billie T. Alban

Several years ago, a manager from a major oil company attended a workshop in which we presented a framework for understanding twelve methods of working with organizational systems as a whole. The next day, he told us that he was so excited about the concept of "getting the whole system into the room" to address important strategic issues that he could not sleep that night. He thought that these methods could help his company solve a crisis: it was the highest-cost, lowest producer on the Gulf Coast. A consulting firm specializing in long-term strategy had told his company that if they could not turn the picture around, they should close down the Gulf Coast operation. This manager was so excited by the potential of these methods that he convinced the company to send a fourteen-person delegation to the next national conference on large group interventions. There, they heard executives describe why they had opted to use these methods for dealing with change in their companies and what results were achieved.

The delegation selected real time-strategic change as a method that could work for them. For the first time in this oil company's history, everyone in this entire system—not only managers and executives, but the roustabouts from the drilling rigs, the contractors, and the suppliers—met in a room large enough to hold them; there were over twelve hundred people. First, they analyzed what was working and what was not working, and what the future would hold if things could not be turned around. Together, they created a vision of the future they desired. Together, they build a common database of information on things that needed to change. As a result, multiple task forces were set up to address the issues. The task forces were always made up of people who were part of the system they were working to change regardless of level or function. A mechanism was established to keep task forces in touch with what was going on in other task forces and deal with overlap. There was communication to the drilling rigs in the gulf so that people who had historically been marginalized could have some voice and influence. The work, which took over two years, resulted in millions of dollars in cost savings and big increases in oil production. It created a new future for this part of the oil company.

What Are Large Group Interventions?

In 1987, Marvin Weisbord's book *Productive Workplaces* (1987) described "getting the whole system into the room" as the best way to ensure that change in organizations would be effective and get commitment. This idea was already in practice in Merrelyn Emery's work on the Search Conference in Australia and in the work of Dannemiller Tyson Associates at Ford with large groups of managers.

The idea of gathering an entire organization (or a diagonal slice representative of it) to talk about, influence, or invent needed changes was new and important because organization development (OD) arose from small groups' research and practice in the 1950s and 1960s and tended to focus on change at the individual or group level. When the whole organization was involved, a waterfall process from top to bottom using groups at various levels was the usual practice. This proved to be both slow and time-consuming.

As the world changed and organizations were hit with more and more global competition, the demand to change faster was urgent. Change involves decisions about what must change and how, as well as a process of implementation. Practitioners knew that old methods were not bringing about change that happened quickly and was implemented quickly. As practitioners ourselves, we began to be aware of interesting developments using much larger groups that included the whole system in the early 1990s. Were these just isolated experiments, or was this a developing social innovation?

We tested our idea that something new in practice was occurring by editing a special issue of the *Journal of Applied Behavioral Science* on large group interventions in 1992. When we issued a call for papers, we were not sure we would be able to fill a whole issue. In fact, more people sent articles for review than we could publish. Reader interest in that issue was enormous and required several printings. We had clearly tapped an important emerging area of practice. As more and more people began to use large groups in their practices, more methods developed. We wrote a book (Bunker & Alban, 1997) that provided a conceptual framework for understanding what had grown to twelve methods. Although there are numerous differences among methods, we choose to organize them by the outcome or work they do. Four methods help organizations (and communities) to plan for the future (see Figure 11.1). Four methods specialize in the redesign of work, making it more effective with attention to the social environment at the same time (see Figure 11.2). And four methods are helpful when an organization needs to solve problems, discuss difficult issues, or make decisions as a whole (see Figure 11.3).

The Importance of Large System Interventions

OD is a process of using applied behavioral science knowledge and systems theory to plan and implement change in organizations. The goal is more effective organizations and a work environment supportive of human needs and development (see Chapter One). Participation by stakeholders during organizational change was demonstrated early to be crucial in effective change processes. One way that people participate is by giving data, usually in survey or interview format, about their life in and their perceptions of the organization and its functioning. Organizations need data from the full range of employees to understand how the system views itself. Unfortunately, many organizations appear not to know how to talk within themselves. These methods often allow what is known to many to become public so that it can be addressed.

Figure 11.1. Large Group Methods
for Creating the Future.

THE SEARCH CONFERENCE
Purpose: To Create a Future Vision
Merrelyn and Fred Emery

- Set Format: Environmental Scan, History, Present, Future
- Criteria for Participants: Within System Boundary
- Theory: Participative Democracy
- Search for Common Ground
- Rationalize Conflict
- No Experts
- Total Community Discussion
- 2.5-Day Minimum
- 35 to 40+ Participants
- Larger Groups = Multisearch Conference
- 1/3 Total Time Is Action Planning

FUTURE SEARCH
Purpose: To Create a Future Vision
Weisbord and Janoff

- Set Format: Past, Present, Future, Action Planning
- Stakeholder Participation, No Experts
- Minimizes Differences
- Search for Common Ground
- Self-Managed Small Groups
- 18 Hours over 3 Days
- 40 to 80+ Participants
- Larger Groups = Multisearch Conference

REAL TIME STRATEGIC CHANGE
Purpose: To Create a Preferred Future with System-Wide Action Planning
Dannemiller and Jacobs

- Format Custom-Designed to Issue
- Highly Structured and Organized
- Theory: Beckhard Change Model
- Common Data Base
- 2 to 3 Days + Follow-Up Events
- Use of Outside Experts as Appropriate
- Use of Small Groups and Total Community
- Self-Managed Small Groups
- 100 to 2,400 Participants
- Logistics Competence Critical
- Daily Participant Feedback
- Planning Committee and Consultants Design Events

ICA STRATEGIC PLANNING PROCESS
Purpose: Strategic Planning

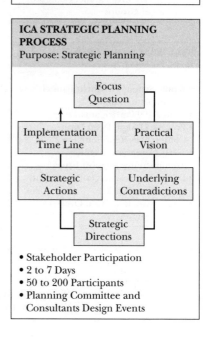

- Stakeholder Participation
- 2 to 7 Days
- 50 to 200 Participants
- Planning Committee and Consultants Design Events

Source: Bunker & Alban, 1997, p. 31. Reprinted by permission of Jossey-Bass, Inc., a subsidiary of John Wiley & Sons, Inc.

Figure 11.2. Large Group Methods for Work Design.

THE CONFERENCE MODEL®
Dick and Emily Axelrod

- System-Wide Preconference Education
- Design Process in Five Conferences
  - Vision
  - Customer
  - Technical
  - Design
  - Implementation
- Three+ Weeks Between Conferences
- 2+ Days for Each Conference
- Data Assist Teams Work Between Meetings to Involve Larger Organization
- 80+ Participants, Parallel Conferences for Larger Groups

REAL TIME WORK DESIGN
Dannemiller and Tolchinsky

- Whole System Present at Launch and Implementation
- 50 to 2,400 Participants
- Process, Design, Deep Dive Conferences Representative
- 1-Day Conferences on Key Administrative Support Issues
- Design Team Manages Process and Does Micro-Work
- Implementation Team Oversees Mini-Conferences

FAST CYCLE FULL PARTICIPATION WORK DESIGN
Pasmore, Fitz, and Frank

- Orientation Events Educate and Include Everyone
- Five Meetings
  - Future Search (2 Days)
  - Meeting External Expectations (1 Day)
  - Work Systems Analysis (2 to 3 Days)
  - Work Life Analysis (1 Day)
  - New Design and Implementation (4+ Days)
- Up to 120 Attend Meetings
- Parallel Design of Support Process Changes
- 1/3 of System Participation Goal
- Design Ratification Events Include Everyone

PARTICIPATIVE DESIGN
Fred and Merrelyn Emery

- Bottom-up Process
- Company-Wide Education Is First Step
- Management Sets Minimum Critical Specifications
- Basic Principle: Each Level Coordinates and Controls Its Own Work
- Each Unit Designs Its Own Work
- Six Design Principles Used to Redesign Work
- Multiskilling Is the Norm

Source: Bunker & Alban, 1997, p. 97. Reprinted by permission of Jossey-Bass, Inc., a subsidiary of John Wiley & Sons, Inc.

Figure 11.3. Whole System Participative Work.

SIMU-REAL Purpose: Real-Time Work on Current Issues, Test Future Designs, Learn About System *Donald and Alan Klein* • Organization Selects Issue for Work • Room Arrangement Reflects Organization's Structure • People Act Their Organizational Role • Periods of Stop Action and Reflection • Decision Process Agreed to in Advance • 1 Day • 50 to 150 People • Facilitator Needs Expertise in Process Consultation	**WORK-OUT (GENERAL ELECTRIC)** Purpose: Problem Identification and Process Improvement • Improvement Target Selected • Employee Cross-Functional Meeting • Process: Discuss and Recommend • Senior Management Responds Immediately • Champions and Sponsors Follow Through to Implementation • Follow-Up as Needed • 1 to 2 Days
LARGE SCALE INTERACTIVE EVENTS Purpose: Problem Solving *Dannemiller and Jacobs* Uses Same Methodology as Real Time Strategic Change. See Description, Part One • Many Different Uses	**OPEN SPACE TECHNOLOGY** Purpose: Discussion and Exploration of System Issues *Harrison Owen* • Least Structured of Large Group Technologies • Divergent Process • Large Group Creates Agenda Topics • Interest Groups Form Around Topics • Periodic Town Meetings for Sharing Information Across Interest Groups • One Facilitator Lays Out Format, Ground Rules, "Holds the Space" • Requires an Understanding of Large Group Dynamics • 1 to 3 Days

Source: Bunker & Alban, 1997, p. 157. Reprinted by permission of Jossey-Bass, Inc., a subsidiary of John Wiley & Sons, Inc.

Large system interventions complete the array of methods needed to intervene at all levels of organizational life. We see this new development as a natural progression in the history of trying to change organizations. Change processes usually target one or possibly two levels of intervention. Change can be planned to target individuals, interpersonal processes, groups, intergroup processes, or the organization.

Some practitioners of OD and industrial/organizational (I/O) psychology have focused at the individual level with interventions about managerial and future competencies, career development, and assessment centers. The theory is that changing the people will also change the organization (see Chapters Two and Three).

Improving the effectiveness of groups also has been thematic over the history of OD (see Chapters Seven and Eight). Early OD capitalized on early T-group research to improve group functioning using interventions such as process consultation, how to run better meetings, and team building. More recently, self-managed teams and global teams have been the focus of attention.

Working on interdepartmental issues (intergroup interventions) developed in the late 1960s, but the methods were few and typically dealt with two or at most three groups. Typical examples are Beckhard's confrontation meeting, union-management structured meetings, and work on interdepartmental tensions within organizations such as marketing and sales or manufacturing and engineering. Because they work with the whole system, large system interventions have developed new methods of working across organizational boundaries.

Until large system interventions were developed, consultants lacked methods for bringing together and working with the whole system at one time. Data-based methods such as survey feedback (see Chapter Four) and generic climate surveys do collect data from and target the whole system for change. However, the intervention process is typically a waterfall from the top that takes months and addresses issues serially from the top of the organization down. Gestalt practitioners have long practiced whole systems thinking and intervention, but even they have been enabled to do much more interactive whole systems work using these new methods.

These methods also make it possible to work with the organization's environment by including stakeholders in events. Furthermore, they can be used for work across groups and organizations in communities and in complex global organizations.

We believe that these methods complete the development of methods in the field of OD practice. They are important because practitioners and clients now have choice among all possible levels of work.

Key Concepts

Data about the system have always been important in organizational change processes. In the early T-group, people shared perceptions of individual and group behavior and used these data to learn about group behavior and development. In team-building interventions, consultants interview team members and feed back summaries of the data they collect for analysis and action (see Chapter Five). At the organizational level, survey feedback, one of the central OD methods, collects data from the whole system and then feeds it back for discussion and action (see Chapter Four). In a somewhat different way, data and the processes for gathering them, analyzing them, and acting on them are central to large system interventions. In the language of these interventions, creating a common database is essential.

Creating and Analyzing the Data

Data are the information, perceptions, beliefs, and values of the people who participate in the large system intervention. This includes all the people or their representatives from the organizational system, a broad selection crossing levels and functions. It often also includes the environment outside the organization, including customers, suppliers, industry experts, regulators, and other relevant stakeholders.

Small groups of seven to ten people sit at round tables, which facilitate interaction, each group composed as a microcosm of the system present at the event. Identifying the key stakeholders for the target issue and making sure that they are present at the event is critical for successful intervention.

In a series of guided activities, these groups take the data that the people present have created and analyze them. Over a series of discussions, they share their perceptions until everyone understands the issues similarly (although they may not all agree, for example, about what should be done). In the language of practitioners, everyone is reading off the same page.

Divergent Views, Conflict, and the Search for Common Ground

People from different parts of the organization come with different perspectives and differing values and beliefs. These differences are acknowledged; however, the strategy for many of these interventions is to search for common ground, or areas where people do agree. The common psychological process in which differences emerge and then everyone focuses on the differences and trying to resolve them is circumvented. The conscious focus is areas of agreement, which often turn out to be bigger than anticipated. This common ground of agreement is the next step in everyone reading off the same page. (For an elaboration of this idea see Bunker, 1999.)

Use of Data and Survey Feedback Use of Data

In general, there are three key differences in the use of data for large system interventions and the more familiar OD survey feedback approach.

Speed and Ownership

In large system interventions, the people who generate the data analyze and interpret them. This is a highly interpersonal process in which people are actively engaged and get immediate reactions to their data, a process that increases ownership and a sense of shared responsibility. Everything happens at one time. In survey feedback, the people who generate the data give them to others to collate and feed back a preliminary analysis (see Chapter Four). This takes time and is a more distant process because the respondents fill out questionnaires for others to analyze. It is slower because a top-to-bottom waterfall process is typically used for the feedback-discussion-action process.

Consulting Role

In the large system intervention, consultants create and facilitate the process in partnership with an active steering committee from the organization. In survey feedback, consultants contract as experts in data collection and analysis. They design questionnaires or do interviews, and they create the initial picture of the data that is fed back to the organization.

Degree of Focus

Typically, the large system intervention has a more focused agenda; people come together around a central theme or issue. Survey feedback has the ability to survey an organization about a wide array of issues at one time. It can be used for a focused issue, but more often it has a broad sweep.

Theory and Methods

By the mid-1990s, the twelve large system intervention methods described in Figures 11.1, 11.2, and 11.3 were very much in practice, and there was a great deal of interest from practitioners in understanding them and getting trained to use them. Among the methods that create the future, Future Search, which was originated by Weisbord from some ideas from the Emerys' Search Conference and methods from the National Training Laboratory, became very popular as a way of creating a vision for the future of organizations and communities. The Search Conference, Future Search, and the Inter-Cultural Affairs methods offer a stable format that can be learned and used by practitioners. Real Time Strategic Change, in contrast, is like a custom-tailored suit. It is designed for each client situation, often using activity modules, some of which were created by Ron Lippitt in his work in the 1970s. Real Time Strategic Change has an advantage in that it is a method that can involve much larger groups, from two hundred to two thousand, than the other future methods. It also routinely creates the option that management can bring in a draft vision of the future that participants react to and influence. In many settings, this allows management to fulfill what they see as their responsibility to lead but also allows for voice from those in the organization. In our view, all of these methods are useful and effective. Choosing the right one for a particular situation is the art form.

Among methods that are used to design work, three methods that were very similar in 1995 in 1995 (the Conference Model, Fast Cycle Full Participation Work Design, and Real Time Work Design) have since become difficult to distinguish as separate methods. This is partly because the inventors of these methods engage in active discussions with each other about the work they are doing from their common theory base in sociotechnical systems theory of work design. It is also true that client needs modify ideal designs. Basically, these methods identify processes in the work flow that need improvement. They create a desired future state, analyze the work, and redesign how it is done and the structure that supports it so that they can create the desired state. This is done in a series of events for large groups supported by smaller task group work. Redesign projects typically take about six months to accomplish, and full implementation is often longer. Because so many people are involved, a wide sense of participation and knowing what is going on is achieved, thus reducing the sense of alienation and secrecy often associated with changes in work process, for example, downsizing.

Participative Design is a radical departure from the methods just discussed. It begins at the bottom of the organization when people design their own work and take responsibility for it. The redesign process then moves up the organization, building on the first units. After they have designed their work, the next level asks, "What is our work?" (now that their subordinates have redesigned their work). They identify what their work is and design it, and so on up to the top of the organization. This totally democratic process must be adopted by management before going forward. In addition, there is a significant period of education before any action, so that everyone in the system understands what is going to happen.

The third set of methods, those for discussion and decision making, emerged at different times and have remained relatively discrete. Simu-Real, invented by Klein in the 1970s, is a process of creating in one place the physical presence for a day of the whole system and exploring in action and stop-action episodes an issue or organizational problem.

Open-Space was invented by Owen in the 1980s as a method to create good conversations about controversial or unexplored issues in organizations and communities. In this least structured of the twelve methods, people create their own agenda in the first hour together and then proceed to explore it using rules and norms that free them from the usual hierarchical constraints.

WorkOut was invented at General Electric in the late 1980s, initially to remove requirements that took up time without adding value. Since then, it has become articulated into a method of addressing serious system problems and making decisions about them within a few months. After the problem is identified, there is intense preparation for a several-day meeting with all the stakeholders off-site. At the end of that meeting, management, including the project champion, comes to hear reports and make decisions about proposed actions. These actions are accomplished within thirty, sixty, or ninety days, by which time the problem should be under control.

Finally, Large Scale Interactive Events are a third form of the Real Time method (Jacobs, 1994) devoted to problem solving. This method, because of its flexibility, can be used for many objectives. For example, when tuberculosis was on the rise in New York City, especially among the poor and homeless, these practitioners designed a three-day meeting that brought together four hundred concerned stakeholders (including police, hospitals, doctors, social agencies, and homeless shelters) to plan for action. In another example, Marriott hotels used this method to deal with problems in specific hotels and to teach the staff Total Quality methods of problem analysis (Jacobs, 1994).

Emerging Trends

We believe that the category system we created is useful and robust as a way of creating a conceptual framework for these methods. In our more detailed examination of the methods (Bunker & Alban, 1997), we also discuss differences among them in structure, decision-making process, number of people who can be involved in any one event, stakeholder involvement, action planning, and type of design. These differences are useful to consider when selecting a method for use (see also Holman & Devane, 1999).

Although we have no hard data on practitioner use of these methods, our central role as people who are interested in all the methods and without favorites among them keeps us in touch with many practitioners. As we move into the decade after the excitement about the discovery of these new methods, it is interesting to consider how they are being used.

Over the past five years, there has been a transition among experienced practitioners from a view that these events can be free-standing and can be counted on to produce enough energy to guarantee change, to a view that these events are part of a change process that needs other support. For example, in the early days of Future Search, Weisbord and Janoff taught that the energy generated in a good Future Search would carry into change processes.

With experience, it is clear that although this sometimes happens, implementation should be planned carefully as the event is planned. Although these events are critical to rapid and system-wide understanding and commitment to change, the stand-alone event emphasis has moved to an understanding of how to work with these events as part of a more sustained process. Systems are difficult to change. These methods add heavy cannon to our array of weapons.

Although there have not been any radical new breakthrough methods emerging, there are practitioners who have taken these ideas and shaped them in line with their particular work and created new names for what they are doing. Most practitioners start out by learning and using one method. Gradually, many of us are using more than one method and using them in combination. For example, a hospital system of five hospitals held Open Space meetings in the five hospital communities before going into a Future Search and then a redesign process within each hospital. These methods are also influencing the design of conferences and meetings. The "talking heads" event typical in many organizations is being transformed into more interactional occasions using small groups around round tables.

Another current trend is experimentation with shorter events for specific client needs. This requires the good judgment of experienced practitioners because methods created and tested over several days have an internal logic and flow that can cause difficulties if they are disrupted. However, when the organizational system is coherent and shares values, there is evidence that some shorter (half- or whole-day) events can be very effective.

People also ask why appreciative inquiry (Ai), a method that developed in the 1980s, is not included in our framework (for a discussion on Ai, see Chapter Ten). The answer is straightforward. Ai is a useful change method that is used in both systems and units of organizations. The methods in our framework all require large group events as the core around which work is done. Ai processes can and do use large groups, but Ai did not emerge as a method based on bringing the whole system together in one room to do its work. In fact, much of Ai work is done in one-on-one interviews. Since the emergence of large system interventions, Ai practitioners, like many others, have incorporated these methods. The basic principle of gathering the whole system to do work has become influential and has stimulated modifications in a number of change methods. For the methods we are discussing, the large group event is core, not optional.

Results of Using These Methods

Although there is distressingly little research about these methods, we propose from anecdotal accounts and our own experience and reflection as practitioners that change occurs in three areas that are measurable.

Measurable Outcomes

Interventions that target increased effectiveness in organizational processes or improved outcomes are most easily quantified by collecting data on the cost of the intervention and the magnitude in hard numbers of the expected changes. Unfortunately for research knowledge, organizations may do this for their own purposes but not make these data widely available. There is a tendency to hear about the success stories in dollars and cents and not to hear the same data about those that did not meet expectations.

Shifts in Perception

People arrive at large system interventions seeing the world from their own perspective and experience. In the event, they engage in focused conversations with a microcosm of the organization in small, self-managing groups. They may hear new views and information from the platform, which they are asked to discuss in these microcosm groups. These conversations build on each other, and the group becomes a unit as it works on its assigned tasks. Perceptions are often widened or changed. Rather than just seeing the organization's situation from a single department's perspective, individuals now can see it as a whole and understand much better how the whole work process, including how heir own function, fits with what others do. They now understand at a new level who the stakeholders are and what their interests are. In short, everyone comes away with a bigger picture of the organization. They may also understand the environment in which the organization is functioning better and why change is critical. Depending on the main issue or theme of the event, people learn from others and enlarge their perspectives.

We recall a manager from Mobil who commented about the impact of working this way on his own way of thinking: "Whenever we have a meeting, I ask myself, 'Who should be here?'" The idea that every issue has a system of stakeholders that need to be involved is experienced so consistently that people who work this way internalize it.

Building Social Capital

A serendipitous result of this way of working is the network of relationships across the organization or community that is created. When people return to their jobs, they have widened their set of contacts across organization boundaries. In *Bowling Alone* (2000), Putnam calls these essential networks that supply information and assistance *social capital*. Knowing how to cross organizational boundaries is an essential skill sorely lacking in many places. A good network helps shift perceptions from *they* to *we*.

A Dearth of Research

Why is there so little research on these important new methods? One reason is clearly the complexity of measurement issues, as well as disentangling them from the many other factors affecting organizational life. Another is the privatization of research.

Most interesting to us is the possibility that this type of intervention, which involves the whole system, cannot be measured by traditional linear methods. Search-Net, an alliance of Future Search practitioners, is engaged in what they call the ripple project—an effort to document changes that happen as a result of the energy for change generated in a large system intervention event flowing in ever widening circles and causing change. Other practitioners report that in "reunions" several months after an event, discussion of what has happened as a result of the event was considerably advanced when people put their individual knowledge together and realized what system effects were occurring. These kinds of data could not have been discovered by sampling individuals. It took the system to understand what had happened in the system.

Emerging Frontiers

In the past few years, several trends have emerged regarding the practice of large system interventions.

Before and After

Early focus was on the event itself, that is, on making gatherings of large groups of people work. A great deal was learned about designing events that engaged everyone and about the logistic requirements to support each design. As practitioners developed enough experience and felt that they had these elements under control, attention has turned to what must happen to ensure that the event and change process are successful.

Before the event, a steering committee is formed that represents a microcosm of those who will be present for the whole system meeting. They serve as a check on whether all the stakeholders have been invited and work with the practitioners who develop the design for the meeting. Their role is to give input to the design— to stand in the shoes of the people who will attend and anticipate issues and problems. Some of the issues can be addressed and resolved during the planning process; others affect how the event is organized. Sometimes the steering committee will go through a practice run of the event in order to get it right. During the event itself, they monitor how well things are going. Each day, the steering committee meets to review the day and the feedback from participants and to make adjustments in the next day's design. The steering committee, in partnership with the large system practitioners, is the control mechanism for the whole process.

Hierarchy and Democratic Participation: A Paradox

There is a history in social science research of repeated demonstrations of the importance of employee participation for commitment to change and implementation effectiveness, but much less success getting organizations' leadership to use these methods.

Why? It is not cost, because companies spend millions on consulting contracts to change organizations.

Someone has said that in America, our values are very democratic but our organizations are very hierarchical. We have found that other cultures, in Scandinavia, Holland, New Zealand, and Canada, seem more comfortable with the use of these methods. Are these cultures more communitarian in nature? Do U.S. executives have a higher need for control and a greater fear of chaos? In many organizations, we experience a tension about issues of authority, a need for management control, and a desire to involve people, to give them voice. Axelrod's *Terms of Engagement* (2000) proposes principles for a new change management paradigm that deals with this tension.

Emery and Purser (1996) have written wisely about the contradictions of trying to run an organization in a mixed mode, that is, both hierarchically and participatively. It creates confusion in people. By contrast, Vroom and Yetton (1973) propose that decision making can work effectively in three different styles. Authoritarian decision making keeps the control with the person in power because he or she alone makes the decision. Group decision making allows group members full participation and equal power in deciding. It is democratic. And consultative decision making, the middle way, involves others in influencing and giving advice to the decision maker while that person still retains the power to decide. Using all three modes makes managers very effective.

The intriguing question is whether both authority and participation can be used in organizations at appropriate times or whether they are orthogonal. Anecdotally, there are stories of the effective use of both styles. For example, Carlson's raiders—a group of U.S. Marines fighting in China in the early 1940s—did the planning for their dramatic air raids around a table where each man, regardless of rank, had an equal voice. Then they went into action and implemented the raids in full military fashion. If both modes are to be used, that level of clarity about authority is essential. Organization leaders have to decide how much participation in decision making they want and at what point in the planning process. We believe many leaders and managers are not clear themselves about this issue, which can create hesitation about employing large system interventions.

Implementation Issues

It is very rare that a single event will change a system. These events are most effective as part of a process of change within an organization. The implementation issue is how decisions get fully carried out, how changes in behaviors, values, and structures become embedded in the organization.

There is a high probability that unless appropriate actions are taken, the propensity of the system will be to fall back into the bureaucratic linear mode and make decisions and do business in the old way, not the new way. For this reason, it is imperative that planning and resourcing of the implementation phase begin in the steering committee at the same time that the event is planned. After most large system intervention events, people are energized and committed to change, but they are also tired. As they go back to their demanding work settings, it is easy for plans to move slowly or erode. Linear planning and responsibility charting are ubiquitous and necessary, but they alone are not sufficient to ensure implementation. Many change efforts fail because the implementation phase is inadequately resourced. We believe that creating dedicated implementation resources is a first step. At the same time, we believe that innovative methods that are less linear and create and support the energy released by the event need more experimentation. People engaged in implementation need "reunions" and occasions to renew commitment and share information. They need to know about implementation activities and have opportunities to participate. Leadership needs to be engaged and visible in support, sending a symbolic message about the importance of this final phase. These processes must be planned in advance and also allow for the creative emergence of new ideas that can be tried to deepen the institutionalization of the change.

Conclusion

Numerous large system interventions are being integrated into more traditional OD practice when the change issue needs to be addressed at the system level. Because these methods are relatively recent, they are being used in change practice in many different ways. We see these experiments as useful and necessary. At the same time, research on outcomes needs development, and the role of leadership needs more attention. Finally, the important issue of implementation is a dilemma of contemporary organizational change practice, not a specific problem of these new methods.

Bibliography for Specific Methods

Appreciative Inquiry

Hammond, S. A. (1998). *The thin book of appreciative inquiry.* Plano, TX: Practical Press.

The Conference Model

Axelrod, R. H. (1993). Using the Conference Model for work design. *Journal for Quality and Participation, 16,* 58–61.

Fast Cycle Full Participation

Fitz, A. S., & Frank, G. (1999). Fast-cycle full participation organization redesign. In P. Holman & T. Devane (Eds.), *The change handbook: Group methods for shaping the future* (pp. 123–137). San Francisco: Berrett-Koehler.

Future Search

Weisbord, M. R., & Janoff, S. (2000). *Future search* (2nd ed.). San Francisco: Berrett-Koehler.

ICA Strategic Planning

Spencer, L. (1989). *Winning though participation: Meeting the challenge of corporate change with the technology of participation.* Dubuque, IA: Kendall/Hunt.

Large Scale Interactive Events

Dannemiller Tyson Associates. (2000a). *Whole-scale change: Unleashing the magic in organizations.* San Francisco: Berrett-Koehler
Dannemiller Tyson Associates. (2000b). *Whole-scale change toolkit.* San Francisco: Berrett-Koehler.

Open Space Technology

Owen, H. (1997). *Open space technology: A user's guide* (2nd ed.). San Francisco: Berrett-Koehler.

Participative Design

Emery, F. (1995). Participative design: Effective, flexible, and successful—now! *Journal for Quality and Participation, 18*(1).

Rehm, R. (1999). *People in charge: Creating self managing workplaces.* Stroud, England: Hawthorn.

Real Time Strategic Change

Jacobs, R. W. (1994). *Real time strategic change: How to involve the entire organization in fast and far-reaching change.* San Francisco: Berrett-Koehler.

Real Time Work Design

Tolchinsky, P. D. (1999, Mar.–Apr.). A redesign of the Central Intelligence Agency. *Journal for Quality and Participation, 22*(2), 31–35.

Search Conference

Emery, M., & Purser, R. E. (1996). *The search conference: A comprehensive guide to theory and practice.* San Francisco: Jossey-Bass.

Simu-Real

Klein, D. C. (1992). Simu-Real: A simulation approach to organizational change. *Journal of Applied Behavioral Science, 28,* 566–578.

WorkOut

Leaders' Guide to WorkOut: Town Meetings. (1999). In R. Ashkenas, T. Jick, D. Ulrich, & C. Paul-Chandhury (Eds.), *The boundaryless organization field book: Practical tools for building the new organization* (Vol. 2, pp. 49–71). San Francisco: Jossey-Bass.

References

Axelrod, R. H. (2000). *Terms of engagement: Changing the way we change organizations.* San Francisco: Berrett-Koehler.

Bunker, B. B., & Alban, B. T. (1997). *Large group interventions: Engaging the whole system for rapid change.* San Francisco: Jossey-Bass.

Holman, P., & Devane, T. (Eds.). (1999). *The change handbook: Group methods for shaping the future.* San Francisco: Jossey-Bass.

Putnam, R. (2000). *Bowling alone: The collapse and revival of American community.* New York: Simon & Schuster.

Vroom, V. H., & Yetton, P. W. (1973). *Leadership and decision making.* Pittsburgh: University of Pittsburgh Press.

Weisbord, M. R. (1987). *Productive workplaces: Organizing and managing for dignity, meaning, and community.* San Francisco: Jossey-Bass.

PART 3

Major Developments in Organization Development

CHAPTER 12

Organization Development and IT
Practicing OD in the Virtual World

Nancy T. Tippins

The technological revolution has touched virtually every American business and changed the way knowledge workers perform their duties. The advent of computers, software, the Internet and the World Wide Web, video, and sophisticated telecommunications provide the foundation for tools that facilitate business and can be easily, quickly, and widely deployed.

These tools have altered the manner in which businesses relate to suppliers, customers, and employees as well as the speed with which these interactions occur. The field of organization development (OD) has felt the effects of this revolution too. OD professionals now have at hand an array of technologically supported tools, ranging from the delivery of training over networked computers, to computerized data collection and analysis packages for succession planning and surveys, to video-teleconferencing for coaching, feedback, and team building.

At the same time that technology has created tools that enhance OD work and expand the delivery of service, it has also provided challenges for OD practitioners, particularly those who are not technologically savvy. In order to use fully the opportunities technology has provided, OD practitioners must now acquire skills associated with acquiring or developing technology-based tools, installing them, and maintaining them. Although OD practitioners may not need to know how actually to do these things, they need to be able to collaborate effectively with information technology (IT) professionals to accomplish them. In addition, OD practitioners may need to adapt their fundamental approach to OD interventions to accomplish the new demands of technology-driven practices. In the future, the most successful OD practitioners are likely to be those who can successfully integrate the diverse fields of OD and IT.

Information Technology and Six OD Practices

In general, six areas of OD practice have been affected by the IT revolution: training, development, surveys, multisource feedback, succession planning, and team building.

Training

Corporate America spends large amounts of money on employee training and constantly seeks ways to deploy training more effectively and efficiently. Computer applications have assisted in developing high-quality materials, making the delivery of training more cost-effective, and enhancing the amount and quality of information about training needs, course use, student achievement, and instructor performance.

• *Communications.* Training often involves extensive communications between the trainer and the trained. Many organizations use intranet or Internet sites that provide course catalogue information and course logistics. Some instructors use e-mail communications to facilitate questions and answers, particularly when distance learning is used. Others use e-mail and Web sites to distribute course materials like lecture notes and reading lists.

• *Course development.* The use of software that assists instructors in developing their courses is increasingly popular. Sophisticated software forces instructors to define learning objectives, relate course content to these objectives, and develop mastery tests that directly reflect course content.

• *Training delivery.* Technology may be used for training delivery in several ways. In some organizations, training is provided through the computer. The advantages of the computer relative to the paper-and-pencil programmed instructions of the 1960s include animation, video and audio clips, and branching based on student performance or interest. Students may review the training modules and measure progress at convenient times. Some computer software programs go beyond simple page turning and provide evaluations of student work, give feedback, and determine what content should be presented next. Another technology application for training is video-teleconferencing: the instructor and students in different locations are linked through a video network. The experience with the advanced equipment is very similar to sitting in a classroom with the instructor and other students.

• *Simulations and work samples.* Simulations and work samples have the advantages of protecting expensive equipment and lives of students and instructors in dangerous situations and providing repeated experiences inexpensively and safely. For example, airplane pilots can practice emergency flight procedures in simulators rather than in actual airplanes, which would be very expensive as well as potentially life threatening.

• *Assessment.* Technology can replace, completely or partially, instructor time spent on evaluation of student performance. A number of organizations have recently developed software to score essays and provide feedback (Burstein, 2001). In some cases where the actual work is a physical product or output, the machine evaluation is more accurate than the instructor's, given the difficulty of observing minuscule parts and distances.

• *Data collection.* Many training organizations use computer applications to collect information about training needs, student progress, and instructor performance. Questionnaires and surveys for needs assessments can be widely deployed and quickly collected and analyzed. Assessments of the student's learning and the instructor's teaching can be administered through computers and stored in computerized databases for future analyses. In some simulations, video or audio recordings of the student can be made for future review and discussion.

The use of technology in training raises many important issues for the OD practitioner. Three significant concerns are the inability of computer-based training to adapt quickly to different learning styles, the lack of opportunities for social interaction, and the discipline required to complete training without frequent human interaction.

Most individuals have preferences for how they learn. Some prefer lectures, for example, and others prefer experiential hands-on instruction. Often preferences are related to the nature of the material to be learned. For many people, knowledge of facts may be best learned from a lecture format, while knowledge of a process or principle might best be learned in a laboratory setting. Instructors in face-to-face training confront similar problems. Because of their presence in the classroom environment, they can adapt to the learners' needs and often use several instructional techniques, particularly with difficult material. Theoretically, computer-based training can be developed so that multiple forms of instruction are presented, but the cost of developing redundant training in different modalities is often prohibitive. Furthermore, required redundant training can be irritating when the student has mastered the material on the first pass.

In many corporate environments, training fills multiple needs. One is certainly to teach information and develop skills. Another important role that training serves is to provide opportunities for social interaction among employees who share at least a common employer and frequently similar responsibilities or interests. Removing the opportunity for informal activities through the use of technology can decrease the desirability of participating in the training.

Finally, many individuals lack the personal discipline to study complex materials on their own. Some sabotage their good intentions by failing to remove intrusions into study time that would not occur if they were in the classroom. Based on experiences with instructorless training, some lack the self-motivation to begin and complete a technology-based training program.

Employee Development

Although there is quite a bit of overlap between the areas of training and development, the topics are separated here so that emphasis can be placed on nontraining-based development activities. Employee development in most organizations involves a cycle of identification of developmental needs, action planning, intervention, and assessment of progress. The developmental intervention may be training or any number of other activities such as coaching in current assignment, new assignments, special projects, mentoring others, and volunteer activities. Technological applications for employee development other than training cover a number of areas:

- *Communications.* Internet and intranet Web pages and e-mail are efficient vehicles for delivering up-to-date information about employee development programs, tools for assessment of need and evaluation of progress, and reporting requirements. An important advantage to using technology is the ability to provide the most current information to large numbers of people.
- *Assessment.* Like other tools, assessments can be presented on the computer. In many cases, assessments can be administered and immediately scored, and feedback promptly provided.
- *Data collection and record keeping.* Technologically based applications allow OD professionals to collect extensive data on what employees' development needs are, the routes they are taking to improve their skills and abilities, how long employees spend on certain activities, and the degree of progress that they make. Analyses can then be conducted to determine the organization's employee capability, the developmental activities that should be provided, and the interventions that are most successful in improving which needs. These applications also provide employees with the tools to record information like evaluation results, personal action plans, and progress. Some tools remind employees of due dates for certification, recertification, required training, and reporting obligations.

One of the biggest concerns about providing tools for individual assessment using the computer and Internet is the ability of untrained individuals to use them successfully. Some people lack the discipline to use assessment tools without aid, others lack the introspective capability to assess their own behavior accurately, and still others are resistant to critical feedback, particularly when the link between the feedback and actual behavior is missing. Of course, the same tool in a more traditional delivery mode, such as paper-and-pencil format, has the same liabilities; however, an important difference is usually the proximity of trained professionals to assist the individual.

A related issue is the question of accuracy of the data, especially in organizations where the data are shared with others in decision-making positions. For an individual conducting a self-assessment to admit to a low level of presentation skills in a sales organization might be fatal to his or her career, so another less sensitive and more easily developed "weakness" (such as financial acumen) may be selected for development. Again, the reluctance of an individual to confront a fatal flaw can occur in more traditional OD approaches. The difference is the presence of an OD practitioner who is skilled in helping individuals face difficult problems.

A second problem with technological applications used in employee development is that some are inappropriate for some kinds of activities. Consider the need for coaching to improve interpersonal skills. Computer applications can recommend coaching as an appropriate development strategy and provide tips on appropriate interpersonal behavior. But no system can actually observe actual behavior, formulate a detailed diagnosis of behavior, and effectively provide the coaching itself in a facilitative manner (see Chapters Two and Three for more on using coaching in an OD context). Although one could argue that coaching could be provided through video-teleconferencing, the question of effectiveness remains.

A number of OD interventions like coaching are highly dependent on interpersonal relationships. The effect of technology on the relationships undoubtedly varies across individuals and remains largely unknown.

Surveys

Organizational survey technologies have increased the speed with which surveys can be administered, analyzed, and reported (see Chapter Four). Surveys can be administered in a variety of methods using computer—among them, e-mail, intranet, and Internet Web-based applications (Church & Waclawski, 2001; Kuhnert & McCauley, 1996; Macey, 1996)—all of which provide instant data capturing. Analysis, report writing, and presentations can be programmed to occur as soon as sufficient numbers of people have responded. Feedback can be distributed widely through computerized sources and discussions and action planning can take place via e-mail, teleconferencing, or video-teleconferencing. Among the specific applications are the following:

- *Communications.* Communications about the survey process, time line, reports, and tools to assist interpretation and action planning can be delivered through Internet technology.
- *Administration.* The physical problems of printing survey booklets and shipping them to remote work sites are reduced when surveys are delivered by computer. Costs for data entry or scanning are eliminated if immediate data recording occurs.
- *Analysis and reporting.* The use of information technologies speeds the analysis of data and reporting back to managers and teams. Although the detailed analysis and reporting of survey data have been computerized since the 1960s, recent developments in word and thought recognition capture write-in comments and categorize them with high levels of reliability.

Perhaps the two most significant dilemmas for OD practitioners using technology for survey work are participant concerns about confidentiality of data and reports and the potential overuse of survey methodology.

All computer data collection applications share the problem of confidentiality. Even the least savvy computer users are aware that submission of personal information and opinions can be easily traced and identified. Virtually all organizations promise confidentiality and anonymity, yet trust is not always present.

A related problem is the confidentiality of survey reports. When survey results are used for important decisions about individuals, a certain level of confidentiality is expected. Computer distribution of reports creates the possibility of unauthorized access.

Technology, particularly in the area of survey research, has streamlined what was once a laborious administrative task. The negative aspect of this improvement, though, is the potential overuse of the survey methodology. Many want to collect opinions on the topic relevant to their project. Overuse may erode participation simply because employees are tired of completing surveys.

Multisource Feedback

Technology has streamlined the administration and reporting of multisource feedback in the same way that it has simplified the administrative tasks associated with surveys. In addition, it has allowed the integration of multisource feedback to other developmental systems (see Chapter Two for more on this topic). Technological applications overlap closely with those already for surveys and include the following areas:

- *Communications.* Communications about the multisource process and tools to assist interpretation and action planning can be delivered through information technology. Theoretically at least, OD practitioners can provide feedback, discuss action plans, and coach through video and audio technologies.
- *Administration.* Distribution and return of questionnaires can be speeded by computer delivery. Costs for data entry or scanning are eliminated if immediate data recording occurs.
- *Analysis and reporting.* The time required for analysis and reporting is decreased when computer software is used.

Although computer-generated interpretive reports can provide factual information about how groups of raters responded, norms, and other general interpretive information, they cannot anticipate reactions to information and assist the rated individual in working through strong emotional responses like anger and disappointment.

A second concern for raters and the rated alike is confidentiality. Ratings of an individual are extremely sensitive and potentially damaging to all parties involved. Despite commitments to confidentiality, many lack the confidence that their ratings are protected (see Bracken, Timmreck, & Church, 2001, for more on the range of issues involved in multisource feedback applications).

Succession Planning

Succession planning in many companies consists of four basic steps: (1) identification of key positions for which succession planning is important; (2) determination of relevant knowledge, skills, and abilities required for the key position; (3) assessment of the talent pool on relevant knowledge, skills, and abilities; and (4) development of employees who are deficient in some area. Technology applications for development have already been discussed. IT applications used for the first three steps include these:

- *Communications.* Succession planning requires a great deal of communication regarding topics like the process to be used, deadlines, the criteria for inclusion or exclusion, and the resolution of conflicts.

- *Data collection.* A number of organizations successfully use computer applications that guide the assessment of individuals and the subsequent nomination process.
- *Reporting.* Preparation of reports for succession planning is often an onerous task because of constantly changing data. One promotion at a high level can create a chain of promotions and developmental moves that alters the underlying structure of the organization, as well as the pool of viable candidates for many positions. Mechanization allows for immediate updates and current reports.
- *Access to data.* Succession planning information is frequently used for staffing activities. Slates of candidates for a position may be developed from the succession plan or lists of high-potential staff. Technology can provide the appropriate people with access to the latest data and with the ability to sort large amounts of information according to the criteria for a specific position.

Perhaps the greatest problem for OD practitioners is controlling who has access to what data (see Chapter Fifteen for more on the ethics of this issue). In most organizations, access to success planning data is limited. In some companies, individuals may not see their own nominations, much less nominate themselves or their peers. Typically, companies establish rules about who sees which data. For example, a common rule is that an individual may make and review nominations of lower-level employees but may not see peer data or higher-level employees' data. This means that OD practitioners must provide the organizational relationships to the computerized application. In large organizations where hundreds of management jobs are considered key positions and thousands of employees are viable candidates for these positions, maintaining the organizational structure is a daunting tasks.

Team Building

Team-building activities (see Chapter Eight) have increased in importance because of the importance of cooperative work in competitive environments and the geographic dispersion of employees.

Much has been written on the use of technology in groups. Hollingshead and McGrath (1995) point out that technology improves access to information and enhances information processing capability while creating opportunities for participation regardless of location or time. However, they also note the limited number of ways to communicate and the reduction in the richness of the information conveyed. OD practitioners use technology primarily to enhance communications:

- *Communications.* Communications of all kinds are fundamental to building teams, and range from the formal exchange of information regarding the job to actual team-building activities that are directed toward establishing productive working relationships. E-mail, teleconferencing, and video-teleconferencing provide alternative methods for communications other than those that are face-to-face.

A central question for OD practitioners is the extent to which teams can be developed and maintained without interaction between the OD practitioner and the team members he or she supports and among the members of the team themselves.

Developing teams solely with technological tools that reduce nonverbal communications completely, such as e-mail, is difficult. Other technological tools, such as video-teleconferencing, preserve some of the nonverbal information but introduce other concerns. For example, the identity of all the participants in a teleconference may not be clear, or the question of taping may not be satisfactorily answered. In addition, because of the expenses associated with teleconferencing alternatives, opportunities for "getting-to-know-you" activities are often omitted, and participants get right to work. The question of the importance of close, interpersonal relationships in team building must be raised.

Advantages and Disadvantages to Using Technology

Many technologies and their applications share common advantages and disadvantages.

Advantages

Common advantages to using IT-related approaches are apparent in a variety of areas, including communications, cost, and speed of delivery.

Communications

A major advantage of using technology for OD applications is the ability to provide detailed, up-to-date information quickly to a large audience. Changes can be quickly made, and employees can gain access to information when they need it.

Delivery

Perhaps the most compelling advantage for using technology in the delivery of an OD tool like training, survey questionnaires and reports, and the communication of information about development tools and programs is the tool's widespread deployment. It is independent of geographic location and individual time restrictions. Learning or data collection can occur on demand and just in time.

Cost

Related to the delivery advantage is the advantage of cost efficiencies. Once developed, a training program (or at least the part that is presented using computer) can be given repeatedly at minimal cost. In contrast, instructor-led training has much higher session-related costs. Training that eliminates travel reduces costs significantly. Similarly, computer software that provides data recording and processing functions for surveys, assessments, and succession planning reduces the costs associated with data entry, report preparation, and presentation development.

Although cost reductions are generally perceived to be an advantage in the long term, nevertheless the cost of entry (for example, the purchase of hardware and software and development of custom applications and templates) can be significant.

Speed

A major advantage to using technological applications is the speed of recording information and processing it. Without laborious data entry tasks for large survey and succession planning projects, data analysis can begin much sooner. Even reporting can be speeded by analysis and reporting programs. Similarly, use of communications vehicles like teleconferencing and video-teleconferencing can hasten progress in team efforts by shortening the time necessary to schedule a team meeting.

Integration with Other Systems

One important advantage to the deployment of technology in OD work is the potential for linking applications and systems (see also Chapters Two and Six). For example, a computerized individual assessment from a succession planning program or feedback from a multisource report can identify developmental needs and point the employee to information about developmental activities, including training opportunities, action planning tools, and registration. Performance in training can be documented, and completion of training can trigger a reassessment of the developmental weakness. Some software records commitments and sends employees reminders to update their action plans and development records. Training data can inform self-assessments as well as supervisory assessments made for the purposes of succession planning.

Disadvantages

Technology-related solutions are not without disadvantages, particularly with respect to hardware, software, and support.

Hardware

All of these technological innovations in OD require hardware, software, and technical support. Despite the technology revolution, hardware can be a significant problem in organizations where computers for personal use have not been widely distributed. Frequently, hourly, nonexempt personnel do not have individual workstations at all or ones that afford enough privacy to work through personal assessments or share opinions of the company or others.

Software that is widely deployed may reside on a central server, making the reliability of the entire system a critical factor in a successful OD application. The OD practitioner must decide how to handle situations in which the technology fails. What happens when data from a survey are lost? How does the practitioner handle lost development records? How does the practitioner protect confidential information during system maintenance?

Another irritating problem to students is difficulty with the quality of transmissions. Although this is primarily an issue with video-teleconferencing, computer training, particularly if it includes video or audio clips, may suffer from technical problems related to transmission or receiving equipment.

Software

Software for OD applications must be purchased or developed. For some applications, such as surveys, a number of options exist, and many meet the specific requirements of many organizations. In contrast, some applications, like succession planning, rarely meet one company's needs exactly. Sometimes the software is incompatible with existing network software or employee information databases. At other times, the report formats are unacceptable. Modifications to purchased software are expensive and sometimes not possible.

Some organizations develop their own software for applications that have very specific requirements. Although the resulting product meets corporate requirements, it also means that the responsible OD professional becomes heavily involved in software design and testing and piloting phases.

Support

Support for hardware and software installation and maintenance is frequently an issue. Few OD practitioners are IT experts, and many find themselves highly dependent on an IT expert to install and keep the application running. OD professionals often make decisions about off-the-shelf software based on the capabilities demonstrated. Unfortunately, there are many technical issues related to the compatibility of the software and the ease with which it can be installed and networked over a large number of computers.

Video-teleconferencing may have the highest demand for IT support. Some video-teleconferencing requires an OD professional, an IT professional to handle the computer software for audiovisuals, a video professional to handle the cameras, and a telecommunications expert to handle the transmission across locations. That support is never inexpensive.

Skill Requirements for OD Professionals

The introduction of technology increases the array of skills required for the OD professional. When OD professionals decide to introduce a technology-based tool into their practice, they become partially responsible for its implementation and maintenance. Yet many lack even the basic knowledge and understanding necessary to collaborate successfully with technical experts. McDonagh and Coghlan (2001) noted that the lack of submissions of papers from OD practitioners for a special issue of the *OD Journal* reflected their view "that the deployment of new ICT [information and communication technologies] is all too frequently not an area of central concern to researchers in the field of OD&C [organization development and change]" (p. 2). The acquisition of technical skills often puts OD practitioners in a quandary. Do they invest in developing and maintaining their OD skills or in acquiring fundamental technical skills? McDonagh and Coghlan suggest that the integration of technical knowledge and expertise with the behavioral science knowledge and expertise may lead to a "career cul-de-sac" (p. 4).

Effects of Technology on Interpersonal Interactions

One disadvantage that OD practitioners must carefully manage is the effect of the technology on the interactions among students, between student and teacher, and among group members. Researchers such as McCauley and Johnson (1998) have emphasized the importance of personal relationships in developmental activities and cite twelve roles that can be played by others in developmental relationships. E-mail communications can lack important information that provides clarifying information or signifies the strength of a feeling depth. In face-to-face interactions, the communicator can observe the listener for cues of understanding and agreement or disagreement. High-quality video-teleconferencing solves many of these problems but leaves open the questions of privacy and self-consciousness.

User Friendliness

Perhaps the biggest disadvantage to computer-based development programs is some employees' discomfort using a computer. Although most programs are typically designed to be user-friendly, problems with software, hardware, or system reliability frustrate users. The idea of conducting some OD activities with technology may have a chilling effect that limits participation.

User Reluctance

Because of their travel schedule, some employees do not have sufficient time in the office in front of a computer to complete assessments and updates. Some who are concerned about their work and family balance resent the lack of flexibility about where the OD activity occurs. Others, particularly at the executive level, simply refuse to use computers. Morris and Venkatesh (2000) report age differences in the adoption and usage of technology in the workplace.

User Appropriateness

The training literature is rich with studies that link individual attributes to various kinds of training performances (Fleishman & Mumford, 1998). An unanswered question for many OD applications is the extent to which individual characteristics and technical applications interact and affect training performance, participation rates, response bias, or assessment accuracy.

Need or Desire for a Human Sounding Board

Another disadvantage that should be noted is the need for a human sounding board when assessing one's own strengths and weaknesses and identifying appropriate developmental activities. Many employees are not introspective enough to perform these kinds of activities without assistance. Others lack objectivity about their own behaviors.

Anonymity and Confidentiality

A potential disadvantage relates to suspicions regarding the anonymity of the person making ratings of himself or herself or others, as well as the confidentiality of the resulting ratings. People know they could easily be identified and may not know the extent to which they should trust the organization. Similarly, many computer users are aware that many stored records are not always kept confidential. The degree to which confidentiality is a problem depends largely on the degree of trust and confidence in the organization for handling these kinds of data.

A related issue is the privacy of the individuals engaged in team building, coaching, or feedback through teleconferencing. Trusting the organization's commitment to privacy and confidentiality becomes extremely important to the successful use of technology in these kinds of OD applications.

Simultaneous Advantages and Disadvantages of Technology

Several aspects of technology applied to OD practices can be both an advantage and a disadvantage.

Limitations of Computer-Based Training

Although computer technologies offer a wide array of written, visual, and audio materials, some kinds of experiences (especially taste, smell, and touch), are difficult to simulate. Thus, medical training for identifying medical problems like diabetes might include a computer-based module with pictures and lab results. It is unlikely that the computer training could give a realistic picture of "fruity breath," a sign of diabetes. Similarly, it is difficult to present realistic scenarios depicting interpersonal conflict or to extract behavior that represents an individual's actual response to a situation.

Coverage of Material

One aspect of technology that is both an advantage and a disadvantage is the coverage of material. Once the investment is made in hardware and support, the amount of information that can be conveyed is practically unlimited if it is formatted properly. Thus, a basic course in electronics can branch to in-depth information for interested, more advanced students. However, if the course materials are constrained to cover only the learning objectives, interested students must find another source for more information. Similarly, it is possible to program a large number of development ideas but impossible to cover all possible approaches for all needs.

Special Needs

Another advantage and disadvantage is the ease with which special needs (for example, large print, extra time, or additional background material) can be accommodated. Once the special accommodations are made to the software, they are easily deployed; however, making changes to many existing programs is not a simple task.

Use of Surveys and Questionnaires

Because technology has become so user friendly, many parts of an organization use surveys and questionnaires as tools (see Chapter Four). This can lead to the collection of lots of data about a number of topics, but overuse can erode participation (Rogelberg, 1998). Employees simply get burned out completing surveys.

Like surveys, multisource feedback (see Chapter Two) can be more widely deployed because of technology, but the risk of overuse increases. Often an organizational leader is so impressed with the value of his or her own feedback that the leader decides to have all direct reports complete the survey. Suddenly, the leader has a questionnaire for all of the direct reports to complete, and each of the direct reports has his or her own survey and others for every peer. The volume of questionnaires to be completed becomes even more unmanageable if subordinates are added to the process. The problem of overuse exists with paper instruments as well, but because distribution is more difficult, overuse is somewhat less likely.

Organizational Structure

An issue that frequently comes up in succession planning is the organizational structure underlying the nominations. While the task of inputting the structure can be a monumental task in a large company, it can also clarify reporting relationships and highlight sources for good candidates.

Impact of Technology on OD Content

The use of technology in OD work has forced practitioners to acquire and use technological skills that once were unnecessary and to revise OD processes to fit technology's restraints. Eight areas seem particularly relevant today and in the future:

- *The development process for computer applications for activities like training, development, and succession planning.* This application requires careful planning and anticipation of problems and questions.

For example, where does a student go with a question that is not answered in the training material? What does an executive do to develop a skill at a level that goes beyond the suggestions in the Internet assessment tools and developmental suggestions? How will two nominations of the same individual with different assessments be handled? When OD interventions are conducted face-to-face without the use of technological tools, these kinds of questions can be addressed as they arise. With technology, the likely questions must be identified beforehand, and the answers must be preprogrammed.

• *The appropriate application of technology for delivery of service.* OD practitioners must determine if some applications are more appropriate for delivery through relatively impersonal means. Which ones require human intervention? That a technological innovation is available does not mean that it is also appropriate. Some applications appear to require more human intervention than others. For example, outplacement counseling, which often includes assessment and development activities similar to employee development, could probably be handled effectively through an Internet application. But is it appropriate? In contrast, training of the sales force on a new product might be well suited for computer presentation.

• *The impact of relatively depersonalized technology driven solutions on outcomes and participation.* OD practitioners have a number of questions to ask. Will the depersonalization of some OD applications through technology limit an individual's use of the application? What could be done to prevent this? How can the OD professional help the individual adapt? How will technology change the group dynamics? How will technology affect the outcomes of a survey or a team-building effort?

• *Learning how to work around the limitations of computer technologies and maximize the opportunities provided.* Too often, the limitations are accepted, and supplements to enhance the technology are not developed. For example, an OD practitioner may recognize the limits of team building through technological tools because of the lack of face-to-face interaction, but fail to develop opportunities for team members to interact informally. Even more often, OD practitioners fail to use the capabilities of computing technologies. For example, many computer-assisted training courses use the computer as a page turner. Why not use branching? Why not force interaction and evaluate the student's work?

- *Development of the ability of OD practitioners to work with IT support personnel.* Although it is improbable that many OD practitioners have the interest or the time to develop IT expertise, it is reasonable to expect them to have a basic knowledge of the tools they must work with and how to work with IT professionals. Superior tools are produced by the collaboration between the OD professional and the IT professional. The innovators of the future are likely to be those who can integrate information from several areas. In the future, being only an OD expert will be insufficient. The real expert will be the person who combines OD knowledge with the latest techniques for implementation.

The question of what kind of education, training, experience, and preparation OD professionals need to develop and implement OD tools that incorporate technology effectively has not been answered. Because there are few programs and courses directed at using IT in OD interventions, the most likely opportunity to acquire these skills is through experience and collaboration with other professionals.

- *The ability to understand basic technologies and anticipate how they are changing.* The one certainty in the technology field seems to be change. OD professionals needs to anticipate that change and incorporate it into practice.

Imagining technology that is similar to what exists today, only faster and cheaper, is not difficult. What would happen if computer technology was so ubiquitous, so portable, and so simple to use that every American worker had immediate access and could handle every OD application? In contrast, visioning completely new technologies is quite difficult and beyond the ability of all but the most gifted seers. OD practitioners will never be prescient of future IT developments, but they must stay up to date with the basics of technological developments.

- *Individual differences and how they affect the use of technology and the success of the OD intervention.* Morris and Venkatesh (2000) found that age makes a difference in individuals' willingness to use technology. What are the other salient variables?

- *What to do with the wealth of data that are being collected.* How can this information be used to make more data-driven decisions? What are the significant research questions for OD practitioners? What kind of research should OD practitioners undertake?

Practice Tips

1. Learn how to manage IT development projects and work closely with the IT professional. OD professionals must develop project management skills for IT projects and learn to collaborate effectively with IT experts.
2. Factor the cost of IT support into the budget for technology-based OD applications. Remember that maintenance will be required even for off-the-shelf packages.
3. Learn to apply the right tools for the right task. Determine when face-to-face interaction is needed, and build it in.
4. Pay attention to user friendliness. Employees cannot use a system they do not understand, and they will not voluntarily use a system they dislike.
5. Practice good OD. Do not be swayed by technologically slick interventions. Bad OD practice is still bad OD practice regardless of how it is delivered.
6. Maintain professional standards and ethics regardless of the medium used. If an assessment is neither valid nor reliable, the mode of delivery makes no difference. Promises of confidentiality must be maintained regardless of how the data were collected.
7. Repeat the corporate message regarding confidentiality, and always practice it. Avoid even the perception of a breach in confidentiality.

References

Bracken, D. W., Timmreck, C. W., & Church, A. H. (Eds.). (2001). *The handbook of multisource feedback*. San Francisco: Jossey-Bass

Burstein, J. C. (2001). *Automated essay evaluation in* Criterion. Paper presented at the meeting of the Association of Test Publishers, Tucson, AZ.

Church, A. H., & Waclawski, J. (2001). *Designing and using organizational surveys: A seven-step process*. San Francisco: Jossey-Bass.

Fleishman, E. A., & Mumford, M. D. (1989). Individual attributes and training performance. In I. L. Goldstein (Ed.), *Training and development in organizations* (pp. 183–255). San Francisco: Jossey-Bass.

Hollingshead, A. B., & McGrath, J. E. (1995). Computer-assisted groups: A critical review of the empirical research. In R. A. Guzzo & E. Salas (Eds.), *Team effectiveness and decision making in organizations* (pp. 46–78). San Francisco: Jossey-Bass.

Kuhnert, K., & McCauley, D. P. (1996). Applying alternative survey methods. In A. I. Kraut (Ed.), *Organizational surveys: Tools for assessment and change* (pp. 233–254). San Francisco: Jossey-Bass.

Macey, W. H. (1996). Dealing with the data: Collection, processing, and analysis. In A. I. Kraut (Ed.), *Organizational surveys: Tools for assessment and change* (pp. 204–232). San Francisco: Jossey-Bass.

McCauley, C. D., & Douglas, C. A. (1998). Developmental relationships. In C. D. McCauley, R. S. Moxley, & E. Van Velsor (Eds.), *The Center for Creative Leadership handbook of leadership development* (pp. 160–193). San Francisco: Jossey-Bass.

McDonagh, J., & Coghlan, D. (2001). Exploiting ICT based capabilities the challenge of integrated change. *Organizational Development Journal, 19*(1), 3–7.

Morris, M. G., & Venkatesh, V. (2000). Age differences in technology adoption decisions: Implications for a changing work force. *Personal Psychology, 53,* 375–403.

Rogelberg, S. G. (Chair). (1998). *Surveys and more surveys: Addressing and dealing with oversurveying.* Symposium conducted at the annual convention of the Society for Industrial and Organizational Psychology, Dallas.

CHAPTER 13

Around the World
Organization Development in the International Context
Michael Marquardt

Successfully practicing the principles of organization development (OD) is challenging and complex enough in one's own culture; it becomes ever more difficult when implementing those competencies on other shores and in other cultures. Yet as more and more organizations extend their global reach, the ability of OD practitioners to operate in other cultures and within global companies becomes ever more commonplace and essential.

Adding to the cultural and global challenges, most of us, as individuals, think and act within the Western cultural mind-set in which we were born and raised; moreover, OD itself is a concept and practice that has been built primarily on Western cultural premises and assumptions, some of which may be inappropriate, if not downright offensive, in non-Western cultures. As Wigglesworth (1987) remarks, "While OD may be popular and effective in Western cultures, it would be a grave mistake to assume that peoples in other cultures are equipped with the learning styles, reasoning preferences, value systems and cultural readiness to cope with OD as it is practiced in either the U.S. or Europe" (p. 17). He further notes that the "roots of OD are inductive, experiential, and direct in its approach which conflicts with deductive, indirect, saving-face cultures of many other parts of the world" (p. 17).

Roberts (cited in Marquardt & Engel, 1993), a senior World Bank consultant, lists some additional challenges for OD practitioners who may have an overreliance on the Western models of OD:

- Inadequate flexibility in understanding the social, political, and cultural contexts in which local organizations operate
- Inadequate flexibility in adjusting to the management and organizational style of non-Western managers
- Overreliance on models, concepts, and materials derived from the consultants' own background that are inappropriate elsewhere
- Lack of long-term commitment to providing adequate follow-through and reinforcement

The final, and perhaps most difficult and overriding, challenge for OD practitioners is the need to assist global companies successfully in reconciling and synergizing the polarizing forces inherent in all global organizations: the forces of globalization (which seek singularity and universalism) versus the forces of cultural localization and differentiation. It is the increased presence of global companies that provides the locus in which most OD practitioners will implement their trade now and in the future. It is critical that we begin this journey of practicing OD around the world by first understanding the dynamics and historical evolution of global companies.

Corporate Evolution Toward Global Enterprises

Global companies are relatively new entities, emerging in the past two decades as a result of advances in technology, unfettered trade agreements, and the ending of the cold war. Historically, most companies have gradually evolved from international to multinational to global status (see Figure 13.1). Each of these stages of corporate evolution has forced organizations to deal with the issues of centralization versus decentralization, of a single corporate culture versus multiple foreign cultures.

Beginning with the industrial age, businesses began to import and export supplies and products to and from other countries,

**Figure 13.1. Corporate Evolution: From
International to Global Status.**

Global
Integrate and centralize operations
Link and leverage all resources
Corporate global culture and synergized local cultures
Global structure and strategies
Local services and customization
Multicultural teams

Multinational
Expanded manufacturing and sales in overseas locations
Separate, semi-independent entities established on-site
Decentralized and close to the customer
Top people are of headquarters cultures; remainder of
    employees of local cultures
Duplications and poor intraorganizational communications

International
Import and export expansion
Corporate headquarters culture dominates
Centralized and run from headquarters
Headquarters separate from other parts of business chain

---

thus moving from the purely domestic stage to the international stage. These companies remained highly centralized and retained the corporate culture of the headquarters office, and suppliers and customers were subject to the operations and values of headquarters. A main weakness of the international stage was the cultural as well as physical distance from the other parts of the business chain.

As customer sales grew in the offshore locations, it became ever more critical for companies to carry out operations such as manufacturing, marketing, and personnel in the local jurisdiction and thereby be more sensitive to local cultural patterns. Companies such as IBM would set up highly decentralized, fairly independent entities, which became IBM-France, IBM-Japan, IBM-South America, and so forth. Hence, in the mid-1900s, companies moved from international to multinational status, operating in many nations so as to capture the benefits of local costs and local tastes. Although this new stage provided companies with the advantage of being more in tune with their customers, it resulted in a variety of corporate disadvantages: duplication, poor intraorganizational communications, each country subsidiary being asked to create and meet its own targets, and competing alone against large and often subsidized local companies (Adler, 1986; Yip, 1992).

Beginning in the 1980s, technology enabled people in organizations to operate worldwide as if residing in one room. This created the possibility of a global company, in which the best of the international (centralized and universal) and multinational (decentralized and differentiated) forms could be combined. Corporate leaders quickly began to recognize the power and competitive advantage of becoming a global company and rushed to globalize. Jack Welch, chief executive officer of General Electric, proclaimed that organizations must "either globalize or die" (p. 27). Ian Mitroff noted that "for all practical purposes, all business today is global. Those individual firms that already understand the new rules of doing business in a world economy will prosper; those that do not will perish" (Marquardt, 1999, p. 241).

A key element of global organizations is that they operate as if the entire world were a single entity. They create a world without walls, made possible by advances in communication and transportation technologies (Moran, Harris, & Stripp, 1993). Global companies are fully integrated; all of their activities link, leverage, and compete on a worldwide scale (Marquardt & Snyder, 1997). They use global sourcing of human resources, capital, technology, facilities, resources, and raw materials. They deem cultural sensitivity to employees, customers, and patterns as critical to the success of the organization (Adler, 1991). Rhinesmith (1993) states that an organization has globalized when it has developed a global corporate culture, strategy, structure, and communications process.

The ability of global companies to take the best of what is global and the best of what is local is what makes them so powerful and leads to such competitive advantages as economies of scope and scale, broader customer base, greater access to human skills and knowledge, as well as financial resources, geographic and political flexibility, and cultural synergies. Very few companies, however, have been able to tap the full potential of being global;

hence, there is a pressing need for competent global OD practitioners who can harness both the universal and the differentiated forces of a global company.

Creating a Global Style for the Organization

The diversity and differentiation created by multicultural, multilocal employees, customers, and suppliers and cause an organizational tension that if left unattended can quickly result in disintegration, conflict, and chaos in the global company. The key challenge for OD practitioners is to build an entity in which there are common values that go beyond culture, universal policies that go beyond local laws, leadership styles that work over boundaries, and operations that can be implemented worldwide and yet retain the cultural richness and diversity of such companies.

An overarching strategy is for OD practitioners to do what systems social psychologists call *structuring*, which provides the connection and order that facilitates the management of and adaptation to the chaos of change inherent in global organizations. Social systems survive when they are able to structure themselves to interact successfully with their environments. A corollary to the systems' ability to differentiate is the corresponding requirement for the system to integrate itself. To maintain its integrity as a system, the global organization must coordinate, communicate, control, and couple its elements.

There is a direct relationship between differentiation and integration. The more that a global company differentiates, the more it has to integrate itself. If it does not, it will lose its identity as a system. Thus, we see a chain of events that has a direct impact on the team and its structuring. The environment becomes more complex and places more demands on the organization. The global organization then responds by increasing its differentiation and increasing the quality and quantity of its integration processes, which results in an increase in the internal system's complexity.

One of the greatest powers of a global company and an important source of its competitive advantage is its diversity. Diversity provides the requisite variety. Without this inherent complexity, global organizations would not survive. They would lack the creativity, energy, and talent to develop the level of problem-solving capability necessary to be successful and thrive in the chaos of the global environment.

These centrifugal forces that create the benefits of diversity must be balanced by a centripetal force that reins in and counterbalances those forces. That centripetal force is the unifying force of globalization. The creation of a global vision and a number of global values, principles, and processes is the structuring glue that holds together the powerful centrifugal forces of diversity.

This global integration can occur through such highly controlling, tightly coupled actions as policy manuals and regulations that are reinforced by aggressive management review. It can also be achieved through loosely coupling mechanisms such as a shared vision and values that allow each element of the system to operate independently within the boundaries of that vision. OD practitioners need to be versatile enough to incorporate as many of these interventions into their OD repertoire.

Although technology enables organizations to be both centralized and decentralized, there are still numerous limitations due to limited, face-to-face contact among members of an organization (see Chapter Twelve). In many cultures, personal contact is essential for the transaction of important business or for any progress in partnerships and promotions. Distance can cause people to feel cut off, be out of the loop, or have a sense of diminished importance. Headquarters culture is often misunderstood or denigrated from afar.

Geographical distance has a clear and direct impact on all forms of communications among team members. It is an impediment to building relationships of trust. Distance obviously makes building trust and good communications much more difficult because people tend to be less direct and more constrained in their personal interactions. Co-located teams are less likely to squabble since colocation usually increases trust and reduces miscommunication.

Distance also affects coordination and control. Problem solving is more difficult as individuals have more difficulty in knowing and understanding each other's styles of decision making. In addition, it becomes much harder to develop cohesiveness and share a common vision of the organization's work and its products.

Most common media are linear, which may be appropriate for certain types of information sharing, such as logical stream-progress reports, data, and logistical information. However, linear modes cannot communicate the collage of information one encounters by walking into another person's office and conversing face to face. Managing and meeting from a distance results in managing by charts rather than by walking about.

And if the communications format chosen is less context rich, then some cultures will find that extremely uncomfortable. Relying on electronic communications that strip everything but the message may leave too much open to inference. High-context cultures will be less comfortable interacting from a distance.

Practice Tips

1. Recognize the polarizing tensions of universalism and differentiation inherent in global companies.
2. Develop interventions and strategies that enable organizations to globalize appropriate operations, functions, processes, and policies.
3. Understand how to use technology to bridge cultural and distance barriers.

Recently, Whirlpool, headquartered in Benton Harbor, Michigan, acquired the $2 billion appliance division of Philips Gloeilampenfabrieken N.V., headquartered in the Netherlands. In one fell swoop, Whirlpool had gone from an almost exclusively domestic company to a company with 40 percent of its operations overseas. With the Philips purchase, it had suddenly become the largest home appliance company in the world.

The significance of the challenge could be seen by the fact that many of the U.S. senior managers did not even have passports. Yet Whirlpool leadership was acutely aware of the critical importance of the Dutch and American companies' becoming an integrated global corporation.

Under the guidance of its president and CEO, Dave Whitwam, and the internal OD staff, Whirlpool quickly began the process of integrating the forces of diverse products, processes, cultures, languages, and people. A key OD intervention was the planning and management of the company's first global conference. Top executives from sixteen countries in Whirlpool's European and North American operations attended. The theme of the conference was "Winning Through Quality Leadership: One Global Vision."

Four major goals were identified:

- Advance a unified vision of the company's future.
- Instill the idea of embracing the future as one global company.
- Establish a keen sense of responsibility within the leadership group for creating the company's future.
- Identify and initiate explicit steps toward integrating various activities and ideas throughout Whirlpool's worldwide operations into a unified whole.

Encouraging cultural mix among the managers was deemed crucial. The problem is that at typical international conferences, managers gravitate toward their own cultural cocoons. Planners built in events to help managers get beyond their own national backgrounds and language. Emphasis was on meeting and getting to know their new global colleagues and developing trust in working with and learning from them. Together, they could better focus on critical, challenging issues such as the Whirlpool vision, strategic planning, and quality.

During the conference, managers were invited to identify which major areas of the company's operations could be improved. Following discussions in small groups, two hundred areas were identified. These were then boiled down to fifteen topics, such as global management reporting systems, global quality initiatives, development of a global corporate talent pool, and concept-to-consumer-product delivery cycles. Fifteen cross-functional and multinational groups, called Whirlpool One Company Challenge Teams, were then formed to examine these fifteen topics.

Whirlpool people felt that this first global conference was so successful that it launched the company ahead in time by an estimated three to five years in the integration of its global management team and saved the company millions of dollars in the process, thanks to planning and interventions of the OD staff.

Incorporating Cultural Components in International OD

The complementary challenge to universalizing elements of the global company is for OD practitioners to encourage and incorporate the differentiating cultures that inhabit the global organization.

Because cultures cause people to see reality very differently, they are a challenge to OD practitioners. Each of us believes that our perception of reality is the correct one. Culture, which we learned at our mother's knee, leads us to believe that our way of thinking, acting, and doing things is the only rational way of thinking, acting, and doing. To suggest or impose another way of seeing and acting can seem strange, ridiculous, or even unfair to someone of another culture (Abdullah, 1996).

Western (the United Sates, Canada, northern Europe, Australia, and New Zealand) and non-Western (the rest of the world) cultures have created a number of clear distinctions in the way people think and act, how they perceive the world around them, and how they live their lives. Table 13.1 lists some of the value differences between these two macrocultures.

These different ways of thinking and acting affect how leaders and workers from different cultures participate in organizational life and accept OD consultation. Five key dimensions have the strongest impact on OD practice.

Leadership Roles and Expectations

Western managers are taught to employ a participative, democratic style of leadership. Everyone is encouraged to express their opinion in order for the goals of the organization to be achieved. We prefer the impersonal authority of mutually agreed-on goals and objectives rather than the arbitrary power of a superior. Disagreeing with a manager is not uncommon, and followers are expected to take the initiative. Attempts are made to minimize inequality through legal and political means. Our organizations tend to be flatter, and power is more decentralized. Managers must earn respect; it is not automatically granted.

Table 13.1. Examples of Western and Non-Western Values.

Western Values	Non-Western Values
Individualism	Collectivism, group
Achievement	Modesty
Equality, egalitarian	Hierarchy
Winning	Collaboration, harmony
Guilt (internal self-control)	Shame (external control)
Pride	Saving face
Respect for results	Respect for status, ascription
Respect for competence	Respect for elders
Time is money	Time is life
Action, doing	Being, acceptance
Systematic, mechanistic	Humanistic
Tasks	Relationships, loyalty
Informal	Formal
Directness, assertiveness	Indirectness
Future, change	Past, tradition
Control	Fate
Specific, linear	Holistic
Verbal	Nonverbal

These roles and expectations relative to leaders are less common in many other parts of world, where leadership may be more hierarchical and accepted. Managers are expected to make decisions rather than work out the problem with subordinates. Work may not easily bypass a chain of command. There may be a clear hierarchy based on status—age, sex, family, or title—that may discourage lower-level workers from airing their views freely lest they be considered as disrespectful or be seen "as the nail that sticks out." Power and authority are centralized, and organizational structure—in terms of highly demarcated levels—is tightly controlled. A leader may need to act in a certain formal way; otherwise, he or she may lose credibility.

> *Practice Tips*
> 1. Recognize that leadership roles and ways of being effective vary from culture to culture and affect the manner in which people and teams work and are led.
> 2. The OD consultant who lacks a high-level title, education, or status may have difficulty working in a hierarchical culture.
> 3. Different cultures have different protocols and action chains for reporting to managers.

Individualism and Groups

A number of cultural research studies have determined that the United States is the most individualistic culture in the world (Hofstede, 1991; Trompenaars, 1994). The rights of individuals are often seen as being more important than the common good of the community. We place a high value on independence, and obligations between people are few. Tasks are valued over relationships. Therefore, the mixing of people of differing ages, genders, roles, and other dimensions fits in with the Western values of egalitarianism, equality, and informality. We like variety, different perspectives, new ideas, and the give-and-take among differing groups. Competence of fellow group members is more important than rank or status.

Most other cultures of the world, however, are more group oriented or collectivist. People in these cultures tend to subordinate individual interests for the good of group interests. Groups protect their members in exchange for loyalty and obedience. Personal identity is based in the social network to which one belongs. Thus, harmony is more valued than speaking one's mind. The mixing of people of differing status groups may oppose their sense of hierarchy and respect or acceptance of differences. Mixing may be seen as a means of undermining authority and power in the workplace. It may even cause embarrassment, confusion, and loss of face.

Practice Tips

1. Although individual rights are important, recognize that the common good of the group supersedes the needs of individuals in many cultures.
2. Mixing individuals regardless of status, age, or gender may prevent data collection or OD interventions from being successful.

Communications

The expressive communication styles found in Latin American, Middle Eastern, and Southern and Eastern European cultures is considered a highly valued art form. People from these countries are less concerned with the precision of communication than with the establishment and maintenance of personal and social connections. People hiding emotions are seen as "dead fish." Voices are raised in joy, anger, and other intense emotions. There is much more hugging and touching than in Western cultures.

The instrumental style of communication found in some other parts of the world is problem centered, impersonal, and goal oriented. What is said is placed above how something is said. Stress is placed on the accuracy of the communication rather than its appropriateness or style. The primary objective is to reach a factual, objective, unemotional conclusion that leads to actions. Displays of emotion are perceived as lacking in professionalism or rationality, as being out of control and thus embarrassing. Informal cultures, on the other hand, are more direct and candid, and they want to establish a friendly, relaxed atmosphere when doing business. Minimal value is placed on custom and hierarchical status.

These different styles of communications result in enormous cultural variability, ranging from exaggeration of desire or intent in the Middle East to silence and pauses during the communication interactions in Asian cultures.

Communications can also range from being high context (environment and nonverbals do much of the communications), as occurs in most Asian, Arab, and Latin cultures, to low context (the words spoken or written are the primary locus of communication), as is the pattern in the United States, Canada, and northern Europe.

Practice Tips

1. A high-context person will find a low-context person's directness uncomfortable and rude. A low-context person will often find a high-context person shrewd, hard to read, and unclear.
2. In elaborate cultures, speakers are expected to produce rich and expressive language, often through the elaborate use of metaphors and similes. In instrumental cultures, the speaker is expected to use silences and pauses to engage in understatement.
3. In personal-style cultures, status plays a back role to informality, whereas in a contextual-style culture, the status and role of the speakers are paramount.
4. Consultants with a direct type of culture must develop a high tolerance for ambiguity when working in an indirect culture.
5. Continued direct eye contact is considered to be rude in many Asian cultures.
6. When gathering or reporting data or suggesting strategy, it is important to consider the amount of context available through different types of interaction.

Decision Making and Handling Conflict

Western culture is much more action oriented than are most other cultures. We encourage people to make decisions and take action. We enjoy tasks more than relationships, achievement more than discussion. We also like to do things that have immediate utilitarian value. Time is money and should not be wasted on anything that does not achieve results.

Other cultures may give people much less authority to act. In Arabic cultures, the leader may consult with others for advice but will then make the decision alone. Those strongly influenced by the Islamic religion are much more aware and respectful of the role of Allah in making decisions. African cultures, partly because of their educational system, tend to be more imitative than creative. Also, the gap in terms of education and skill level between management and other employees in African firms has been the widest in the world (Hellreigel, Slocum, & Woodman, 2001). These factors may cause African managers to be reluctant sometimes to delegate authority, share information, or involve subordinates in decision-making process.

In many Asian cultures, people are much more circuitous in selecting a course of action. Social and political sensitivity may influence the choice of a solution, and the action taken cannot cause someone to lose face. Hence, even if the group thought it a proper decision, they would desert or disavow the decision later.

Direct cultures like that in the United States tend to be explicit and frank when presenting facts or negotiating and dealing with conflict. We encourage individual opinions to be stated and view conflict as natural. We say, "Let's deal with this now," or, "Give it to me straight." Conflict is dealt with from the top by means of power and force.

Many other cultures of the world are much more indirect in conveying disagreement or criticism (see Table 13.2). There is a preference for implicit communication and conflict avoidance. Indirect cultures use a mix of conflict avoidance and third parties to handle conflict. Much indirectness in communication is made in the desire to save face, protect honor, and avoid shame. In such cultures, to say no directly, whether in negotiations or in rejecting ideas and advice from a consultant, is very difficult, if not impossible. The desire to avoid direct refusal is a cultural trait rooted in courtesy and respect. Wigglesworth (1987), for example, notes the relative absence of dialogue and debate in China and Japan.

Status is also important in determining the degree to which a person can state an opinion. Many African societies have a rigid, hierarchical, bureaucratic structure with great status differences and extreme deference to authority. In conservative Islamic cultures, men and women cannot even be in the same room, much less exchange ideas on an equal level. Age almost always comes before competence when deciding who is to be the most important member in the group.

Table 13.2. Indirect Communication Strategies.

Strategy	Description
Mediation	A third person is used as a go-between.
Refraction	Statements intended for person A are made to person B while person A is present.
Covert revelation	The person portrays himself or herself as a messenger for someone else or allows notes to fall into the hands of another party.
Correspondence	Communication is written so as to avoid direct interaction.
Anticipation	Being understated, unobtrusive, and empathetic accommodates the unspoken needs of the other person.
Ritual	Rituals help maintain control of uncertain situations.

Practice Tips

1. Be culturally and politically sensitive to the membership in groups. If in doubt, check with a local member of the organization.
2. Recognize hierarchy and individual status when seeking data and giving feedback.
3. Criticism can be taken very personally in many cultures. Personal relationships can become strained as the criticized person has lost face.
4. In some cultures, young people in a group will hesitate to speak out if older people are in the group because age may be seen as being more important than competence.
5. Status may be important in determining the degree to which a person can state an opinion.

Balancing Competitive and Cooperative Styles

What motivates workers and learners differs significantly from culture to culture. How we work and learn with each other varies from being very competitive to being cooperative. Competitive cultures place an emphasis on being assertive and focus on results, success, and achievements, especially as they relate to tasks and rewards. Work is highly valued and determines one's worth, value, and importance. Cooperative cultures place a high value and emphasis on consensual decision making. Employees are hired not only for their skills but also for their ability to fit into the group, promote its shared values, facilitate communication, demonstrate loyalty, and contribute to the overall work environment.

Practice Tips

1. Identify the motivating factors of the culture in which you are working.
2. Develop appropriate activities that build on the work styles of all the different members of the organization, and not necessarily on what motivates you.
3. Competition between groups may be much more comfortable than competition within groups.

Building Cultural Synergies at Nokia

Nokia leaders and OD staff recognize the importance sensitizing all of its employees to operating in the multicultural world of a global telecommunications company. Being able to work with people from other cultural backgrounds is crucial to the company's success, according to Pentti Sydanmaanlakka, a senior OD manager at Nokia. A key OD intervention has been to increase global job rotation, which is considered the best way to acculturate and globalize employees. A global human resource steering committee meets regularly to establish global as well as local policies and procedures.

Impact of Culture on the OD Process

Cultural values and practices affect every step of the OD process. How the OD practitioner communicates, facilitates, handles conflict is affected by the cultural context. OD practitioners must be cognizant of some specific cultural nuances when implementing the entry, data collection, and feedback stages of consulting.

Entry and Agreement

In the United States, parties may quite quickly reach agreement, and a written contract is immediately prepared. In many other cultures, such as Arab, Chinese, and Japanese, this entry agreement can last months and require approvals from numerous levels and individuals within the organization. Global OD consultants must be exceedingly patient, allowing plenty of time for laying the groundwork and being ready to show trust and acceptance in numerous ways. A person shows sincerity and seriousness by observing appropriate customs and rituals, such as dress, greetings, business card exchange, forms of address, and gift giving. Relationships tend to build more slowly, but once they are developed, they may be deep and permanent. Chinese people, for example, have highly formalized business communications, whereas Americans are more informal.

Practice Tips

1. Recognize the importance of formality and hierarchy at the entry and contracting stages.
2. Be patient, and accept differing perspectives on time.
3. Communications should follow explicit protocols, commonly understood definitions of business processes, jargon, and cultural symbols.

Data Collection and Delivery

The collection and presentation of data for American OD practitioners is quite clear, direct, and straightforward. However, in many other cultures, people may be much more inhibited relative to providing information that might be construed as being negative about another person and will appear to be evasive in their responses. For Arabs, "Allah loveth not the speaking ill of anyone."

Hence, there may be difficulty in getting accurate information, especially bad news.

Asking for feedback and encouraging self-analysis may work among Westerners who value frankness and openness (see Chapters Two and Three), but would be disastrous in Asia, where a much higher value is placed on hiding one's feelings and thoughts and not prying into the feelings and thoughts of others. For example, it may be very difficult for members of some Asian cultures to tell Westerners that things are going wrong.

Conveying of the data may also be affected by cultural norms and expectations. Due to protocol and hierarchical norms, data may sometimes need to be provided first, if not only, to senior members of the organization; in many Asian, Arab, and Latin cultures, they are traditionally the ones who go behind closed doors to make the final decisions after acquiring information from others.

Practice Tips

1. Participants may tend to base their response on what they think you want rather than what they actually believe or feel.
2. Avoid forcing people to respond with a no. Rather, through the use of questions, professionals need to distinguish a variety of contextual cues as to the level of agreement or disagreement felt by the clients.
3. The use of organizational surveys (see Chapter Four), which are more anonymous and not so precise about individual behaviors, may be more effective than one-on-one interviews (see Chapter Five).
4. Be aware of the cultural priorities of being clear and being polite. Polite cultures are concerned about hurting feelings, minimizing imposition, and avoiding negative evaluation by the other person. Clear culture wants clarity and effectiveness.

Feedback and Collaboration

Leading proponents of process consultation such as Schein (1988) and Block (1999) emphasize the importance of the collaborative process (fifty-fifty sharing of responsibility throughout the consulting stages) and authenticity about what one is observing or has discovered. These behaviors may be less effective with cultures in which the consultant is expected to be the expert who will tell clients what the right thing to do is, who should be fully responsible for the various stages of consultation, and who should not be so direct and confrontational as to cause people to lose face and dignity.

Practice Tips

1. Understand the importance of maintaining harmony.
2. Discuss and explain your approach to consulting, and develop arrangements that allow you to maintain your integrity and skills and yet respect the needs and values of your client.
3. Appreciate the indirectness and formality of many cultures.
4. Be careful not to be seen as too threatening or a source for causing anyone to lose face.
5. Pose questions to the group as a whole rather than to individuals.
6. Emphasize the individual and group disclosures and feedback are confidential to the group.

Conclusion

Practicing OD around the world is difficult and complex because of the challenges in attempting to understand and work in a cultural setting that might be quite different from one's own and using a methodology that is built on different premises and values. Nevertheless, cultural differences need not diminish the use of OD or its potency across all cultures and in all global organizations. By modifying and adapting elements of OD without losing their purpose and power, practitioners can work anywhere. Instead of seeing these cultural differences as barriers, we should see them as the source of synergy that contributes to new perspectives and new ways for OD to be globally successful.

References

Abdullah, A. (1996). *Going "glocal."* Kuala Lumpur, Malaysia: MIM Press.
Adler, N. (1986). *International dimensions of organizational behavior.* Boston: Kent.

Block, P. (1999). *Flawless consulting.* San Francisco: Jossey-Bass.

Hellreigel, D., Slocum, J., & Woodman, R. W. (2001). *Organizational behavior* (9th ed.). Cincinnati, OH: South-Western.

Hofstede, G. (1991). *Cultures and organizations.* New York: McGraw-Hill.

Marquardt, M. (1999). *The global advantage.* Houston: Gulf.

Marquardt, M., & Engel, D. (1993). *Global human resource development.* Upper Saddle River, NJ: Prentice Hall.

Marquardt, M., & Snyder, N. (1997). How companies go global. *International Journal of Training and Development, 1,* 104–117.

Moran, R., Harris, P., & Stripp, W. (1993). *Developing the global organization.* Houston: Gulf.

Rhinesmith, S. (1993). *A manager's guide to globalization.* Burr Ridge, IL: Irwin.

Schein, E. (1988). *Process consultation.* Reading, MA: Addison-Wesley.

Trompenaars, F. (1994). *Riding the waves of culture: Understanding diversity in global business.* Burr Ridge, IL: Irwin.

Wigglesworth, D. (1987). Is OD basically Anglo-Saxon? *Leadership and Organization Development Journal, 8*(2), 29–31.

Yip, G. (1992). *Total global strategy.* Upper Saddle River, NJ: Prentice Hall.

CHAPTER 14

Evaluating the Impact of Organization Development Interventions

Jennifer W. Martineau
Hallie Preskill

One of the most important yet often overlooked elements of any organization development (OD) intervention is the evaluation of impact. Research has shown that the evaluation of OD interventions is sorely lacking (Golembiewski & Sun, 1990; Woodman & Wayne, 1985). This chapter will address some of the challenges associated with the evaluation of OD interventions and will provide strategies for designing effective OD evaluation measures and systems. We hope that readers will, after reading this chapter, be able and motivated to employee evaluation effectively and appropriately with their own OD interventions.

Why is it so difficult to find high-quality evaluation in OD interventions? That question has been noted particularly by Golembiewski and Sun (1990) in a report regarding quality of working life (QWL) implementation, where the rigor of evaluations in QWL interventions was questioned. In the cases studied, the authors cited the evaluations as lacking rigor and being poorly designed, resulting in the findings being significantly biased toward being positive, or supportive, of the intervention. More often than not, the lack of high-quality evaluation is due to misconceptions on the part of OD practitioners.

Why is it important to evaluate the impact of OD efforts? As with other emerging fields of practice, the competition is increasing for those who perform OD services. In addition, clients are growing more sophisticated regarding their expectations for change initiatives, such as those characterized as OD. Therefore, evaluating the impact of these initiatives enables managers of OD efforts to demonstrate their value, resulting in a greater understanding of what does and does not work with OD efforts in general, as well as providing specific evidence that can lend an OD initiative's designers a leg up on the competition.

Challenges to Evaluating OD Efforts

As we have reviewed the literature and considered the status and nature of OD in today's organizations, we have come to understand that there are many reasons that OD efforts have not often been evaluated. Comments such as the following have not served evaluation well:

> Evaluation can be a consultant's least favorite part of an OD project. Some consultants have difficulty finding the time and energy to evaluate their work. . . . Evaluation can divert consultants from their intervention tasks, reduce their income opportunities, or even eliminate some of their favorite programs and activities from the entire change program. . . . The safest course seen by consultants in some situations . . . is to carefully limit, if not eliminate, evaluation efforts [Jackson & Manning, 1994, p. 5].

> The evaluation process of OD practice can be compared to an annual physical examination—everyone agrees that it should be done, but no one, except a highly motivated researcher, wants to go to the trouble and expense of making it happen [Burke, 1987, p. 138].

To understand better how some OD consultants have come to these beliefs, we discuss several challenges that have influenced the field's interest in and ability to conduct credible and useful evaluations.

Consultants' Lack of Evaluation Training

Most OD consultants learn their craft either through graduate education or by working in the field and taking workshops from time to time. However, OD practitioners rarely receive education and training in the discipline of evaluation; many may not even be aware that there is such a discipline. For example, it is likely that few OD consultants know that the American Evaluation Association, the Canadian Evaluation Association, and the Australasian Evaluation Association exist (as do as many others in Africa, Latin America, and Europe). Nor are many aware that the evaluation profession has developed its own set of ethical guidelines for practice (Sanders, 1994; Newman, Scheirer, Shadish, & Wye, 1995). Although those who obtain graduate degrees in OD most likely have a good grounding in action research designs and methods (see Chapter One), it is unlikely that they have been introduced to the theories, philosophies, models, and practices of evaluation.

In fact, several published articles on evaluation and OD use the words *research* and *evaluation* interchangeably. As a result, when OD consultants conduct what they refer to as evaluations, their approach typically exemplifies a research study rather than an evaluation. This confusion leads to a muddying of the purposes and uses of the evaluation's processes and results. Hence, the goals of evaluation will be harder to achieve when an OD intervention is evaluated using a research mental model and approach. Without understanding the differences between research and evaluation and how their practices differ, evaluation studies are less likely to produce useful information for the client.

Overreliance on Quantitative, Experimental, and Positivist Designs

OD's foundation in the behavioral sciences has significantly affected (and limited) how research and evaluation studies are approached. As French and Bell (1995) write, "OD programs apply scientific and practice principles from the behavioral sciences to intervene in the human and social processes of organizations. Although human behavior in organizations is far from being an exact science, there are lawful patterns of events that produce effectiveness and ineffectiveness" (p. 104). The assumptions underlying this definition of OD have led researchers and evaluators to use primarily a quantitative, experimental, and positivist approach to understanding the impact of their interventions. In this respect, the evaluator or OD practitioner develops hypotheses, establishes comparison groups randomizing where possible, controls variables, and designs the study for replication and generalization purposes. In their quest to prove the impact of their interventions, OD researchers have consistently called for improvements in statistical tests, determining which variables to control, and the elimination of bias (Woodman & Wayne, 1985). The use of qualitative approaches and methods has typically been discounted as not being scientific enough.

Articles written about evaluations of OD interventions most often mirror a research perspective and approach, and seldom explain the purpose of the evaluation, the key evaluation questions, the political context of the evaluation, or how the evaluation's results will be (or were) used, and they do not refer to evaluation models. The normative stance that has guided evaluation in the OD field has assumed that evaluations should be objective and scientific and lead to the generation of knowledge (Burke, 1987). Taking such a narrow view of evaluation has limited the usefulness of the resulting information and OD consultants' ability to understand and demonstrate the impact of their work.

Perceived Lack of Time for Conducting Evaluations

When evaluation is perceived to be an add-on activity, done at the end of an OD intervention and costing extra, it will fall victim to the "there's no time" and "there's no money" mantras. Although it is certainly true that evaluation work takes time and resources, saying that there is no time is more a function of viewing evaluation as a low priority than in not having the time or resources. We have discovered that when certain tasks and activities are considered high priority within an organization, the time and money are usually found. The perceived lack of these resources is generally related to a lack of understanding about the value of evaluation.

On the other hand, those who do understand and appreciate the role and value of evaluation may be challenged by the fact that the impact of many OD interventions may not be realized for months or years after the intervention, long after the OD consultant has moved on to other projects. As Rothwell, Sullivan, and McLean (1995) remind us, "OD is long range in perspective. It is not a 'quick-fix' strategy for solving short-term performance problems" (p. 7). For external OD consultants in particular, this poses a formidable challenge if there is no long-term relationship with the client organization.

No Request by the Client

Evaluation within organizations is a relatively new concept. It grew up in the 1960s, born out of federal social program legislation, and has since become increasingly widespread in nonprofit, educational, and other government programs and organizations. It is slowly making its way into the corporate sector and becoming a more common function within human resource development (HRD) and other departments in many Fortune 500 companies. In smaller organizations, HRD practitioners are being asked to demonstrate their own evaluation knowledge and skills. Yet most corporate clients are unaware of the field of evaluation, the usefulness of evaluation processes, or what constitutes good evaluation practice. As a result, many are unclear about the potential benefits of evaluation and are unlikely to commission evaluations of OD interventions. In addition, those interested in organizational learning have not quite made the connection between evaluation and learning. Thus, it is easy for OD consultants to ignore this important component of practice.

Change: A Moving Target

When and what to evaluate pose several challenges for OD practitioners. For example, the following questions need to be addressed:

- At what point might we expect the intervention to affect change?
- Do we evaluate the intervention while it is in progress or only afterward?
- Is the evaluation formative (for improvement purposes, dur-

ing or after the intervention) or summative (to determine outcomes, once the intervention has concluded)?

- Should the focus be on individual, group, or organizational effects—or both?
- When might change be detected? What will it look like? Will we know it when we see it?

In addition to nailing down the answers to these questions, identifying all the measurable variables in advance is problematic. Inherent in OD work is the unpredictability of the effects of any intervention. Often the implementation of one intervention causes ripples throughout the organization far beyond what was planned for or anticipated. This can be a very exciting and rewarding effect, but it makes the job of evaluation even more complicated. Such a situation begs the question, "How do we evaluate those things we can't anticipate?"

The Nature of OD Work: A Solo Act

The "lone ranger" approach to evaluation has been enjoying less popularity recently. Increasingly, evaluators are calling for more collaborative, participatory, and empowerment approaches and methods of evaluation where intended users and other stakeholders are closely involved in the evaluation's design and implementation (Preskill & Caracelli, 1997). Studies have shown that evaluation results are more likely to be used if intended users and stakeholders understand the evaluation process and have developed a vested interest in making sure the findings will be useful (Patton, 1997). This is true for both internal and external evaluators. OD, however, is still conducted by individuals, who rarely seek to empower others with OD skills and knowledge. This shift to working more collaboratively with organization members in evaluating OD interventions could be challenging if OD practitioners are used to working alone.

Fear of Evaluation

The very word *evaluation* causes some people to cringe, shrink with fear, or even hide. It is often perceived to be something that is done *to* them rather than *for* them. This feeling might be valid when program evaluation is confused with personnel evaluation or when organization members fear that the results of an OD intervention or program evaluation will be used to terminate their employment or reposition them in the organization. Certainly, a fear of evaluation is sometimes warranted, but it has significantly limited the positive role that evaluation can play.

OD consultants might also shy away from evaluation if they worry that the evaluation results might not show a positive change or impact, which could ultimately affect their future employment or status. When evaluation is not well designed and does not involve stakeholders in its design, this fear is quite understandable.

The Fuzziness of Some OD Intervention Goals

Many OD interventions are initiated because of some trigger event: an imminent merger, a change in leadership, a new product or service, persistent low employee morale, or organizational restructuring, for example. If the OD intervention's goals and objectives are unclear or unfocused, evaluating the impact and effects of the intervention will be difficult. Determining what to evaluate can be the greatest challenge. The good news is that in designing the evaluation, the goals of the initiative are usually greatly clarified.

Nature of OD Theories and Models

A quick perusal of most planned change or OD theories and models will show that evaluation has never been a central construct in OD theory and practice. Although some OD approaches mention evaluation as one phase of an intervention, it is often relegated to the end of the OD cycle (Burke 1987; Rothwell et al., 1995) rather than being integrated into OD practice. Thus, evaluation becomes an event, is product oriented, and is done only if time and money are available. McLean, Sullivan, and Rothwell (1995) observe that although evaluation is part of the action research model that is often used to assess the impact of OD, "it is most often omitted or abbreviated" (p. 311). Nonetheless, they stress the importance of evaluation of OD interventions and are one of the few who provide an OD evaluation model.

Best Practices for Designing Evaluation Measures and Systems

As organizational life becomes more dynamic and complex, it is incumbent on OD practitioners and researchers to consider the role of evaluation in OD more seriously. If "organizational development is concerned with helping organizations manage and live with change," then "they must have the information and tools required to address the existing organizational challenges" (Walumbwa, 1999, p. 213). Evaluation can easily serve such a role.

Given the many obstacles to evaluating OD initiatives, what is an OD practitioner to do? Some of the best practices for evaluation can be incorporated into OD initiatives in ways that lead to a greater likelihood that the findings will provide useful information on which to make decisions. We examine these practices and provide examples to illustrate how to (and how not to) implement them.

Evaluation Is an Integrated Component of OD Initiatives

The typical timeline of OD interventions looks like this:

NEEDS ASSESSMENT ➤ DESIGN ➤ IMPLEMENTATION

or this:

NEEDS ASSESSMENT ➤ DESIGN ➤ IMPLEMENTATION ➤ EVALUATION

Both leave evaluation out or relegate it to the end of the initiative. Often this framework permits OD practitioners to put off thinking about evaluation until the initiative is well under way.

Contrary to the common perspective that evaluation is something to do at the end of the process, and only if time and money are available, evaluation can most strongly contribute to OD interventions if it is held as a positive, necessary component when designing any OD initiative. It is not something that occurs at the end or something that is done by someone other than the OD team. Rather, it is a piece of the OD initiative that must have the necessary resources to accomplish it, just like any other component.

An example speaks to the value of evaluation in almost every type of intervention. Picture an organizational restructuring that has been under way for six months. In this case, the organization sought the assistance of OD consultants to redesign their organization in a way that was more customer focused. The restructuring was expected to take one year to implement fully, with many interdependent areas of the organization needing to change at different paces from others in order to maintain the level of quality of customer service.

At the early stages of their relationship with the OD consultants, the executive staff said that the organization was losing customers due to lack of flexibility when asked to customize services to meet client needs and the many levels of decision making that must occur before a change from normal service could be made. After spending time interviewing the executive staff and others in the organization, the consultants began work on the plan for restructuring. As requested, the intervention progressed slowly and intentionally, ensuring that each interdependent set of departments was aware of changes to each department and the potential implications for their own department.

At the six-month point, with approximately 75 percent of the restructuring complete, the executive staff wanted to know whether it was making any difference. To accomplish this, the executives began asking customers about their perceptions of the organization's responsiveness. The results indicated that although customers were pleased with the changes they had experienced in the organization's willingness to customize services, the length of time between making a request and receiving the desired services had not improved. In fact, in some cases, it had worsened. What had happened?

Turning the clock back to their early work with the executive staff, the OD consultants realized that they had failed to include key organizational members in the needs assessment and failed to uncover some of the underlying issues. They had no spoken with customers either. By employing an evaluation framework at the outset of the initiative, the consultants would have identified the critical stakeholders and asked, "If the restructuring is successful, what will you be doing differently when it is complete?" and "What factors might stand in the way of a successful organization?" Had they asked these questions, they would have discovered that the organization's structure was only part of the problem. Another part of the problem was that in some areas, decision makers lacked the experience to make quick decisions, regardless of the way in which decisions were handed to them. In addition, the organization was less clear regarding how to customize some of their services even when they could make a quick decision to do it. Therefore, training and design of services were needed in addition to the restructuring. By asking the questions that focused attention on the concrete, desirable results, the consultants were able to uncover problems that had not surfaced when they had addressed the issue from a more abstract, future-focused perspective.

Once these problems were uncovered, they were addressed through a slight redesign of the initiative. The costs of the initiative and its duration increased somewhat, but the organization was able to achieve its goals in the end.

In this case, the act of designing an evaluation prior to the initiative could have saved the organization both time and money on the initiative itself, in addition to hastening its effective customer service, which undoubtedly would have increased client revenues down the road. According to Jackson and Manning (1994), an evaluation designed at the outset of an OD intervention can fill the needs for clarity and validity in assessing the results of the initiative. In the example, evaluation could have shaped the OD initiative at all stages, allowing the OD professionals to improve the services rendered and learn about how the initiative was being implemented at various points during its life cycle.

Evaluation Takes an Inquiry Approach

A second best practice in evaluating OD initiatives is to use an approach that integrates the evaluation and allows full buy-in by the key stakeholders. To truly integrate evaluation into practice, evaluation becomes a process of asking questions and learning continuously within an organization. Sometimes evaluation is seen as an activity that levies a judgment on the OD intervention. An expert comes in and designs an evaluation that describes the relative success or failure of an intervention. Following a presentation of the evaluation results, the outcomes and suggestions from the evaluation go unused. The reason is that the evaluation typically ends there. But when an evaluation is used to its full value, its results can inform an organization regarding next steps rather than become a report that sits on a shelf. To get there, evaluation must begin by understanding the needs of the various key stakeholders around an organization and designing a process to assess change relevant to these needs. The previous example demonstrated just that and could have been improved using a process known as evaluative inquiry, which is

> an ongoing process for investigating and understanding critical organizational issues. It is an approach to learning that is fully integrated with an organization's work practices, and as such, it engenders (a) organization members' interest and ability in exploring critical issues using evaluation logic, (b) organization members' involvement in evaluative processes, and (c) the personal and professional growth of individuals within the organization [Preskill & Torres, 1999, p. 1–2].

In performing evaluation in an inquiry mode, say Preskill and Torres, both the evaluator and the intervention's sponsors become key stakeholders in the evaluation, designing and carrying out the evaluation and then interpreting and making use of the results. They become partners in the evaluation in an effort to improve the intervention and make decisions for action. Both the evaluation and the OD initiative are richer when this type of process is used.

Evaluation Is Both Summative and Formative

Whereas most OD interventions place evaluation at the end, best practice would employ a design that assesses the intervention at multiple points in time and provides different types of feedback. Patton (1994) discusses developmental evaluation: evaluation begun before a program is designed, with the evaluator working side by side with the design team to collect the data necessary for making design decisions (including, but not limited to, needs assessment information). Evaluation should also provide feedback to the OD initiative throughout (formative) as well as after (summative) its application.

It is possible to take the appropriate steps in designing an evaluation prior to the start of an initiative, but then design the evaluation in a way that does not help the development of the initiative. Such evaluations are known as summative; they provide data that illustrate only whether the initiative succeeded at its conclusion. The most valuable evaluations contain both summative and formative components, with the latter providing feedback along the way that can help modify the initiative as it is being implemented. In the previous example, the interviews conducted at the six-month point were formative. The feedback enabled key stakeholders and the consultants to get a sense of customers' current experiences with the organization and make additional interventions that would be necessary to implement the initiative fully.

Truly effective evaluations are designed in a multiphase manner that allows key stakeholders to (1) assess needs, (2) check along the way and make any necessary changes to the initiative while it is still under way, and (3) demonstrate the success of the initiative. This design allows for improved chances for the success of this initiative, over and above what was possible when the initiative began.

Evaluation Captures All Relevant Aspects of Change

Evaluation should address the qualitative as well as the quantitative, the subjective as well as the objective. The methods used should be selected to fit the OD initiative and its objectives. Some OD professionals tend to overrely on quantitative, experimental, positivist evaluation designs. These evaluations seek proof of the impact of the intervention, but this evidence is often evasive. Nevertheless, certain situations may call for particular types of evaluation. For example, evaluators may want to use group discussions (see Chapter Five) or open-ended questionnaires when clients are available and willing to discuss or write their perspectives openly and when trust and safety have been established (Jackson & Manning, 1994). On the other hand, when the data presented need to be visibly objective and impartial, methods such as standardized survey questionnaires (such as Likert-type scales; see Chapter Four) or objective performance outcome measures (such as a decrease in customer service complaints, as in the example) might be the preferred method (Jackson & Manning, 1994). In most situations, however, it is likely that the OD initiative can benefit from a combination of qualitative and quantitative, as well as objective and subjective, evaluation methods.

In the case example, a promising evaluation would include interviews with customers, customer satisfaction questionnaires, counts of customer complaints filed, interviews with relevant employees and key stakeholders, and observations of customer service interactions by the evaluator. The blend of methods and linkages among the types of data collected (see Chapters Two and Six) serves to provide a more complete and balanced picture of the changes that occur (or do not occur) as a result of the OD initiative.

Evaluation Takes a Systems Approach

Although using the appropriate evaluation methods is important, evaluation is really more about the process of learning than about the specific methods being used. It examines the impact of the initiative on individuals, groups, and organizations, including the relationships among them. A comprehensive, systems-oriented evaluation begins with the objectives of the initiative. These objectives address the ways in which the initiative is intended to change individuals and groups within the organization, as well as the organization itself. Once the objectives are identified, it is necessary to break them down into observable or measurable outcomes at each level. Through this process, it is possible to identify the overall system of learning and change.

In the case example, the overall objective of the initiative is to improve customer service through increasing the ability to meet customer-specific requests and reduce time spent in decision making. Drilling down another level, we find that individuals are expected to receive, process, and respond to client requests in a timely manner. In some cases, these three steps may be fairly simple and straightforward; in others, the requests may require customization of services to meet clients' needs. To accomplish this, the organization must first have determined types of allowable customization, enabling the individual client representatives to put together a customized client service without going before a decision-making body. In the few cases where the client request goes beyond the bounds of these allowable types of customization, the organization needs to have teams of decision makers readily available to create and approve the desired service. Hence, the evaluation design needs to be able to capture not only the extent to which client requests yield appropriate responses more efficiently, but also where and how this response is being enabled. This assessment must also examine the relationship among the steps in the process and determine how one step affects the others. This systems approach to the evaluation will produce learnings that are useful; any possible modifications to the initiative can be easily targeted and identified.

Evaluation Is Different for Every OD Intervention

Finally, it is important to know that there is no single best evaluation plan that works across the board; evaluation always must be customized to the organization and the initiative. Hence, it is not possible to produce here the ideal evaluation plan for all OD initiatives. Therefore, we have provided best practices that describe how an evaluation's design, implementation, and findings can contribute to understanding the impact of an OD intervention.

Critical to identifying the most appropriate evaluation for a situation is knowing the key stakeholders, the objectives of the initiative, and the types of data that will answer the key evaluation questions. It certainly is not necessary to create an extremely comprehensive evaluation when the key stakeholders are using the evaluation only to show that they have attempted to demonstrate the initiative's value and know that there are few pressures to truly understanding the process or the outcomes of the initiative. In this case, a simple evaluation demanding only low effort may be most appropriate. However, when an initiative is the first in a multiphase process, a more comprehensive evaluation would be in order—one that can reveal the effective and ineffective components of the process, as well as its outcomes in an effort to inform the subsequent phases.

Conclusion

The intent of this chapter was twofold: to unmask some of the myths that prevent OD practitioners from using evaluation in their initiatives and to provide best practices as a means of helping OD practitioners consider the effective use of evaluation. We also highlighted a few additional tips for conducting evaluation.

Organization development and evaluation are complementary activities. If they are used appropriately, OD practitioners may discover that evaluation is an invaluable component of OD work.

Practice Tips

1. Identify all key stakeholders while the initiative is still being designed. These people should have a stake in the success of the initiative, as well as in the effectiveness and use of the findings of the evaluation.
2. Ask critical questions of all key stakeholders, enabling them to determine the desired results of the initiative and steps they will take depending on the results of the evaluation.
3. Identify the objectives of the initiative—both the overall, intended outcomes as well as any outcomes that may appear along the way.
4. Determine the needs for the evaluation. What are key stakeholders expecting to learn from it?
5. Work with key stakeholders to design the evaluation.
6. Select evaluation methods that make the most sense for the initiative and for the context within which it resides.
7. Whenever possible, use a combination of evaluation methods.
8. Design the evaluation to assess the effects of the intervention using a systems framework, including all intended targets of change as well as the relationships among these targets.
9. Include key stakeholders in the interpretation of the evaluation data.
10. Use the evaluation data to create an action plan for modifications to the initiative, as well as parameters for future initiatives.

References

Burke, W. W. (1987). *Organization development: A normative view.* Reading, MA: Addison-Wesley.

French, W. L., & Bell, C. H., Jr. (1995). *Organization development: Behavioral science interventions for organization improvement* (5th ed.). Upper Saddle River, NJ: Prentice Hall.

Golembiewski, R. T., & Sun, B. (1990). Positive-findings bias in QWL studies: Rigor and outcomes in a large sample. *Journal of Management, 16,* 665–674.

Jackson, C. N., & Manning, M. R. (1994). Evaluation fundamentals and realities. In C. N. Jackson & M. R. Manning (Eds.), *Evaluating organization development interventions* (pp. 5–17). Alexandria, VA: American Society for Training and Development.

McLean, G. N., Sullivan, R., & Rothwell, W. J. (1995). Evaluation. In W. J. Rothwell, R. Sullivan, & G. N. McLean (Eds.), *Practicing organization development: A guide for consultants* (pp. 311–368). San Francisco: Jossey-Bass/Pfeiffer.

Newman, D., Scheirer, M. A., Shadish, W., & Wye, C. (1995). *Guiding principles for evaluators: A report from the AEA task force on guiding principles for evaluators.* Magnolia, AR: American Evaluation Association.

Patton, M. Q. (1994). Developmental evaluation. *Evaluation Practice, 15,* 311–319.

Patton, M. Q. (1997). *Utilization-focused evaluation: The new century text.* Thousand Oaks, CA: Sage.

Preskill, H., & Caracelli, V. (1997). Current and developing conceptions of use: Evaluation and use of topical interest group survey results. *Evaluation Practice, 18,* 209–226.

Preskill, H., & Torres, R. T. (1999). *Evaluative inquiry for learning in organizations.* Thousand Oaks, CA: Sage.

Rothwell, W. J., Sullivan, R., & McLean, G. N. (1995). Introduction. In W. J. Rothwell, R. Sullivan, & G. N. McLean (Eds.), *Practicing organization development: A guide for consultants* (pp. 13–45). San Francisco: Jossey-Bass/Pfeiffer.

Sanders, J. R. (1994). *Joint committee standards for educational evaluation: The program evaluation standards: How to assess evaluations of educational programs* (2nd ed.). Thousand Oaks, CA: Sage.

Walumbwa, F. O. (1999). Power and politics in organizations: Implications for OD professional practice. *Human Resource Development International, 2,* 205–216.

Woodman, R. W., & Wayne, S. J. (1985). An investigation of positive-findings bias in evaluation of organization development interventions. *Academy of Management Journal, 28,* 889–913.

CHAPTER 15

Organization Development Ethics
Reconciling Tensions in OD Values

Gary N. McLean
Susan H. DeVogel

The historical roots of organization development (OD) are found in the social and behavioral sciences, reflecting humanistic values and concerns. Recently, an increased focus on business results has led to changes in how OD is practiced and who practices it, which has invited a reexamination of the assumed set of beliefs of the field. The disconnect between the espoused humanistic values of OD and the bottom-line orientation of most organizations in which the OD consultant practices can often lead to a series of personal conflicts and ethical dilemmas that practitioners must confront and overcome.

In working through these ethical dilemmas, OD practitioners must maintain their integrity while meeting client needs within this changing context, for delivering on both of these conditions is necessary for an OD effort to be truly successful; that is, practitioners must act with integrity *and* provide the client system with value-added services, not one or the other. Therefore, throughout this chapter, the nature of ambiguity and ethical dilemmas in OD will be described, frameworks for thinking about them will be presented, and strategies for resolution will be proposed.

This chapter is based on several premises. First, there are new and increasing pressures on internal and external OD consultants to support interventions aimed at affecting desired business outcomes (for example, sales or profit), sometimes at the expense of individual or team well-being. This extreme bottom-line focus has understandably had an impact on the nature of OD work, since practitioners fundamentally are service providers and must at some level work to please their clients. Unfortunately, this pervasive and heightened focus on business performance, often at all costs, has led to somewhat of a perceived values shift within the field of OD. Many practitioners feel that the focus of their work has shifted away from humanistic values and more toward hard or bottom-line results (Margulies & Raia, 1990), and research conducted with practitioners in the field has supported this assertion (Allen, Crossman, Lane, Power, & Svendsen, 1993; Church, Burke, & Van Eynde, 1994).

Moreover, this shift in values has been exacerbated by changes in the backgrounds of people entering the field of OD. The lucrative nature of OD work has led to an influx of practitioners who have not been formally trained in or exposed to traditional OD values. In fact, many of them are not even aware of the basic tenets of OD (see Chapter One) and how it is differentiated from other types of organizational consulting. This disturbing trend has led many to question the true nature of OD and has been the source of continuing debates within the field (Church, Waclawski, & Siegal, 1996; Golembiewski, 1990; Miles, 1977; Weidner & Kulick, 1999).

Despite these changes in focus, basic professional ethics have not changed. In the end, the fundamentals of ethical reasoning should provide the guideposts for OD professionals in their quest to resolve the values dilemma. For example, if a client requests a practitioner's involvement in using multisource feedback data (see Chapter Two and McLean, 1997) collected under a purely development context for a set of termination decisions, the ethics involved should dedicate the appropriate response; that is, sensitive data should not be used for purposes for which they were not originally intended. Unfortunately, ethics codes are of little use in making difficult decisions, particularly in the midst of tensions between conflicting values that on the one hand are espoused by the founders of the field and on the other demanded from clients (and successful performance in the service role as they have defined it). Furthermore, without sanctioning power from a governing body of like-minded professionals, detailed ethical codes in OD, or any standards for practice, for that matter, are weak and lack consequences for those who might violate them (Weidner & Kulick, 1999).

In sum, there is a need to educate newcomers to the field and remind veteran practitioners as well about the ethics of the consulting profession and to critique and refine our approach to engaging in OD work that balances yet supports both humanistic and business-related values. Given the absence of structure and standardization in the OD field, this means that the ensuing dialogue will be messy and at times difficult to resolve. Nonetheless, such a discourse is critical to our collective understanding of the field of OD and what it means to work under this professional label.

The Shift from Concern for People to Concern for Profit

Nearly all of the historical OD literature focuses on values of human dignity, autonomy, and intrinsic value (Margulies & Raia, 1990). Underlying this belief structure is a concurrent general assumption that humans should not be harmed for organizational or business purposes. The ethical dilemma arises when competing values (say, human versus business) must be reconciled. If a business is losing money, it may need to decide whether to lay people off (harming some individuals in the short run) or keep everyone employed until bankruptcy (which harms more people but delays the pain). *Downsizing, right-sizing,* and other euphemisms for layoffs have always brought pain to the faces of employees and OD practitioners (Noer, 1993), even when they brought smiles to the faces of stockholders.

OD was founded largely by people from the social sciences or humanities, many of them trained in individual or organizational psychology. Yet the field has always attracted people from a wide variety of disciplines, including psychology, theology, education, literature, social work, and business. Initially, group process consultation, quality of worklife (QWL), and team building were almost synonymous with "doing OD work." Although practitioners have always operated within the business framework as internal agents or external consultants, the value system promoted a sense of not doing anything at the expense of an individual. Hence, it is often expected that OD practitioners might refuse to participate in any intervention that could cost other people their jobs.

A Case Example

We were involved in an OD consultation effort with a dairy company interested in Continuous Quality Improvement (CQI). The dairy industry is very competitive; a fraction of a cent reduction in the production cost of a half-gallon of milk can affect competitive survival. Everyone involved in the intervention was aware that one of the goals of CQI was to improve processes overall, with the specific objectives of increasing quality and efficiency. Increases in efficiency often translate in business to a reduced need for personnel; fewer employees means less personnel overhead and thus lower production costs overall. Because a frequent first step in CQI is process documentation, which requires the participation of knowledgeable employees, a natural question for employees to ask is, "Why should I participate in eliminating my own job?"

When this very question arose in our work, it created an apparent business versus human needs conflict for us. As it turned out, a review of employee demographics across the company revealed that many personnel were approaching retirement, and thus natural attrition rather than forced terminations could be used to reduce head count for this improvement process. Thus, management committed that no employee would lose a job; personnel reductions would be managed solely through retirement. Fortunately, the union cooperated with this decision as well because of their conviction that failure to improve productivity would result in job loss for other reasons. So in the end, it all worked out for the best, at least with respect to the values dilemma. But what if these conflicting goals could not have been met? What then would be the ethical responsibilities of the consultants?

Has the OD World Really Changed?

In the 1980s and 1990s, major business trends, such as mergers and acquisitions, leveraged buyouts, downsizing, Total Quality Management, business process reengineering, Six Sigma, and other profit-driven, large-scale changes began to dominate the lives of many OD practitioners. As OD professionals became involved in these initiatives, they found that the cultural rules had changed, and sometimes these initiatives caused obvious harm to individuals. This trend continues.

Furthermore, large accounting firms have spawned consulting businesses operating under the broad rubric of organizational effectiveness. These are intended to complement and add value to their accounting and information technology services. As Church and Waclawski (1998) have noted, however, the growth and diversification of the consulting industry have led to the emergence of "vendors" whose primary objective is to "make the sale" and a shift in the client expectation and experience from a personal relationship with a professional expert to a consumer relationship with a interchangeable vendor. As a result, OD professionals may more frequently be in the position of competitive bidding, being tempted to cut corners, avoiding a thorough diagnosis (which might produce a different recommendation from the one most appropriate to the situation), engaging in creative pricing, and generally hard-pressed to differentiate themselves from the mass of other consultants.

In addition, some business schools have begun offering OD as an emphasis or formal field of concentration in their programs, which is likely to instill an entirely different set of values and skills in students. Given these trends, it appears as though the focus of OD may indeed be shifting from the human input side to the business results side of the organizational effectiveness equation.

All of these changes exacerbate the already complex ethical environment in which OD professionals work. Moreover, the academic side of the field has failed to provide support and assistance in helping professionals understand what the ethical dilemmas are or providing them with meaningful and practical tools for addressing these critical dilemmas.

The Definitional Issue: What Is Ethical?

Trevino and Nelson (1995) defined ethical dilemmas as "situations concerning right and wrong where values are in conflict" (p. 4), based on "the principles, norms, and standards of conduct governing an individual or group" (p. 12). Although helpful, this is somewhat of a simplistic view, ignoring any distinctions in how ethics are viewed in individual, group, or organizational contexts.

Individual Values and Moral Judgment

For an individual, a *value* is a principle or quality that is intrinsically desirable. It reflects a personal belief and is part of an internalized value system. A *moral,* in comparison, represents a standard that dictates the difference between right and wrong behavior (that is, the manifestation of a value in action). Both values and morals can be derived from a variety of sources, including individuals, family, and society.

Because morals reflect the evaluation of behavior, morals and moral dilemmas are fundamentally interpersonal in nature. While values reflect an internal belief and therefore do not require an outward expression, moral judgment is the process of determination as to whether that value has been acted on appropriately according to some standard. Thus, individuals confronted with an ethical dilemma make a choice of action based on the importance and congruence of their personal belief systems weighted against the moral standards to which they are accustomed. Typically, moral dilemmas are resolved at the level of the individual conscience.

In the practice of OD, a moral dilemma might be a request to facilitate meetings for a team developing biological weapons. In this case, the consultant must weigh the importance of the value of helping the team be more effective with the belief that biological weapons should not be developed and used on people. In this scenario, individual and societal-level values and morals interact. The final decision, however, rests with the individual.

Group Norms and Professional Ethics

As a profession grows and develops, group values and norms begin to arise that define good and "bad" practice. Nearly all consulting professions (law, medicine, accounting, psychology) have developed traditions as to what constitutes good or bad behavior. These group norms and expectations are so strong that they often overshadow individual values and moral judgment. In some professions, these norms and values are transformed into formally articulated and even legally sanctionable guidelines that are used to enforce adherence to their standards.

Although somewhat similar, professional ethics can also emerge that represent a system of ethical reasoning adopted by a distinct group of professionals with similar practice approaches or academic preparation. This reasoning is a logical process by which people evaluate options and select behaviors or courses of action. "Do no harm" in the medical profession, for example, represents an ethical imperative. Few state licensing boards, however, would use this criterion to evaluate whether a physician is fit to practice medicine. Ethics represent a signpost; morals and values represent more personal internalizations.

For example, the counseling profession has developed a taboo on sexual relationships with clients. Even if a psychologist falls in love with a client, the profession has determined that a social relationship may not develop until the professional relationship has been terminated for a prescribed length of time. Violation of this principle may lead to the loss of professional license. People who conform to those expectations are ethical practitioners; those who do not may face formal or informal sanctions.

The Role of Ambiguity

The dilemma of ethical behavior is how to resolve conflicts in situations of high ambiguity when there are no easily identifiable standards. Ambiguity results in "The Ethic of Right vs. Right" (Kidder, 1995, p. 13), or as Tom MacLean in the novel *China White* (Maas, 1994) said, "The world's a hell of a lot more gray than black and white" (p. 12). Kidder (1995) emphasized the dilemmas that exist in the gray area by constructing four dichotomies or extremes:

Justice versus mercy: Fairness, equity, and even-handed application of the law versus compassion, empathy, and love

Short term versus long term: Immediate needs or desires versus future goals

Individual versus community: Us versus them, self versus others

Truth versus loyalty: honesty or integrity versus commitment, responsibility, or promise keeping

Most ethical decisions lie in the gray area between the poles of these dichotomies.

The source of this ambiguity is that "individuals and groups have to make decisions in a highly complex context where roles and norms, authority and power relationships, competitive pressures, profit motives, and organizational structures all come into play" (Trevino & Nelson, 1995, p. 13). In spite of the proliferation of codes of ethics, according to Toffler (1986), "There is no agreement on the substance of right and wrong, its source, or on the universality of application" (p. 10). As Tillich (1963) stated, "Life at every moment is ambiguous" (p. 32). The result of this situation is that professional practice is by default defined by ambiguity.

Ethical Dilemmas Confronting OD Practitioners

It is impossible to provide a complete list of all of the ethical dilemmas faced in the field. However, there are some common dilemmas that most OD professionals face at some point in their career. In order to ascertain the central nature of these issues, DeVogel (1992) conducted a series of interviews with practitioners that revealed the following major themes or types of dilemmas:

- *Uses of information.* How much should the practitioner control the flow of information? What should a practitioner do with information that might benefit employees but management intends to keep from them? Does a consultant reveal individual capability assessment information to a client even if that assessment was collected (and communicated to employees) for other purposes, such as using multisource feedback for employee evaluation or performance appraisal (see Chapter Two and McLean, 1997)?
- *Intervention choice.* What happens when a consultant is tempted to use an intervention that might stretch beyond one's competency level? Should one initiate an intervention as requested by a client without having completed a needs assessment first? What happens if a practitioner is asked to conduct an intervention that seems to be totally inappropriate? Should the consultant continue if he or she believes a deeper intervention is needed than the client is able to understand or wishes to undertake?
- *Role conflict.* Is it okay to involve friends or family members in an OD process? Where is the balance between having one's own

needs met and the needs of the client? Should a practitioner develop social relationships with client members?

• *Fees.* How much is reasonable and ethical to charge the client for services rendered? Is it fair to base this decision on what this client can afford to pay? What are the services provided really worth? Is it acceptable to charge for a project that was not successful? Is it appropriate for a consultant to sell a workshop based on a specific instrument because the consultant is certified and receives a commission on the sale of the instruments?

• *Competency of the team.* What should be done about the perceived incompetence of a co-consultant or an internal or external counterpart? What should be done when a consulting contract is sold by a senior consultant but the work is done by junior-level consultants? How should technical ineptness be handled, which can result in inappropriate application of OD processes and techniques (Wooten & White, 1983)?

• *Collusion and assimilation.* How should a practitioner prevent the potential loss of objectivity that can occur through personal involvement with the company or the threat of loss of income? How long should the consulting process continue? How should lack of interest in evaluating the efficacy of the OD intervention be dealt with?

• *Who is the client?* What happens when there is difficulty in determining to whom one is accountable or for whose welfare one is responsible? How should the practitioner respond if the client passes responsibility for the entire change effort to someone else?

• *Values.* How does one resolve a situation in which the consultant's values are in direct conflict with client values or practices (such as production of hazardous waste or deleterious effects of downsizing on the local economy)? How are internal value conflicts with oneself resolved (for example, demoting a person for the larger good of the company)?

Clearly, these are some challenging issues. In dynamic consulting relationships, it is impossible to predict the emergence of any one of these dilemmas, but OD practitioners should not be as surprised when they emerge. Unfortunately, these seem to be a normal outcome of the process of working with individuals and organizations. Moreover, if left unacknowledged and unresolved, they can create stress in the relationship between client and consultant, which can lead to poor business decisions, ineffective interventions, and potentially moral and legal even concerns.

In the end, it is the moral responsibility of the OD practitioner to be sensitive to the ethical aspects of the consulting process and to work through these issues as they arise. Although everyone can benefit from such a reminder, this message may be especially needed by those who have entered the field of OD through a pathway other than the traditional, humanistically oriented fields.

How Do OD Professionals Respond to Ethical Dilemmas?

DeVogel (1992) also identified the most frequently used responses by OD professionals to these types of ethical dilemmas. These "theories in use" as opposed to "espoused theories" (Argyris, 1990, 1993) are presented in Table 15.1 in descending order.

Despite all the philosophy in the literature on professional ethics and despite efforts by professional associations to describe appropriate reasoning and guidelines for ethical decision making, interviewees typically chose as their preferred response, "I rely on my inner resources." Moreover, this was nearly always accompanied by the explanation, "I am an INFP," that is, relying on their Myers-Briggs type (see Chapter Three). The second most frequent process cited was discussion with colleagues. In sum, the research that DeVogel (1992) carried out would suggest that OD practitioners make choices that are driven primarily by their inner values and refer little to external authorities for wisdom in making these decisions.

Models for Ethical Decision Making

Research is not the only approach for understanding the decision-making process when faced with an ethical dilemma. Several models posit how individuals make decisions in these difficult situations. Kidder (1995, p. 154) suggested "three principles for resolving dilemmas":

1. Do what's best for the greatest number of people (ends-based thinking).

**Table 15.1. How Practitioners Respond
to Ethical Dilemmas.**

Ranking (1 = most frequent)	Strategy and Typical Consultant Response
1	Strategy: Negotiate to reach a resolution, including possibility of compromise.
	Typical response to the client: "I'm not comfortable doing this, but how about an alternative such as . . ."
2	Strategy: Open confrontation.
	Typical response to the client: "This is wrong. These people were promised confidentiality, and I won't violate the promise."
3	Strategy: Conduct action research.
	Typical response to the client: "Let's get some more data before we go to the next step and see where it takes us. Then we can plan a more appropriate intervention."
4	Strategy: Take independent action, perhaps covertly.
	Typical response to a person who is likely to be fired: "It looks to me as though some people might be losing their jobs. Have you given any thought to what you might do if you were affected?"
5	Strategy: Indirect response.
	Typical response to the client: "Well, team building might be a good idea. Can we talk about training first?"

2. Follow your highest sense of principle (rule-based thinking).
3. Do what you want others to do to you (care-based thinking).

The third principle, in spite of its universality, can be critiqued for assuming a homogeneous world culture. It might better be rephrased as, "Do unto others what they want you to do to them." Kung (1993) also raised the question of whether it is possible to have an ethic that is valid for all people everywhere.

These three principles are similar to a three-perspective model often used within religious studies using a time-based approach:

- Deontology, or past based (law, rules, standards, religion, codes of conduct, values statements)
- Teleology, or future based (vision, mission, purpose)
- Situational, or present based (what is best for me now)

Other models have suggested that ethical decisions exist within the actor. Thus, Schön (1983) encouraged the development of a "reflective practitioner," and Kidder (1995) called for "energetic self-reflection" (p. 13). Still others suggest a step-by-step, prescriptive approach (Hall, 1993; Trevino & Nelson, 1995). According to Hall (1993), the following steps should occur in the decision-making process: (1) define the problem, (2) identify the stakeholders, (3) identify the practical alternatives, (4) determine the measurable economic impact of each alternative, (5) identify the immeasurable economic consequences of each alternative, (6) arrive at a tentative decision, and (7) decide how to implement the decision.

In the end, as much as some would like to have a straightforward model of how to make ethical decisions, the ambiguity in which we live and the variations that exist in individual value sets make this extremely difficult, and probably impossible.

Ethical Obligations of OD Professionals

Given that OD originated in the social sciences, it should not be surprising that much has been written in the field regarding practitioners' ethical obligations to their clients. In particular, several authors have outlined principles related to this issue (Bayles, 1981; Gellermann, Frankel, & Ladenson, 1990; LeBacqz, 1985; Lippitt & Lippitt, 1978). Bayles (1981) specified the following obligations to clients:

- Honesty: Not stealing from the client; no kickbacks; no provision of unneeded services.
- Candor: Disclosure and open truthfulness, including full explanations. (Candor might sometimes conflict with confidentiality.)
- Competence: Accept only work that is within one's capabilities; do not charge during the learning process.

- Diligence: Work should be done quickly and promptly; do not take on more work than you have time to do well.
- Loyalty: Examine all potential conflicts of interest and be honest with the client about the conflicts.
- Discretion: General consideration of the client's right to privacy.

Unfortunately, statements of values and ethics of this nature are somewhat limited in utility. Typically, these lists go on and on, sometimes, it seems, endlessly. Moreover, many of them are so all encompassing as to appear to be written at the motherhood and apple pie level. Although they can be helpful in reminding us of the basics of ethical behavior in OD, they provide little if any guidance about what actual course of action a practitioner should take when confronted with an ethical dilemma. More specifically, these lists are generally phrased as detailed normative statements and are much too long to memorize, let alone have available in the midst of practice, to be useful in ethical decision making.

Creating a Code of Ethics for OD?

One way to go about creating a workable code of ethics for the field is to look to the literature on group formation. There is a well-known framework among OD practitioners that can be used to describe the process by which groups develop: forming, storming, norming, and performing (Ross, 1989). That is, once a group has been established (formed), it enters the storming phase, which is characterized by the surfacing and resolution of conflicts. Often these conflicts stem from disputes over group norms that have not yet been established. As a result of these conflicts and how they are settled, the group begins to develop a set of norms based on belief, attitudes, and opinions to guide its behaviors (norming). Until a process for settling conflict has been determined, the group cannot begin to engage successfully in the tasks it has set out to accomplish (performing).

Applying this framework to the field of OD, when a norm (or taboo) becomes well entrenched within a group of professionals, it represents a standard of practice. Violating this norm can carry with it heavy or light sanctions depending on the group's process for dealing with norm violations. In order to avoid arbitrary or idiosyncratic methods for conflict resolution, when professional groups form, they often write an explicit code of ethics based on the norms established within the group. Entry into the profession can involve swearing loyalty to the code, and exit from the profession may result from violating it. Some professional organizations (for example, the medical and legal professions) have explicit codes of ethics that when violated carry with them harsh penalties (respectively, revocation of one's medical license and disbarment). As might be expected from this analogy, the field of OD is still in the storming phase and has been for nearly forty years.

As Church et al. (1996) have noted, the OD profession remains loosely organized. There are many avenues into the field, and nearly anybody can be a self-proclaimed OD practitioner. Moreover, there are no controls for entry into or exit from the profession. Within some in OD, there are common understandings of what constitutes "good" or "bad" practice, but there is no formal system for enforcing these beliefs, and not everyone agrees on what exactly these rules are. In fact, absolutely no formal licensing body exists to regulate the practice of OD.

Voluntary professional associations, such as the Organization Development Network (1996), the Organization Development Institute (1991), and the Academy of Human Resource Development (1999), have developed their own codes of ethics in an effort to respond to this need in practice. However, none of these groups defines and enforces standards of professional practice, because none has the power to control professional entry or exit. Gellermann et al. (1990) also provided a very well-thought-out document and detailed list of principles, similar to an ethics code, but this has never been fully accepted or enforced in any way by a professional organization.

Of course, adoption of a code of ethics does not ensure ethical reasoning. Public discourse about ethics frequently revolves around determining to what extent a rule has been broken, not about the balancing of conflicting or competing interests or values. In the final analysis, if there is no decision to be made, we are not "doing" ethics.

It is not clear whether or how ethical behavior can be developed, especially among adults. Moreover, changing one's value system or moral views is unlikely to happen after childhood. So perhaps the best we can do is to provide people who already have strong values with tools for making ethical decisions. What can be taught, for example, is ethical analysis (Hall, 1993). Some of approaches are set out in Exhibit 15.1.

Some in the field have called for stronger actions than an ethical analysis process for gaining awareness about ethical consideration in practicing OD, (Church et al., 1996; Weidner & Kulick, 1999). A number of OD professionals have called for the establishment of clear standards for the discipline and the adoption of an accreditation process. This accreditation process would be based on criteria such as the following:

- Demonstrated competence in the behavioral science technologies and interventions used for OD
- An understanding of the behavioral science theories that have contributed and continue to contribute to the OD perspective
- Experience and competence in working with interpersonal issues, group dynamics, and human relations
- Understanding, accepting, and committing to established values, ethics, and ideals of the field

Exhibit 15.1. Some Approaches to Fostering Ethics.

Ethics games that generate conversation about organizational ethical dilemmas

Case studies (print and video)

Cognitive approaches

Meditation and reflection

Discussion with a mentor or peer review

Force-field analysis

Interviews with people who have faced ethical dilemmas

Role playing

Mentoring and coaching

Placing persons in difficult ethical situations and observing them in assessment centers or through workplace experiences

Self-analysis instruments

Development of a personal values statement

Moreover, in order to accomplish these goals, some authors (Church, 1996; Weidner & Kullick, 1999) have recommended that the field formally regulate or license OD practitioners, with prescribed training and pathways. This would mean instituting a formal review process for educational and disciplinary purposes. In addition, they advocate the active promotion through such means as conferences and publications of the desired values and behaviors of OD practitioners. As an incentive, they suggest providing awards to practitioners who model the desired behaviors and values.

It seems unlikely that any of these recommendations can be successful. First, licensing of professionals is generally managed by state governments, making the first two recommendations very difficult to implement. If it were not managed by the state, then it would need buy-in from everyone involved in the process, very unlikely in the OD field. In spite of this, the exploration of licensure or certification continues to be raised as a possibility (Tippins, 2001; Sackett, Thomas, Borman & Campion, 1995).

Conclusion

A variety of models, frameworks, and approaches exist for fostering ethical practice in OD. Unfortunately, there has been no wide acceptance or adoption of any of these methods, just as there is no consistency in theory or practice. OD is still very much a fragmented field of solo practitioners who do not agree on a common definition of OD, let alone OD ethics. In the end, ethical behavior rests heavily on the shoulders of individual OD practitioners. Nevertheless, the picture is not as bleak is it may appear. We think that it is reasonable to assume that OD professionals will understand and use the tools available in their decision-making process. Those committed to ethical OD are obligated to remind colleagues of their ethical obligations to the profession, their clients, and themselves.

Practice Tips

1. Establish a set of personal principles of integrity before the difficult or complicated circumstances arise.
2. Develop a formal list of values statements, but only if you intend to strive to live up to the statements. Statements produced only for public consumption lead to more cynicism than ethical practice.
3. Ask yourself, "Would I want to see this behavior on the front page of the newspaper?" or, "Could I justify this line of reasoning to a disinterested colleague?"
4. Meet regularly with colleagues to discuss the ethical issues you are confronting (while maintaining confidentiality). It is difficult for unethical behavior to exist in an open environment.
5. Set aside regular time to reflect on decisions that you are making; meditate.
6. Use force-field analysis techniques to identify potential consequences of actions or options (see Chapter Five for a description of a force-field analysis).
7. Participate in conferences of professional organizations that hold up ethical standards.
8. Use role clarification to minimize ambiguity.
9. Openly discuss with clients any problematic issues with potential ethical implications.
10. Maintain a systems perspective. Work to align corporate cultures with ethical behavior, examine reward and punishment systems, and focus on both formal and informal systems.
11. Be aware of your whole self. Pay attention to your feelings and your thoughts and how they interact.

References

Academy of Human Resource Development. (1999). *Standards on ethics and integrity*. Baton Rouge, LA: Academy of Human Resource Development, Standard Committee on Ethics and Integrity. Available at: http://ahrd.org/publications/publications_mail.html.

Allen, K., Crossman, D., Lane, L., Power, G., & Svendsen, D. S. (1993). The future of OD: Conversations with "living legends." *OD Practitioner, 25*, 28–32.

Argyris, C. (1990). *Overcoming organizational defenses: Facilitating organizational learning*. Needham Heights, MA: Allyn & Bacon.

Argyris, C. (1993). *Knowledge for action: A guide to overcoming barriers to organizational change*. San Francisco: Jossey-Bass.

Bayles, M. D. (1981). *Professional ethics*. Belmont, CA: Wadsworth.

Church, A. H. (1996). Values and the wayward profession: An exploration of the changing nature of OD. *Vision/Action, 15*, 3–6.

Church, A. H., Burke, W. W., & Van Eynde, D. F. (1994). Values, motives, and interventions of organization development practitioners. *Group and Organization Management, 19*, 5–50.

Church, A. H., & Waclawski, J. (1998). The vendor mind-set: The devolution from organizational consultant to street peddler. *Consulting Psychology Journal, 50*(2), 87–100.

Church, A. H., Waclawski, J., & Siegal, W. (1996). Will the real OD practitioner please stand up? A call for change in the field. *Organization Development Journal, 14*, 5–14.

DeVogel, S. H. (1992). *Ethical decision making in organization development: Current theory and practice*. Unpublished Ph.D. dissertation, University of Minnesota, St. Paul.

Gellermann, W., Frankel, M. W., & Ladenson, R. F. (1990). *Values and ethics in organizations and human system development: Responding to dilemmas in professional life*. San Francisco: Jossey-Bass.

Golembiewski, R. T. (1990). Is OD dying, or even ill? Testing alleged problems against success rates. *OD Practitioner, 22*, 16–20.

Hall, W. D. (1993). *Making the right decision: Ethics for managers*. New York: Wiley.

Kidder, R. M. (1995). *Good people make tough choices: Resolving the dilemmas of ethical living*. New York: Morrow.

Kung, H. (Ed.) (1993). *A global ethic: The declaration of the parliament of the world's religions*. New York: Continuum.

LeBacqz, K. (1985). *Professional ethics: Power and paradox*. Nashville, TN: Abingdon Press.

Lippitt, G. L., & Lippitt, R. (1978). *The consulting process in action*. San Francisco: Jossey-Bass/Pfeiffer.

Maas, P. (1994). *China white*. Rockland, MA: Wheeler.

Margulies, N., & Raia, A. (1990). The significance of core values on the theory and practice of organization development. In F. Massarik (Ed.), *Advances in organization development* (Vol. 1, pp. 27–41). Norwood, NJ: Ablex.

McLean, G. N. (1997). Multirater 360-degree feedback. In L. J. Bassi & D. Russ-Eft (Eds.), *What works: Assessment, development, and measurement* (pp. 87–108). Alexandria, VA: American Society for Training and Development.

Miles, R. E. (1977). OD: Can it survive? And should it? *OD Practitioner, 9*, 4–7.

Noer, D. M. (1993). *Healing the wounds: Overcoming the trauma of layoffs and revitalizing downsized organizations.* San Francisco: Jossey-Bass.

Organization Development Institute. (1991). *The International Organization Development code of ethics* (22nd rev. ed.). Cleveland, OH: Author.

Organization Development Network. (1996). *Organization and human systems development credo.* Available at: www.odnetwork.org/credo.html.

Ross, R. S. (1989). *Small groups in organizational settings.* Upper Saddle River, NJ: Prentice Hall.

Sackett, P., Thomas, J., Borman, W., & Campion, M. (1995). Proposed revision of SIOP policy on licensure: Call for comments. *Industrial-Organizational Psychologist, 33,* 12–20.

Schön, D. A. (1983). *Reflective practitioner.* New York: Basic Books.

Tillich, P. (1963). *Systematic theology: Vol. 3. Life and the spirit, history and the kingdom of God.* Chicago: University of Chicago Press.

Tippins, N. T. (2001). A message from your president. *Industrial-Organizational Psychologist, 38,* 7–12.

Toffler, B. L. (1986). *Tough choices: Managers talk ethics.* New York: Wiley.

Trevino, L. K., & Nelson, K. A. (1995). *Managing business ethics: Straight talk about how to do it right.* New York: Wiley.

Weidner, C. K., II, & Kulick, O. A. (1999). The professionalization of organization development: A status report and look to the future. In W. A. Pasmore & R. W. Woodman (Eds.), *Research in organizational change and development* (Vol. 12, pp. 319–371). Greenwich, CT: JAI Press.

Wooten, K. C., & White, L. P. (1983). Ethical problems in the practice of organization development. *Training and Development Journal, 37,* 16–23.

CHAPTER 16

Voices from the Field
Future Directions for Organization Development

Allan H. Church
Janine Waclawski
Seth A. Berr

At the beginning of this book, we wrote that the field of organization development (OD) has evolved somewhat haphazardly from an eclectic combination of social science theories, applied techniques, and a set of underlying values and beliefs about what it means to, and why we work with, people and organizations to facilitate change. In part, because of these influences, the field is in a constant state of flux regarding both its current identity (What exactly is OD? Is OD a trade or a profession?), as well as its future direction (Where is OD going? Can OD survive, and should it?).

Although we do not propose to have all the answers to these difficult yet frequently asked questions about the field (Church, Waclawski, & Siegal, 1996; Golembiewski, 1990; Miles, 1977; Weisbord, 1982), we have offered a new contextual framework that encompasses what we consider to be the quintessential components

Note: We thank the following individuals for their responses to our survey questions: Terry Armstrong, Matt Barney, Michael Beer, David Boje, Wayne Boswell, Frans Cilliers, David Coghlan, Richard Engdahl, Stan Herman, Jay Morris, William Pasmore, Karen Paul, Jeff Schippmann, Ron Shepps, Peter Sorensen, Jennifer Tuman, Vicki Vandaveer, Glenn Varney, William Verdi, Therese Yaeger, Ken Weidner, and David White.

of doing OD work: an action research framework, a systems mindset, and a normative values stance (see Chapter One). We have also used this framework to guide the content of chapters in this book.

The one area that has yet to be directly addressed is the future. What are the biggest trends and key challenges in the field today? How do practitioners see the field evolving? What new types of skills will be needed? What will OD look like in ten years?

Although we could certainly speculate on these issues (and indeed have elsewhere), given one of the central tenets of this book that OD is a data-driven process, we felt that the best solution was to practice what we preach and go directly to where OD work is done in the organizational trenches every day. In short, we asked practitioners.

Comments from the Field

We canvassed over twenty respected individuals, representing both external and internal practitioners, as well as consulting academics, regarding the trends and challenges they face today and their insights into the future of the field. More specifically, we asked them to respond to four specific questions about their experiences and predictions. Their responses are summarized below by major themes. Given the diversity in the field today (in terms of experience, formal education, knowledge of various tools and techniques, and other parameters), it should come as no surprise that although some consistent messages did emerge, the responses from these practitioners were as wide as they were deep.

What Types of OD-Related Services Are Most in Demand Now?

Responses to this question described many different types of practitioners and the OD work they engage in. Overall, comments fell into five general categories or themes. To some extent, these mirrored the three basic levels of focus or analysis that different types of practitioners have: individual, team, and organization. Moreover, many of these services are described in more detail in other chapters in this book.

Executive Coaching and Development

A number of professionals noted that executive coaching and development has become a major industry (some might even say a field) and that many OD practitioners are moving into this area of practice. In addition, this trend is reflected in the increasing demand to help organizations develop more senior leadership talent. While primarily focused on the individual, one-on-one coaching was seen as a key means for enhancing self-awareness and learning and ultimately driving behavioral change and follow-through (see related discussions in Chapters Two and Three). Although technically this is not an OD approach, a formal coaching framework systematically applied can be an important tool for practitioners, particularly when various sources of individual and organizational data are to be used as inputs into the process (Waclawski & Church, 1999). Moreover, process consultation, which is indeed a classic OD method, represents a related form of individual coaching, although the focus is somewhat different (see Chapter Seven and Schein, 1988).

Team Building and Team Effectiveness

Many respondents indicated a strong demand for so-called soft skills development work at the team level as well. Considered by some practitioners to represent more traditional or quintessential OD, efforts directed at helping people listen, communicate, and generally work together more effectively in groups and teams was seen as a key aspect of contemporary OD practice (see Chapters Seven and Eight). Such facilitation services were also seen as being of particular importance when working with senior management to ensure proper alignment when planning and moving forward on change initiatives. Clearly, if the leadership of an organization is not in agreement and support of the strategy of a given change effort, it will be difficult, and perhaps impossible, to implement effectively.

Facilitating Strategic Organizational Change

Related to the issue of alignment, OD practitioners were also seen as being called on to help facilitate the acceptance and implementation of large-scale changes such as those affecting an organization's structure, strategy, values, or direction. Examples included developing communication plans to reduce confusion and anxiety in times of chaos (such as during mergers and acquisitions), building the human perspective into the reengineering process, facilitating the strategic planning process, and positioning data collection tools (for example, surveys, feedback, and performance management systems) to help employees understand what is expected of them.

Systemic Integration

Several individuals noted a demand for OD-related assistance in integrating the plethora of existing change interventions and initiatives typically in place in organizations. By applying a broader social systems perspective, it was thought that OD professionals could help bring some order to the chaos of competing initiatives and directives. Practitioners were also seen as being called on to help link existing human resource initiatives to business strategy. Moreover, some people felt that many organizations were finally ready to build greater connectivity among corporate strategy, leadership, and bottom-line results, an area in which OD has not always been particularly strong (see Chapters Six and Fourteen).

Diversity and Multiculturalism

The final area of contemporary practice reflected the rise of supporting efforts directed at diversity-related change efforts in organizations. Comments described these efforts as existing on a multicultural diversity continuum, where concerns on the diversity side result in OD efforts focused on individual differences, while multiculturalism interventions tend to focus more on group identity. Although diversity training has long been a related offshoot of OD, given the changing nature of work, the workforce, and the organization-employee contract (Howard, 1995; Jackson, 1992), it is not surprising that this element of practice is now increasing. The most recent application of this construct centers around not differences or diversity per se but rather on creating an inclusive culture and working environment where everyone's unique talents, backgrounds, and personal characteristics are valued.

What Are the Biggest Challenges You Face on a Day-to-Day Basis as an OD Practitioner?

Respondents identified four sets of challenges. These reflected both time- and priority-related issues—for example, the need to pack more impact (and decision making) into less time and the pressures associated with having too much going on at once—as well as communicating and applying some of the unique components of the field to the world of work.

The Need for Speed

A number of practitioners noted that while project responsibilities have expanded for many OD professionals in organizations, the time frames for these efforts have actually contracted. The result is an increasing need for speed in all phases of the OD effort. This means finding ways to perform a quick (but accurate) diagnosis, review and select an intervention or tool to address the need, implement the process with diligence, and demonstrate the impact in both the short and long term. Given all of the information and issues bombarding people in organizations today, working in this hectic environment requires learning to identify which projects are important and effective and which ones should clearly not be pursued.

Unfortunately, as some individuals noted, practitioners and clients alike often fall victim to the time crunch by trying to do too much at once without discerning what is truly important. As one respondent observed, "It's as though we have gotten stuck on a treadmill and are afraid to step off, take a short break, and make sense out of all the activity that is going on around us." Moreover, the need for speed also appears to be affecting some practitioners' ability to have a balanced work-family life. It is also impeding their ability to pursue other important self-development activities, such as engaging in pro bono projects, writing articles, engaging in consulting work on the side, attending conferences, and generally keeping up with changes in the field.

Resistance to Change

Dealing with resistance to change was cited as a constant challenge and concern in OD work. One person noted that as long as people are invested in and have emotion for their work, there will be some resistance. For example, shifting power dynamics associated with pending changes to culture, systems, or structures (such as following a merger or restructuring), and particularly at senior management levels, can fuel resistance. Other sources mentioned include functional silo mentalities and an overly transactional focus on the part of some leaders, even in the face of business challenges and external threats. Whatever the underlying cause, the challenge of OD professionals is to use their facilitation skills to help identify and surface these issues and then work with various constituents to try to resolve them.

Differentiating OD

Considering the lack of agreement in the underlying definition of OD among practitioners, it makes perfect sense that conveying the unique nature and contribution of the field to clients would be just as problematic. Often the difference between an OD approach and a management consulting one is unclear to people (Weidner & Kulick, 1999). For example, in the interest of speed, many managers and executives focus on finding the quickest (and not necessarily the best) solution to their problems. Because of this emphasis, it is often hard to convey the importance of using an OD approach such as action research or a data collection framework to identify the right solution, that is, one that will be embraced by the key constituents because they participated in the diagnosis and action planning phases. The OD professional suggesting such a reflective solution in this context will often be dismissed for a more expedient quick-fix or cookie-cutter solution. Although not all interventions require extensive diagnosis, in general, the more customized a solution is to the needs of the organization and the people involved, the greater the likelihood is that it will have an impact over time.

Practitioners also indicated that much of their work involved first trying to get buy-in from the top of the organization, especially from "old-school executives" for the "soft stuff." Because making the case for OD efforts often means convincing management that OD work does positively affect people and business results, the notion of demonstrating these linkages through applied research and evaluation is critical (see Chapters Two, Four, Six, and Fourteen).

Interpersonal Skill and Awareness

Practitioners also noted some frustration with the level of interpersonal skills and awareness on the part of many managers and executives in organizations today. Between personal agendas, a general lack of sensitivity to individual differences (including race, gender, and cultural diversity—see Chapter Thirteen), and conflict-averse management styles, some practitioners felt that far too much time is spent negotiating these issues. Moreover, dealing with the barrier of politeness that exists in some organizations can impede effectiveness as well because people are not comfortable in giving honest and open feedback. As one individual commented, the result is that individuals frequently talk *about* one another instead of *with* each other. Clearly, this is an area where some personality assessment and processes consultation might yield some results (see Chapters Three and Seven).

What Are the Three Biggest Emerging Trends in OD?

Responses to this forward-looking question were quite mixed, reflecting several different themes. Interestingly enough, however, most of the comments focused on emerging potential problem areas for the field rather than new techniques, applications, or theoretical contributions that might influence practice. Although the issues raised are consistent with concerns voiced in the literature about the state of OD (Church & Burke, 1995; Margulies & Raia, 1990; Weidner & Kulick, 1999), it was somewhat disconcerting to see this same pattern emerge from this group as well.

Lack of Professionalism

The first major trend (and indeed concern) noted by practitioners was the perception of a general decrease in professionalism in the field of OD. One practitioner, for example, jokingly complained about seeing his favorite OD guru wearing shabbier and shabbier clothes at conferences and in professional settings. When the practitioners were pressed, however, the primary concern they expressed was one of boundaries. Although practitioners have never collectively been able to define what is and what is not part of the field, that interest in OD continues to grow in the absence of a clear, consistent set of standards—or baseline, entry-level competencies and skills—is a significant concern for many in the field. As one individual put it, "There are simply too many unskilled people calling themselves OD practitioners today." Although some in the field have argued vehemently to professionalize (and legitimize) the use of the OD label through formal educational requirements, certification, or even state licensure (Church, Waclawski, & Siegal, 1996; Weidner & Kulick, 1999), there appears to be little interest in or appetite for such regulation among the larger collective of practitioners who would likely be excluded (also see Chapter Fifteen). Clearly, however, some feel that if these are unaddressed, they may foreshadow an even greater decline in credibility for the field.

Changing Nature of OD

While issues of professionalism and lack of appropriate or consistent background and training in OD often arise in such discussions of the future, so too does the typical call to delineate the boundaries of practice better. This is to be expected, and it occurred here as well. What was somewhat surprising, however, was exactly *what* boundaries these practitioners suggested including. Typically, the argument is made to be less inclusive, citing the need for a background in specific content areas such as group dynamics, organizational theory, leadership, or applied research (as well as many of the approaches outlined in this book), to name a few. Several of the respondents, however, suggested instead a trend toward casting the boundaries wider to reflect a more business-focused, holistic, and multidisciplinary approach to doing OD. Although they noted that standard types of OD efforts are still popular, they felt that the OD perspective needs to change in order to adapt better to a changing world. They cited the emergence of a new wave of leaders who have moved their practice away from traditional one-sided (that is, soft) OD interventions to those more grounded in a combination of the organization sciences with business strategy, financial indicators, global trends, market, and customer research.

In addition, a few individuals saw a shift in practice from less reliance on the facilitative process consulting approach (Block, 1981; Schein, 1988) and more on the expert model using performance metrics, technology, and knowledge of business models to drive their interventions of choice. Interestingly, this expert model is the approach used by non-OD-trained management consultants today. One explanation for this trend is that it may be a direct reflection of the emergence of nontraditional types of management consultants into the OD and change management arena, as some OD professionals have noted (Church et al., 1996; Weidner & Kulick, 1999). Whether this shift ultimately portends a move toward greater relevance for the field or the end of the unique contribution of the OD approach remains to be seen.

Impact of Technology

The third biggest trend in the field concerns the potential impact of technology. Respondents were almost evenly split in their opinions on the subject. Half of the group felt strongly that changing information technology will have a deeply profound and lasting effect on the practice of OD. Some felt that practitioners are blind to the potential impact of the Internet and e-business. One person even went so far as to comment, "The next generation of enterprise resource management tools will have a greater influence on the way we work in the world of HR than any event in the last twenty years."

In contrast to such proclamations, however, the other half of practitioners indicated that although technology will indeed have a major impact on some core OD tools (see Chapter Twelve) and the way in which data are collected, analyzed, and delivered, fundamentally the impact of the information technology and e-business explosion is largely another "flavor of the month." These individuals argued that rather than jumping on the e-bandwagon and discarding everything we know about people at work, OD practitioners should focus their efforts instead on exploring how employees adapt and learn from new technology and evaluate which areas are appropriate for focused interventions. A few people in this camp even felt that no matter how technologically advanced we get as a society, OD work fundamentally cannot be done without the warmth of human interaction. Others have echoed this sentiment (see, for example, Church, 2000).

Whatever the outcome of this trend, what is clear is that practitioners will need to increase their technical facility with OD-related information technology applications.

What Will the Field of OD Look Like in Ten Years?

As might be anticipated, many of the descriptions of the future state of OD in ten years mirror the potential outcomes of the three trends already outlined. Comments reflected the underlying values debate that has plagued OD since its inception (Church, Burke, & Van Eynde, 1996; Greiner, 1980; Murrell, 1999): the interdisciplinary nature of the field, the potential for even more new influences, and the role of technology.

The End of the Great Values Debate

Although many would like to see the values issue resolved (see Chapter One), predictions about the future fell into two distinct groups. The first set of practitioners envisioned a resurgence in the recognition and importance of organizational humanistic values in organizations, heralded by a new generation of leaders who would recognize the benefits of getting the "people part" right (Roddick, 1994). These individuals also thought that as a result of this shift, the field of OD would finally be able to center itself on the more human aspects of facilitation and change management.

Furthermore, although some individuals anticipated a new focus in OD on how to redesign work itself to provide more inherent meaning for people in this lifelong pursuit, others painted a picture in which organizations would have to understand their raison d'être better in order to succeed. This means having an overriding ecological or anthropological purpose or reason for existence that goes well beyond a business-driven vision or mission. In short, these individuals are looking at organizations as being more than just social systems; they are evolving communities (Murrell, 1999).

Far from a unanimous perspective, however, a divergent group of practitioners saw businesses focusing even more in the future on squeezing every ounce of productivity out of employees, placing financial performance well above all other metrics and concerns. In short, pulling all sense of community and humanity out of the workplace (Bellah et al., 1985). The result in this scenario would be that the role of OD professionals would be minimized to just another disempowered staff function struggling to justify its existence. Clearly this vision is not a warm and fuzzy one for the field of OD or for society in general.

A Truly Interdisciplinary Approach

Another theme that emerged was that practitioners in the future will be expected to address complex organizational issues through the synthesis of information from a variety of fields, including international relations, history, psychology, sociology, education, anthropology, strategic management, and organizational behavior. Although the basic eclectic core we know today is expected to remain intact, a number of these individuals believed that OD ultimately would emerge as the key approach that spans the boundaries and makes the linkages apparent between the plethora of social and behavioral sciences. In essence, OD practitioners of the future would become the center of integration for the entire realm of organizational sciences, placing them at the strategic nexus of every organizational change process. As a result, several individuals saw practitioners as being more involved with chief executive officers and their immediate staff in communicating and facilitating large-scale change.

Technology as a Way of Life

Given the reality that advances in information technology will transform many existing OD tools, practitioners saw the field in ten years as being increasingly Web based and computer driven. As one individual noted, the flip chart will be nowhere in sight. Instead, OD facilitators will be speaking their focus group notes aloud into a voice-recognition and parsing program on a laptop that summarizes, content codes, and subsequently displays the key messages on a large screen.

Although this scenario may perhaps be a little too forward looking, it is safe to predict that OD practitioners and clients alike will need to adjust to working with and through various information technology systems. Just as the days of executives' having their administrative assistants print out their e-mails in paper copy for review will soon be at an end, so too will the acceptability of a flustered OD practitioner who is not fully Web savvy or technology enabled. In short, facility with information technology and data-based systems and tools will represent a greater part of everyone's lives, and thus OD practitioners will need to be ready to respond to and converse in this arena. There will be no more hiding behind the phase, "I'm no good with technology, I'm an OD people person."

Globalization and Multicultural Acumen

Just as awareness of and skills for diversity and multiculturalism are important trends today, these practitioners predicted that the future will see even more global businesses competing for scarce resources. Some identified process consultation skills as absolutely critical for networking in the global economy across multiple geographies and time zones. Several respondents also stressed the importance of having international work experience and exposure to a multiplicity of cultures, which would have an impact on practitioners' ability to relate to and work with the evolving global workforce. Others felt that more targeted efforts directed at creating global culture were the wave of the future.

The End of the Identity Crisis

The final prediction for the future state of OD in ten years concerned the identity and visibility of the field. Several less optimistic individuals felt that OD's continued inability to address its unresolved identity crisis would ultimately result in the further decay of the field. As a result, they predicted that in ten years, OD efforts would be less visible, less effective, and therefore less viable. Although a few felt that OD tools and techniques would be absorbed into the day-to-day behaviors of managers, making the role of the OD specialist essentially obsolete, others were more cynical, as expressed in one person's final comment: "The charlatans in the field are now selling their schlock at a fever pitch."

Fortunately, there was varying opinion as to this outcome. Another group of individuals felt that the future would yield a rapid expansion in terms of OD membership and demonstrated impact on organizations, with greater visibility and higher standards of professionalism. They credited such change to the increasing presence of more doctoral and master's programs focused specifically on producing OD professionals (as opposed to applied organizational psychologists or human resource development practitioners). In short, these individuals believed that as long as we work to define the field and ground new entrants in the skills and knowledge needed, the field will only get better.

Conclusion

Clearly, and consistent with prior surveys of the field (Church & Burke, 1995; Allen, Crossman, Lane, Power, & Svendsen, 1993), opinions were quite mixed about both the current and future state of OD. Moreover, as Table 16.1 highlights, some of the major themes were in direct opposition to one another.

While some practitioners saw the field in a state of confusion and decline, others saw a more positive evolution, with the future reflecting either greater integration and power for OD professionals as the center of the emergence of an enhanced focus in organizations on humanistic concerns that would finally help to resolve the ongoing OD values debate. In addition, while most practitioners agreed that professionalism and the importance of defining the core theories, practices, and skill sets for the field is a major issue, the directionality of the boundaries that need to be drawn (either more or less exclusively) was not clear. Even the impact of technology, now and in the future, drew mixed levels of concern from representing foundational change for the field to being just another new tool to learn. About the only major theme practitioners agreed on was the importance of diversity and multiculturalism.

So what does this say about the future of the field of OD? It would appear that not much has truly changed in the past twenty years. Despite the rise in the number and complexity of tools in practice and the names that accompany them, most of the same methods still exist in some more evolved form today. Moreover, despite all the years of debate about the underlying value structure in the field, there are clearly still some practitioners who believe in helping people have more meaningful lives at work, helping people in organizations be more effective, or helping organizations be more successful. Thus, as was the case in each decade of practice since the origin of the field, there is concerned debate and disagreement about the goals and methods behind OD.

In the end, what this all means is truly up to each reader. For some, the fractured and inconsistent state of the field suggests that

**Table 16.1. Questions and Themes
from OD Practitioners.**

Question	Major Themes
What types of OD-related services are most in demand now?	Team building and team effectiveness
	Executive coaching and development
	Facilitating strategic organizational change
	Systemic integration
	Diversity and multiculturalism
What are the biggest challenges you face on a day-to-day basis as an OD practitioner?	Need for speed
	Resistance to change
	Differentiating OD
	Interpersonal skill and awareness
What are the three biggest emerging trends in OD?	Lack of professionalism
	Changing nature of OD
	Impact of technology
What will the field of OD look like in ten years?	The end of the great values debate
	A truly interdisciplinary approach
	Technology as a way of life
	Globalization and multicultural acumen
	The end of the identity crisis

the OD glass is half empty and sour. For others, OD's fluidity and welcoming of new ideas, influences, and practitioners is a glass that is half, and maybe completely, full. The reality is that practitioners come from different backgrounds, with different experiences, various suites of skills and tools at their disposal, and their own point of view on why and how organizations change. Given this situation, we hope that this book and the framework it offers, along with the consistent messages and themes throughout, will help shape the field into a more consistent and cohesive approach toward working with people in organizations.

References

Allen, K., Crossman, D., Lane, L., Power, G., & Svendsen, D. S. (1993). The future of OD: Conversations with "living legends." *OD Practitioner, 25*, 28–32.

Bellah, R. N., Madsen, R., Sullivan, W. M., Swidler, A., & Tipton, S. M. (1985). *Habits of the heart: Individualism and commitment in American life.* New York: HarperCollins.

Block, P. (1981). *Flawless consulting: A guide to getting your expertise used.* San Francisco: Jossey-Bass/Pfeiffer.

Church, A. H. (2000, Fall). Managing change in the new millennium: Old dog or new tricks? *Performance in Practice,* pp. 9–10.

Church, A. H., & Burke, W. W. (1995). Practitioner attitudes about the field of organization development. In W. A. Pasmore & R. W. Woodman (Eds.), *Research in organizational change and development* (Vol. 8, pp. 1–46). Greenwich CT: JAI Press.

Church, A. H., Burke, W. W., & Van Eynde, D. F. (1994). Values, motives, and interventions of organization development practitioners. *Group and Organization Management, 19*, 5–50.

Church, A. H., Waclawski, J., & Siegal, W. (1996). Will the real OD practitioner please stand up? A call for change in the field. *Organization Development Journal, 14*, 5–14.

Golembiewski, R. T. (1990). Is OD dying, or even ill? Testing alleged problems against success rates. *OD Practitioner, 22*, 16–20.

Greiner, L. (1980). OD values and the "bottom line." In W. W. Burke & L. D. Goodstein (Eds.), *Trends and issues in organization development* (pp. 319–332) San Diego, CA: University Associates.

Howard, A. (Ed.). (1995). *The changing nature of work.* San Francisco: Jossey-Bass.

Jackson, S. E. (1992). *Diversity in the workplace: Human resource initiatives.* New York: Guilford Press.

Margulies, N., & Raia, A. (1990). The significance of core values on the theory and practice of organization development. In F. Massarik (Ed.), *Advances in organization development* (Vol. 1, pp. 27–41). Norwood, NJ: Ablex.

Miles, R. E. (1977). OD: Can it survive? And should it? *OD Practitioner, 9*, 4–7.

Murrell, K. L. (1999). New century organization development: The five core components of spirit, community, work, wisdom and transformation. *Organization Development Journal, 17*, 49–60.

Roddick, A. (1994). *Body and soul: Profits with principles—the amazing success story of Anita Roddick.* New York: Crown.

Schein, E. H. (1988). *Process consultation: Vol. 1. Its role in organizational development* (2nd ed.). Reading, MA: Addison-Wesley.

Waclawski, J., & Church, A. H. (1999, Summer). Four easy steps to performance coaching. *Performance in Practice,* pp. 4–5.

Weisbord, M. R. (1982). The cat in the hat breaks through: Reflections on OD's past, present, and future. In D. D. Warrick (Ed.), *Contemporary organization development: Current thinking and applications* (pp. 2–11). Glenview, IL: Scott, Foresman.

Weidner, C. K., II, & Kulick, O. A. (1999). The professionalization of organization development: A status report and look to the future. In W. A. Pasmore & R. W. Woodman (Eds.), *Research in organizational change and development* (Vol. 12, pp. 319–371). Greenwich, CT: JAI Press.

Name Index

337

Subject Index